Korean Workers

Korean Workers

The Culture and Politics of Class Formation

HAGEN KOO

CORNELL UNIVERSITY PRESS

ITHACA AND LONDON

First published 2001 by Cornell University Press
First printing, Cornell Paperbacks, 2001

Printed in the United States of America

Library of Congress Cataloging-in-Publication Data

Koo, Hagen, 1941–
    Korean workers: the culture and politics of class formation / Hagen Koo.
        p. cm.
    Includes bibliographical references (p.   ) and index.
    ISBN 978-0-8014-3835-6 (cloth : alk. paper) — ISBN 978-0-8014-8696-8
(pbk. : alk. paper)
        1. Working class—Korea.   2. Industrial organization—Korea.   3. Labor
movement—Korea.   4. Labor disputes—Korea.   I. Title.
HD8730.5 .K66 2001
305.5′62′095 19–dc21   2001002813

Cornell University Press strives to use environmentally responsible
suppliers and materials to the fullest extent possible in the publishing
of its books. Such materials include vegetable-based, low-VOC inks
and acid-free papers that are recycled, totally chlorine-free, or partly
composed of nonwood fibers. For further information, visit
our website at www.cornellpress.cornell.edu.

Cloth printing   10   9   8   7   6   5   4   3   2   1

Paperback printing   10   9   8   7   6   5   4   3   2

To my mother and the memory
of my father

Contents

Preface

I began this book as a study of South Korean development from a broad sociological perspective, focusing on the social and cultural dimensions of rapid industrialization. I was particularly interested in the class dynamics of this process and in the ways in which social classes have shaped the pattern of industrial transformation in South Korea. I wrote a few articles along these lines, but soon realized that I was dealing with too large a phenomenon for one book. I also discovered the important role that industrial workers played in this process of rapid industrialization, and how little attention has been paid to their experiences in the literature. More alarming was the discovery of the incredible injustices that the Korean factory workers had been subjected to and the amazing spirit of resistance they demonstrated against oppressive power. I realized that their struggles for a more just society deserve several thorough books, as their experiences and reactions constitute the core of the industrial transformation in South Korea from the 1960s to the 1990s.

Having convinced myself that it would be an eminently worthwhile project to write a book on the Korean working class, I nevertheless had considerable hesitation because I felt that I was not the most qualified person to write about the experiences of industrial workers. There are many people in South Korea who have been deeply involved in the labor movement and have written many books and articles about it from the perspective of their in-depth knowledge and deep commitment to the cause of the emancipatory labor movement. As described in this book, one of the most distinctive aspects of the labor struggles in South Korea was the involve-

ment of a large number of students and intellectuals in the labor movement. These intellectual labor activists have produced a large amount of
descriptive and analytic material on the labor movement during the 1980s
and 1990s. Furthermore, many factory workers themselves have written
about their experiences in the forms of personal essays, poems, union reports, and strike leaflets. Many of them are more qualified than I am, I
thought, to write about labor problems in South Korea's development process. But then I realized that I had the advantage of being able to look at the
Korean experience from a distance and from a comparative perspective,
and that I am better able to present the Korean workers' story to an
English-speaking audience.

At the early stage of my research, I discovered that an adequate amount
of material on the South Korean labor movement exists, although available
mostly in Korean, but that there was an absolute paucity of work on the
formation of the Korean working class, leaving many interesting questions
largely unaddressed and unanswered. How have Korean workers interpreted their experiences in the factories, how have they realized the common interest shared among themselves, how have they forged a collective
identity as workers, how have they obtained a clear awareness of the
importance of worker solidarity and representative unions, and how have
they developed a higher level of political consciousness in opposition to
the authoritarian state? These are the key questions to be answered if we
are to understand the workers' struggles not simply as a trade union movement but as a process of creating a collectivity with a distinct class identity and consciousness.

In this book, I present the development of the South Korean labor movement from the beginning of export-oriented industrialization to the end of
the 1990s and analyze the process of the formation of the working class in
South Korea from a comparative perspective. The South Korean experience
of labor struggle and class formation is a fascinating case for comparative
study and has much to offer that moves beyond the current Euro-centered
theories of class formation, and this book is a first step toward this
comparison.

In presenting the narrative of Korean working-class struggles, I pay special attention to the ways in which culture and politics impinged on the
experiences of the first generation of industrial workers and shaped the patterns of their struggles. As is widely accepted in current scholarship on
class formation, social class is formed ultimately on the basis of the lived
experiences of the workers. But these lived experiences are formed not simply by production relations but also by culture and political power that exert influence from outside, as well as from inside, work relations. In the
context of South Korea, it is very important to understand that workers'
lived experiences are shaped by Confucian cultural tradition and patriar-

chal ideology, as well as by authoritarian state power. Both culture and political power worked to suppress the development of a new class identity
and consciousness among Korean industrial workers. But at the same time,
the ways in which culture and political power collaborated with capital to
suppress workers generated intense worker resentment and resistance.
One of the most interesting aspects of the working-class struggle in South
Korea was the dual and contradictory roles of culture and power in simultaneously suppressing and facilitating worker identity and consciousness.

THIS book took nearly a decade to complete, and I have accumulated numerous debts along the way. My deepest gratitude goes to the many workers and union activists who shared their experiences and insights in the
course of my research: Suk Jung-nam, Kim Ji-sun, Pang Yong-suk, Kim Jun-
yong, Han Myung-hee, Yang Seung-hwa, Cha Un-nyon, Kim Sook-ja, Park
Da-rye, Park Jae-ku, Kim Ho-kyu, Park Joon-suk, Lee Sang-do, Kim Hae-
yoon, Kim Hyung-kwang, Kim Kang-hee, Hur Dong-wook, and several others whose names I regretfully forgot to record. They helped me understand
the deep human dimensions of the labor struggles and taught me how to
read and make better sense of the large amount of material on Korean labor produced by the government, media, labor experts, and labor unions.
Talking with them over a period of several years, I could not help thinking
what intelligent, sincere, and dignified human beings they were and how
unfair and unjust the Korean industrial system, as well as Korean society
as a whole, were to these people who deserved respect. I sincerely hope that
these workers find some satisfaction in this book; that would be my
partial payment to them for the many things they taught me.

I feel very fortunate to have met and learned from several students-
turned-workers who played an important role in facilitating the democratic union movement in the 1980s: Park Dong, Lee Sun-ju, Shim
Sang-jung, Um In-hee, Chung Kwang-pil, Roh Hoe-chan, Kim Ho-kyu, Lee
Soo-kyung, and Chung Ju-Eun. Some of the most courageous and unselfish
people I have met in my life, they gave up far more comfortable and lucrative careers in order to devote themselves to the causes of equality, justice,
and democracy. I would like to express special thanks to Roh Hoe-chan,
currently vice president of the Democratic Labor Party, for sharing his insights and intimate knowledge of the role of activist organizations. I am
also grateful to Kim Ho-kyu and Lee Soo-kyung for inviting me to stay in
their home at the Hyundai apartment complex in Ulsan and allowing me
to get in touch with the personal space of a worker's family life. They also
introduced several of their wonderful colleagues and friends, who kindly
shared their experiences with me.

I would probably not have undertaken this project had there not existed
a large amount of documentary materials produced by unions, church or-

ganizations, and other activist groups. I would like to thank all those who were involved in compiling these data, making them easily available to interested people. Also essential to my research were many well-informed analyses written by Korean labor experts who stayed close to the day-to-day development of the labor movement. Some were written by anonymous writers or by writers using pseudonyms. Of the many who produced valuable works on the South Korean labor movement, I am especially indebted to several scholars who helped my work tremendously through their personal advice and through their written works. Choi Jang Jip helped me greatly by commenting on portions of my earlier writings, sharing his unpublished papers, and confirming the worthiness of my endeavor. Kim Dong-Choon, Lim Young-Il, Song Ho Keun, Shin Kwang-Yeong, and Park Joon-Shik kindly sent me their newly published books, which allowed me a better grasp of the post-1987 trend of the democratic union movement. The works of Kim Hyung-Ki and Lim Ho similarly helped me. All of them represent the cohort of the most thoughtful, bright, and committed scholars produced by 1980s political activism. I am very proud of this younger generation of Korean sociologists.

Several colleagues read and commented on various parts of this book: Ravi Palat, Arif Dirlik, Alvin So, John Lie, Eun Mee Kim, Kyung-Sup Chang, Jonathan Goldberg-Hiller, Frederic Deyo, Guobin Yang, Elizabeth Perry, Andrew Gordon, Akira Suzuki, Richard Boyd, Tak-Wing Ngo, Nancy Abelmann, and Elisabeth Lamoureux. I also appreciated the excellent review provided by an anonymous reader for Cornell University Press, and I would like to thank two other anonymous reviewers who provided very helpful comments on another occasion. I extend my warm appreciation to our graduate students at the University of Hawaii, especially to those who took my social stratification seminar in spring 1999, for reading and critiquing an earlier draft of this book. I am particularly thankful to Shi-jen He, who helped me with computer problems, with the tables and figures included in this book, and indexing, as well as providing sharp critiques of some chapters. Hae-Jin Koh, Stella Hookano, and Jane Kim read portions of the manuscript and gave me editorial help.

I am indebted to several institutions for funding various phases of my research: The Center for Korean Studies at the University of Hawaii, the Korea Foundation, the East-West Center, and the Asia Research Fund. I am most grateful to the Netherlands Institute for Advanced Studies in Humanities and Social Sciences for inviting me to spend a wonderful year as a fellow-in-residence at the institute. My year at the NIAS in 1998–1999 allowed me to finish the first draft of the book manuscript and to reshape its theoretical framework. One of the nicest people I met in the Netherlands is Anne Simpson, the editor at the NIAS. She was kind enough to copyedit all the chapters of my book manuscript while I was there and was willing to help me with my writings even after I returned to the United States.

Several other people, who had no particular interest in the subject of my book, assisted me in one way or another. Chun Kyung-ja translated Park No-Hae's poem into English for me, and Jennifer Lee translated a worker's song at my request. Jung Hee-nam kindly drew a map of industrial estates for me. I wish to express my appreciation to the *JoongAng Daily News*, where I worked as a reporter before leaving Korea to study in North America, for allowing me to use several photos in this book. I am also grateful to Dongkwang Publishing Company for giving me permission to use several photos taken from their book and to Oh Sook-Hee for allowing me to use two pictures of her brother, the late Oh Yoon.

I would like to extend special thanks to Roger Haydon, my editor at Cornell University Press, for his long interest in my work on the South Korean working class and for his enthusiastic support for getting the book published. He is just about the best editor to work with: prompt, efficient, courteous, and with an excellent sense of judgement and humor. I would also like to thank Julie Nemer for her superb and scrupulous copyediting and Ange Romeo-Hall for her most responsive and judicious management of the editorial process.

Finally, I thank my wife and two daughters for their unfailing love and support. I know they are as happy as I am in seeing this prolonged project come to the end.

At this time, I would also like to express my eternal gratitude to my mother and to my deceased father for their bottomless love and devotion to their son; and to my sister for sacrificing her own education for the sake of her brother's, just as most of the factory women I portray in this book did for their siblings. I received much of the inspiration for this work from my parents—from their hard work, self-sacrifice, tenderness toward other people, resilience, constant striving for an improved status, and *han* of not receiving much formal education. These are the same themes running through the lives of the factory workers. I dedicate this book to my mother and to the memory of my father.

Korean Workers

1 Introduction: The Making of the Korean Working Class

> And class happens when some men, as a result of common experiences (inherited or shared), feel and articulate the identity of their interests as between themselves, and as against other men whose interests are different from (and usually opposed to) theirs.
>
> (Thompson 1963: 9)

In January 1997, ten years after the eruption of a huge wave of worker protests, South Korean workers caught the world's attention once again by staging a massive nationwide strike to protest newly passed labor laws. These controversial new labor laws were designed to give employers more power to lay off workers and hire temporary workers and scabs, while disallowing the formation of competing unions in a single workplace for another few years. The strike mobilized some three million workers and shut down production in the automobile, shipbuilding, and other major industries; it also disrupted television news broadcasts and services in many hospital wards and in the subways. Despite unfavorable seasonal factors—the New Year holidays and cold weather—the three-week-long strike maintained a consistently high level of worker participation and a surprisingly high level of public support. It ended in late January when the government reluctantly agreed to revise the new labor laws.

The general strike demonstrated how much South Korea's organized labor had matured since the massive wave of labor unrest in 1987. No longer was labor unrest a consequence of spontaneous worker protests during a period of political turmoil; no longer were workers interested primarily in making economic gains or in venting their suppressed resentment against managerial despotism. Now workers were more concerned with long-term job stability than with short-term economic gains, with legal and institutional issues than with enterprise-level concerns. It was a political struggle rather than an economic one, and the main target of the struggle was the state rather than individual capitalists.

As job stability was the central issue, the January 1997 strike represented the interests not only of blue-collar workers but also of many white-collar and managerial workers (thus the broad public support). By fighting for job stability, an issue that concerned many people in diverse occupations, organized labor assumed a new societal role: representing cross sections of the population and defending the widely shared values of job security and fairness in employment relations.

Although the general strike achieved only minimal concessions from policy makers, it demonstrated worldwide the rise of labor militancy in South Korea. Major international newspapers were united in describing the South Korean workers as "militant," "aggressive," and "combative." The *Los Angeles Times* (January 21, 1997) described the South Korean labor movement as "world-renowned for its passion and fury," and the *New York Times* (January 17, 1997) described South Korea as "a nation of endemic strikes." Clearly, South Korea's image as a nation with a docile and pliable labor force had almost completely changed. The South Korean working class, as Walden Bello and Stephanie Rosenfeld note, "evoked images of the European working classes in the nineteenth century: rebellious, uncompromising, and passionately class conscious" (1990, 23).

This was an amazing development. Until recently, Korean workers had been known, like their counterparts in other East Asian countries, for their industry, discipline, and submissiveness. Rapid economic growth in South Korea had been achieved thanks to the nation's industrious labor force and a high level of "industrial peace" that had prevailed during the first two and a half decades of export-oriented industrialization. The number of labor disputes from the early 1960s to the mid-1980s rarely exceeded one hundred a year, and most of them were concerned with such defensive issues as arbitrary layoffs, wage delays, and intolerable working conditions. One highly publicized labor protest that occurred in 1976 was indicative of the workers' weak position—the protest organized by women workers employed at Haetai Bakery, Inc., one of the largest baking factories employing some 2,500 workers. An appeal filed at the Bureau of Labor by these Haetai workers includes the following:

> Please let us work just 12 hours a day. We are forced to work more than 12 hours a day. We know that the Labor Law prescribes 8-hour work, but con-

> sidering the company's situation we are willing to work up to 12 hours. But
> more than 12 hours is just too much for us to bear with. . . . On top of this,
> we are frequently assigned to a double shift and are forced to work 18 hours
> on consecutive days suffering enormous physical and mental pain. (Soon
> Jum-soon 1984, 21–22)

It is well known that South Korean workers worked extremely long hours; in fact, they worked the world's longest workweek during the 1980s. As this petition indicates, a 12-hour workday was even a desideratum for many workers employed in the labor-intensive sector in the 1970s. Most workers quietly suffered the pains of long work hours during this period, but these Haetai workers were courageous enough to organize a union and fight to reduce their work hours. Similar struggles began to occur in the garment, textile, and other export industries beginning in the mid-1970s; however, Korean labor overall remained submissive, unorganized, and politically quiescent.

The general strike in winter 1996–1997 and the Haetai workers' struggle in 1976 occurred only two decades apart. In this relatively short time, South Korean labor changed substantially. Whereas Korean factory workers in the 1970s took 10- to 12-hour workdays as normal and were even willing to work 15–18 hours with a little extra pay, many of the blue-collar workers in large industrial firms in the late 1990s regard 8 hours as a normal day and are unwilling to work extra hours unless the overtime pay is satisfactory. Whereas wages in the 1970s were set unilaterally by employers, in the late 1990s they are determined by serious negotiations between capital and labor. Whereas labor struggles in the 1970s and the 1980s were primarily against long hours and inhumane working conditions, the 1990s labor movement has focused on protecting job stability and enhancing the organizational power of labor.

What accounts for this drastic change in South Korean labor relations? What made South Korea's once-docile labor force rapidly become a militant social force? What made South Korean workers far more successful than their counterparts elsewhere in East Asia in developing a strong and aggressive labor movement? These are the questions my book seeks to answer. This book tells how the first generation of South Korean industrial workers adapted to the proletarian world of work and tried to make sense of their new industrial experiences.[1] It looks at the ways they struggled to

---

1. Although the 1960s was not the first time a large number of industrial workers appeared—wage workers began to appear in large numbers during the colonial period in the 1920s—export-oriented industrialization produced a new generation of factory workers on a massive scale, most of whom were recruited directly from the countryside and had no prior experience of wage employment. In this sense, it seems appropriate to regard this new industrial proletariat as the first generation of the Korean working class.

organize independent unions in order to protect themselves against a highly exploitative and abusive system of industrial production. It explores how they developed a new collective identity as workers and a sense of solidarity based on their shared interest. It examines how Korean workers developed a distinctive class consciousness and the ways in which this class consciousness was expressed in diverse forms of organizational, cultural, and institutional activities. In short, this is a study of the formation of the working class in South Korea. This is also a study of South Korean industrialization as seen from the standpoint of the workers, rather than from the perspective of industrialists or policy makers.

Much has been written about South Korean economic development, but almost all of the stories about this economic change have been told from the perspective of developmental economists. (See, for example, Cole and Lyman 1971; Kuznets 1977; Jones and Sakong 1980; Amsden 1989; Steinberg 1989; Song Byung-Nak 1990; Woo 1991; World Bank 1993; Sakong 1993; Cho Soon 1994.) Their primary concern in this extensive literature is to explain how South Korea and the other East Asian tigers (Taiwan, Singapore, and Hong Kong) were able to achieve such remarkable economic performance. The economic crisis of 1997 has dampened the fascination with East Asian economic miracles and provoked a search for the causes of the meltdown of Asian economies. Yet the South Korean economy recovered from the crisis faster than every economist had predicted, and so the old debate over the taproots of the South Korean economy's exceptional performance is likely to continue.

Whether the debate concerns the economic miracle or the financial crisis, conspicuously absent is any serious attention to the people—those millions of working men and women who made the spectacular economic growth possible with their blood and sweat. Accounts of the East Asian miracle have much to say about the role of the developmental state, market mechanisms, growth-promoting institutions, and abstract notions of Confucian culture, but very little to say about the workers and their concrete experiences. This is not necessarily because economists have failed to recognize the important role played by labor in economic development. They clearly acknowledge that successful export-oriented industrialization in the East Asian newly industrialized countries (NICs) depended on a low-wage, hard-working labor force. The abundant supply of cheap, high-quality labor at the early stage of industrialization, they agree, was the key source of comparative advantage of these economies in the world economic system. Notwithstanding this recognition, developmental economists have rarely looked at labor as more than a factor of production or a factor of comparative advantage. What concerns them is not the human experiences of working people but the wages and productivity levels of the labor force as a basis of national economic competition.

To the extent that developmental economists have paid attention to the social consequences of economic development for the workers, they have largely confined their analyses to the issues of wages and income distribution. It has been noted that economic development in the East Asian NICs has been associated with a relatively equitable distribution of income, and thus has been praised as a case of "growth with equity" (World Bank 1993). South Korea's record of income distribution does not equal that of Taiwan or Singapore, but nonetheless is very good compared with other Third World countries. Korean workers received one of the highest rates of wage increases in the world, and the rapid wage increase since the 1980s significantly reduced the competitive strength of Korean businesses.

A big puzzle, therefore, is thus why the workers who benefited so much from this economic growth were so discontented with the economic system that brought such a dramatic improvement in their standards of living. The well-known phenomenon of relative deprivation, resulting from rising expectations outpacing actual economic improvement, must have played an important role. However, a far more important factor was workers' daily experiences in the factory as a highly exploited and abused workforce. It was not so much the lagging income as the brutal experiences at work that bred so much anger and resentment among Korean factory workers and nurtured the rise of a strong labor movement in South Korea.

The East Asian development literature has given little attention to labor issues largely because labor has played a very passive and submissive role in development. In all the four East Asian tigers, labor had been demobilized and politically controlled well before the initiation of export-oriented industrialization and had been kept under tight state control throughout the period of rapid export-led industrialization. In this regard, a sharp contrast is found between East Asia and Latin America. Latin American labor had already made a powerful appearance in the political arena in the first decades of the twentieth century, and even after its incorporation into a corporatist system in many countries labor continued to play an important role in the evolution of the political system. As Ruth Collier and David Collier (1991) argue, the mode of incorporation of labor has determined the trajectory of political development in most Latin American countries in the second half of the twentieth century (see also Bergquist 1986).

The political mobilization of labor also occurred in the East Asian tigers during a short period after World War II, but leftist labor was completely destroyed by the emergence of the strong anti-communist states and has left no trace of organizational or ideological influence. Collier and Collier suggest that in Latin America political elites continued to have the "duel dilemma" of controlling organized labor on the one hand and seeking support from influential labor groups on the other hand (1991, 48–50). Such a dilemma has never existed in East Asia. Labor has always been an object of control and exclusion and has never been considered a major political ally or constituency. Without a historical legacy of organization and without support from political parties, the labor force in the East Asian tigers was incorporated into export-oriented industrialization as atomized workers. They worked hard, made few demands on their employers, and posed no serious challenge to the implementation of the state's development policies.

The dominant theme in writings on East Asian labor is, therefore, its docility, its organizational weakness, and its exclusion from politics. In the only systematic comparative study of East Asian labor, Frederic Deyo describes the dominant character of labor in the East Asian NICs as follows: "organized labor plays a politically marginal and insignificant role in national affairs. Labor organizations confront employers from a position of weakness in collective bargaining, industrial work stoppages are few and generally easily suppressed, and there is rarely more than symbolic labor participation in economic policy-making" (1989, 3–4). He further observes that "Rapid, sustained industrialization has not altered the weak political position of labor" and that "despite the creation of a vast factory work force over a period of three decades, labor movements in general remain controlled and inconsequential" (4–5).

Thus, the main issue in the study of East Asian labor is about its passivity and its political quiescence. What accounts for this distinctive quality of East Asian labor? Deyo (1989, 5–6) identifies three popular explanations of labor acquiescence in the East Asian economies. The most frequently mentioned explanation is cultural: Confucian culture, with its emphasis on hierarchy, respect for authority, cooperation, industriousness, and familism, is widely understood to encourage worker submissiveness and cooperation with management and to discourage worker solidarity and collective action. It is true that industrialists in Japan and the four tigers have consciously used Confucian tradition to produce industrial systems that generated far fewer labor conflicts than in most Western industrial societies. Industrial authority in these East Asian organizations often assumes a paternalistic and patriarchal form, and familistic ideology has often been employed to ensure worker submissiveness and commitment to company goals.

The second explanation is economic: rapid economic growth in the East Asian tigers has substantially improved the standard of living of ordinary workers. The job market has improved continuously and so have the levels of wages and other compensations. Although workers' organizations and collective action have been suppressed, such a substantial improvement in standard of living is assumed to have discouraged workers' interest in collective action as a means of upward social mobility. In the continuously growing economy and expanding job market, workers can seek individual advancement and have little interest in joining unions, especially as this would involve great personal risk.

The third explanation focuses on the role of the state. As is well known, the state in South Korea, Taiwan, and Singapore are exceptionally power-ful and autonomous of other societal groups. They possess extensive appa-ratuses of social control and are willing to use them to maintain political and social stability. The state elites in these countries have identified eco-nomic growth as the main basis for the legitimacy of the regime and have regarded autonomous labor organizations as inimical to economic devel-opment and political stability. Although the forms of labor control vary among the East Asian tigers, all of them have maintained tight control over labor organizations and labor activities. Unions have been controlled by the government and companies, the scope of collective bargaining has been severely restricted, and worker protests have been harshly suppressed. East Asian labor's docility and quiescence thus seem hardly surprising given such a repressive labor regime, especially when repression is compensated by rapid economic growth and improvement in the workers' standards of living.

These economic, cultural, and political explanations apply equally to all four East Asian tigers. However, as Deyo (1989, 77–81) notes, South Korean workers have been far more resistant to the exploitative system of indus-trial production and more aggressive in organizing independent unions in opposition to the official unions controlled by the government. Conse-quently, South Korea's labor regime has been far more unstable and conflict-ridden than those of other East Asian countries. So an interesting question is why South Korean workers reacted to their industrial experi-ences far more aggressively and how they were able to develop a stronger labor movement than their counterparts in the other East Asian tigers.

It would require a systematic comparative analysis to answer this ques-tion satisfactorily, but the narrative of the South Korean working-class struggle presented in this book can provide a clue to explaining the unique-ness of the South Korean experience in a comparative perspective.[2] My

2. Deyo suggests that the differential strength of the labor movements in the four East Asian tigers is mainly due to the differential structural characteristics of the working classes. He argues that labor-intensive light manufacturing for exports tends to produce a structurally weak and predominantly female labor force, while heavy industries or import-substitution industries produce a structurally stronger and predominantly male workforce. Deyo explains the general weakness of East Asian labor as a whole in terms of this "struc-tural capacity" factor and also explains the intraregional difference using the same factor. As he points out, the South Korean industrial development has been oriented more toward heavy and chemical industries and has been more geographically and organizationally con-centrated than the other East Asian tigers (Deyo 1989, 167–96). My analysis here and in Koo (1989) agrees with Deyo on this point, but stresses political factors as more important in explaining the differences between South Korea and other East Asian tigers.

analysis demonstrates that the South Korean pattern of economic and political change has generated among workers an intense feeling of grievance and resentment against the industrial system and has also provided them with the organizational and discursive resources to resist the dominant structure of social control. The same cultural and political factors that are often assumed to have produced labor subordination, such as traditional culture and state oppression, have also worked to facilitate a strong working-class movement in South Korea. A major thesis of this study is that culture and politics have interacted closely to facilitate the rapid formation of the working class in South Korea.

The distinctive pattern of the working-class formation in South Korea is put in sharp relief when it is compared with the experiences of the early industrializing countries in Europe. Of course, late twentieth-century South Korea and nineteenth-century Europe are far removed from one another, not only in time but also in cultural, social, and political contexts. However, they share the dramatic experiences of rapid industrial transformation and the consequent rise of the working class. Bringing the early experiences of European working-class formation to bear on the recent South Korean experience can help us isolate interesting aspects of class formation in South Korea and raise important questions about this process. After all, practically all class theories have been derived from the European or American experiences, so it is useful to compare our case with these prototypes in order to gain comparative and theoretical insights.

In recent years, many excellent studies of nineteenth-century working-class formation in Europe have been done, inspired by E. P. Thompson's seminal work, *The Making of the English Working Class* (1963). In this book, Thompson establishes what is called a historicist or constructivist perspective, in contrast to the structural-reductionist or determinist conception of class. In his masterful study of the nineteenth-century English working class, he demonstrates that the working class in England, as an entity with a definite class disposition and consciousness, did not emerge automatically from its structural position in the production system. Stressing that class must be understood as "an historical phenomenon," he argues, "I do not see class as a 'structure', nor even as a 'category', but as something which in fact happens (and can be shown to have happened) in human relationships" (Thompson 1963, 9). Thompson's conception of class gives primacy to the role of human agency, to the self-activity of "making" a class, rather than to the passive process of a class being created by structural conditions. As he eloquently writes, "class is defined by men as they live their own history, and, in the end, this is its only definition" (11).

Thompson's historical and agency-oriented conception of class stresses the role of culture and institutions in shaping people's "lived experiences" within the production process and outside of it. How people perceive and interpret their material condition and how they react against it, he argues, are influenced by cultural factors "embodied in traditions, value-systems, ideas, and institutional forms" (1963, 10). In his oft-quoted phrase, Thompson writes:

> Class is a social and cultural formation (often finding institutional expression) which cannot be defined abstractly, or in isolation, but only in terms of relationship with other classes; and, ultimately, the definition can only be made in the medium of time—that is, action and reaction, change and conflict. When we speak of a class we are thinking of a very loosely-defined body of people who share the same congeries of interests, social experiences, traditions, and value-system, who have a disposition to behave as a class, to define themselves in their actions and in their consciousness in relation to other groups of people in class ways (1966, 357).

Strongly influenced by Thompson's inspiring work, many recent studies of nineteenth-century working-class formation in Europe take his historicist and constructivist perspective (e.g., Aminzade 1981, 1993; Biernacki 1995; Calhoun 1981; Hanagan 1989; Jones 1983; Moore 1978; Sewell 1980). These studies contain historically grounded explanations that emphasize the institutional and cultural determinants of class dispositions and class actions. They demonstrate that class interest is not unproblematic—that is, not determined by a structural position in a straightforward manner— and that its translation into political action is contingent on institutional and political processes. These studies suggest "an alternative approach that takes the identities and perceived interests of actors as problematic, and as constituted through political activity, via organizational and ideological mechanisms that link social structures, including class structures, to political behavior" (Aminzade 1993, 6).

Several findings made by these studies of early working-class formation in Europe are of relevance to our study of the South Korean class formation. The first is the role played by the artisans and the artisan culture and organization. It has been demonstrated that it was the artisans who played a leading role in the working-class protest in nineteenth-century Europe, not factory workers (e.g., Aminzade 1981, 1993; Biernacki 1995; Calhoun 1981; Hanagan 1989; Jones 1983; Moore 1978; Sewell 1980). In France, England, and, to a lesser extent, Germany, artisans led the working-class movement by providing the leadership, organizational resources, and language for worker struggles. As Thompson observes, "in many towns the actual nucleus from which the labour movement derived ideas, organization, and leadership, was made of such men as shoemakers, weavers, saddlers and harnessmakers, booksellers, printers, building workers, small tradesmen, and the like" (1963, 193). William Sewell argues similarly that

"The nineteenth-century labor movement was born in the craft workshop, not on the dark, satanic mill" (1980, 1).

Why did artisans play such an important role in protest? Barrington Moore explains that "The artisans felt moral outrage at an attack on their rights as human beings. The loss of allegedly ancient rights constituted the core of their grievances" (1978, 152). Sewell also argues that artisans' reactions were primarily social and moral rather than economic, and that "the artisans' proclivity for class-conscious action was largely a consequence of a social understanding of their labor that derived from the corporate or guild system of the medieval and early modern cities" (1986, 53). From their culture of mutuality, artisans drew material, social, and organizational resources to forge strong collective actions in response to proletarianization.

A second aspect of the nineteenth-century class formation in France and England that is relevant to Korean class formation is the major impact of the French Revolution of 1830, especially its ideological and political discursive impact. "The French Revolution of 1830," Thompson notes, "had a profound impact upon the people, electrifying not only the London Radicals but working-class reformers in distant industrial villages" (1963, 829). Ronald Aminzade argues that the political and ideological impact of the Revolution was to place "the democratic vision at the center of European political life" (1993, 3). Many scholars suggest that the most important consequence of the French Revolution was the introduction of a new political culture and language, embracing equality, freedom, contract, individualism, and citizenship rights. Ira Katznelson writes, "The Revolution fundamentally altered the ways workers conceived and talked of class. It created new categories of citizen and rights; it made concrete new versions of contract and sovereignty; and it spawned new vocabularies of political justification" (1986, 34). Sewell also argues that "the transformations of the early 1830s created the intellectual, linguistic, and organizational space on which the subsequent workers' movement was built. These transformations established for the first time a class-conscious discourse and institutional practice that was further elaborated by workers over the following decades" (1986, 64).

A third relevant aspect of class formation, stressed in studies of class politics, is the key role played by political institutions, especially political parties, in shaping class organization and class actions. The studies point out that groups do not act out predetermined political roles consistent with their class positions.[3] Instead, political identities and allegiances

---

3. Katznelson (1986) argues that the most problematic link in the multilayered processes of class formation is the translation of class disposition to class actions, and that at this critical juncture political institutions tend to play a determining role.

are created by a political process in which political parties and the state structure play critical roles. Thompson's study (1963) describes how various political groups, although not parties yet, contributed to the development of workers' political dispositions and collective identities. A study of class politics in France by Aminzade suggests that "the mid-nineteenth-century Republican party played a decisive role in working-class formation by fostering workers' capacities for collective action and by encouraging certain forms of political participation" (1993, 14). In Europe and America, political parties played varying roles in determining the saliency of potential sources of political identity, but in general they provided important organizational resources for the incipient working-class movements (Hobsbawm 1984; Katznelson 1986; Kocka 1986; Zolberg 1986).

Compared with the early European experiences, the Korean working class was born in an extremely unfavorable cultural and political environment. Many of the cultural and institutional factors that are identified as critical facilitating factors for working-class formation in Europe have been absent in South Korea. First of all, it is important to note that the Korean working class had no strong artisan culture. Artisan production was not only insignificant in traditional Korea, but artisans occupied a very low status in the Confucian system. In fact, many artisans were recruited from slaves during the Chosun dynasty to produce paper, utensils, special garments, and other luxury goods for the court and aristocracy. Thus, a generation of Korean industrial workers experienced proletarianization without cultural and organizational heritage. There was no culture of mutuality, no sense of pride in workmanship, no cherishing of autonomy and independence, in short, no cultural and institutional basis on which to form a positive self-identity.

What the past bequeathed to the Korean proletarians was the contemptuous status attached to those engaged in physical labor other than independent farming. Without a corporate idiom and culture of sociability, South Korea's neophyte proletarians were thus incorporated into the new industrial system as atomized and uprooted workers. On the other hand, the tremendous social and political changes that Korea underwent, from the end of the nineteenth century on, made Koreans highly adaptable and flexible, and thereby made Korean workers' adaptation to industrial wage work much easier. The workers brought with them mental alertness, habits of hard work, small expectations, and no sense of collective identity beyond family or kinship circles.

The political, ideological, and discursive environment in South Korea was even more unfriendly to the working-class formation than the cultural factors. The Korean peninsula was at the center of the Cold War since the end of the World War II. Political turmoil in Korea in the immediate postwar period ended with the formation of two mutually hostile states, and with the complete destruction of the leftist forces in the south (Cumings 1981). In this state-formation process, militant leftist unions (which had emerged right after liberation from Japanese colonial rule in August 1945) were completely destroyed by right-wing forces and the U.S. military government, leaving the new generation of Korean factory workers no organizational base on which to build their movement. What this early post-war experience left behind was an unfortunate legacy for the future working-class movement—an equation of labor mobilization with communist agitation and the fear of persecution for being involved in activities suspected of being pro-communist. In the intense Cold War environment, anti-communism was always an overarching ideology (for an excellent analysis, see Choi Jang Jip 1989). It provided a ready justification for the suppression of political freedom and civil liberty, and it served as a powerful tool in controlling labor activities and dissident movements. This political environment also deprived labor of political party support. No party in South Korea, even at the end of the 1990s, sought to identify itself with labor or to render organizational support to the working-class movement for fear of being branded as sympathetic to communism.

The dominant language effecting Korean workers' perceptions of their industrial experiences was provided by the state, including the language of nationalism, familism, harmony, and national security. The state defined economic development in terms of the national goal of "modernization of the fatherland," as a project to make the nation rich and powerful so as to protect itself from the hostile communist north and other foreign powers. It praised workers' hard work and sacrifices as patriotic behavior, while characterizing militant unions as disrupting industrial peace and damaging the nation's economic development process. Factory workers were called industrial warriors (*sanŏp chŏnsa*), builders of industry (*sanŏp ŭi yŏkkun*), and the leading force of exports (*suchul ŭi kisu*). The label industrial warriors represented the state's attempt to define the identity of factory workers as soldiers involved in an economic war against foreign competitors, willing to sacrifice themselves for the glory of the nation. Industrial relations were also frequently equated to family relations, based on mutual trust and sacrifice for the good of the collectivity. The state-created slogan, "Treat workers like family members, Do factory work like my own work," was a frequently heard phrase in South Korean factories, displayed at almost every factory gate across the country. The state also propagated the traditional Confucian ethics of diligence, loyalty, and worker-management harmony through the state's educational program.

It is thus evident that South Korea's working-class movement developed in an extremely hostile cultural and political environment. Both cultural and political factors discouraged the development of worker identity. Workers were looked down on as menial and contemptible objects, and they inherited no language of collective identity and organization from their culture. Until the mid-1980s, Korean factory workers were often called *kongsuni* (factory girl) or *kongdoli* (factory boy), with the connotation that their menial and contemptible status was comparable to servants. The political and ideological environment also discouraged workers from identifying themselves on the basis of shared occupational interest. In such an environment, it is natural that South Korean workers' dominant orientation was "exit" rather than "voice," to use Albert Hirschman's (1971) extremely useful terms. They wanted to get out of the wretched world of factory work and shed the despicable status of factory laborer as soon as possible. Identifying themselves in a positive way as workers or as members of the working class was extremely difficult in this cultural and social environment.

A crucial aspect of working-class formation in South Korea is, therefore, the ways in which Korean factory workers overcame the cultural image of despised laborers (as *kongsuni* and *kongdoli*) and the state-imposed label of industrial warriors (*sanŏp chŏnsa*) and developed their own collective identity as workers (*nodongja*). A major assumption in this study is that working-class identity is far more problematic in societies such as South Korea, where culture and politics suppress and distort its development. The central questions to explore are therefore: How were Korean workers able to overcome these cultural and political obstacles and forge a strong worker identity? What structural and demographic conditions facilitated this process? What were workers' lived experiences in the factory that made them resist patriarchal authority with such surprising courage and intensity? From where did they draw the cultural and organizational resources to forge a new collective identity and political consciousness?

This book describes the development of the working-class movement and collective identity in South Korea during the past three decades of rapid industrialization. The 1980s was a particularly important period for the formation of the Korean working class. In investigating these issues, my approach does not assume that working-class formation in South Korea was completed by the end of the 1980s or even by the late 1990s. Class formation, understood as "the emergence of a relatively cohesive working class, self-conscious of its position in the social structure and willing and capable of acting to affect it" (Katznelson 1986, 11), is an open-ended process, and it is futile, in my view, to try to determine when class formation has occurred or not occurred. It is important to realize, as Jürgen Kocka argues, that "classes are always in the process of becoming or disappearing, of evolution or devolution" (1986, 283). What seems certain is that during the 1980s a significant change occurred in Korean workers' collective identity and consciousness and that this change was expressed not only in the pattern of their struggles for unionization but also in the language they used and in the cultural activities they engaged in. In short, I assume that the significant changes in the process of Korea's working-class formation had occurred during the 1980s and that these changes were the result of cumulative changes that began in the 1970s.

The major sources for my study are a wealth of materials produced by workers and labor activists in South Korea. Fortunately, the active and highly politicized labor movement in South Korea during the 1980s produced a large amount of material on the development of worker struggles. The bulk of this material was written by the intellectuals and political activists who were directly or indirectly involved in the Korean labor movement. Activist students and dissident intellectuals became closely linked to the grassroots union movement from the late 1970s, and they wrote a great deal about the union movement and the repressive actions by the employers and the government. In addition, Korean factory workers, themselves, wrote much of the material, in the form of personal essays, poems, play scripts, and collective reports on their protest actions. Fortunately, much of what they wrote is available in print thanks to several small publishers that collected workers' scattered writings and published them in collections of essays or reports in the 1980s (e.g., Chang Nam-soo 1984; Chun Chum-suk 1985; Kim Kyŏng-sook et al. 1986; Suk Jung-nam 1984; Song Hyo-soon 1982; Yu Dong-wu 1984; Lee Dal-hyuk 1985).

I have also conducted many informal interviews with factory workers, unionists, and labor experts over the past ten years. My understanding of worker protest and class formation in Korea has evolved slowly from these interviews and from reading and reflecting on what they wrote. In addition, I have also drawn extensively on many scattered writings produced by Korean intellectuals who were involved in the democratic union movement in the 1980s. Their analyses tend to be narrowly focused, reflecting the viewpoints of the activists, and often written for a practical rather than an analytical purpose. Nonetheless, their writings provide invaluable information and insightful observations for students of Korean working-class formation.

In contrast to the rich material available in Korean on the South Korean labor movement, the English literature on the topic is extremely scanty. As of this writing, there are only three books that are concerned exclusively with the contemporary Korean labor movement in addition to Deyo's (1989) comparative study. The first book, Choi Jang Jip (1989), presents an excellent analysis of the evolution of the corporatist system of labor control in South Korea from the 1960s through the end of the 1970s. The second book, Ogle (1990), was written by an American former clergyman who played a key role in establishing labor-oriented missionary work in South Korea and presents a vivid firsthand description of the plight of Korean workers under the military authoritarian regimes. The third book,

Seung-kyung Kim (1997), describes the women factory workers' struggles in the Masan export processing zone in the late 1980s, based on the author's experiences in an electronics factory. There are a few other books that address the issues of labor oppression and labor struggles in South Korea as part of a broader study of economic development in South Korea or the East Asian NICs, but their focuses are usually limited to certain aspects of Korean labor and are generally wanting in analytic depth (e.g., Bello and Rosenfeld 1990; Kearney 1991; Hart-Landsberg 1993). Several Ph.D. dissertations on South Korean labor have also been written in the United States and elsewhere (e.g., Cho Soon-Kyoung 1987; Kim Yong Cheol 1994; Lee Jeong Taik 1987; Lee Eun-Jin 1989; Suh Doowon 1998). Taken all together, the literature on South Korean labor represents only a tiny fraction of the huge literature on South Korean development.

The dominant tendency in the literature on South Korean labor, in an interesting contrast to the general conception of East Asian labor in the development literature, is to take the rise of labor militancy in South Korea more or less for granted. This is particularly the case in writings by Koreans, most of whom had close ties with the union activists and social-movement communities. Given the enormous amount of exploitation and abuse that factory workers were subjected to in their daily lives, the workers' proclivity to class antagonism and collective action must have appeared to these intellectual observers as only natural and inevitable. Most writings by Korean analysts are thus primarily interested in highlighting the extraordinary degree of labor exploitation and harsh state oppression of labor actions. In their writings, the independent union movement tends to be taken as a natural consequence of the state's oppressive labor policy and the inability of the government-controlled official union to represent the workers. Therefore, the dominant conception of class relations revealed in this literature is a reductionist or essentialist assumption, assuming that classes emerge, more or less automatically, from the structure of the capitalist relations of production.

I regard this reductionist or essentialist perspective as inadequate in the study of the development of the working-class movement in South Korea, as well as in other societies. The same pattern of capitalist industrialization in other East Asian NICs did not produce the same kind of class response, despite practically the same intensity of labor exploitation and oppression. This teaches us not to assume that class actions based on shared class identity emerge naturally from the process of state-led capitalist development. Both a comparative perspective and current theories of class formation suggest that the development of class identity and class consciousness must be understood as a problematic phenomenon, something that may or may not occur depending on how other factors mediate between work-based experiences and consciousness. This is clearly the most important point suggested by the literature on European and American working-class formation that we reviewed previously.

The narrative presented in this book demonstrates that the ultimate source of labor militancy and the high level of workers' political consciousness in South Korea was the extremely abusive and despotic work relations in the factories. Factory workers experienced a keen sense of injustice and harbored intense resentment against managerial despotism. Factory workers were also deeply affected by the contemptuous treatment they received from their superiors, as well as from other members of the community. Korean workers' grievances and resentment were thus derived from multiple sources of oppression rather than simply from low wages and poor working conditions, and this was particularly so for women workers. They were not only economically exploited but also culturally and symbolically oppressed. Thus, in the Korean factory, class exploitation, gender oppression, and status subjugation combined to produce the workers' intense frustration and resentment against the despotic management. Korean workers' reactions, therefore, tended to be highly emotional and morally based. The sporadic outbursts of worker protest during the 1970s sprang more from their cultural reactions to their experiences than from a rational effort to improve economic conditions in the factory. Their most urgent demands were *humane treatment* and *justice* rather than higher wages or better working conditions. In this regard, we see some similarities between Korean and earlier European workers; for both, a moral sense of justice played a critical role in defining workers' reactions to their proletarian work relations (Thompson 1963; Moore 1978).

The labor protests that occurred during the 1960s and 1970s were very few in number and were also largely unorganized, spontaneous, and defensive. These protests were rarely backed by a strong sense of collective identity and solidarity, and they were easily controlled. Starting in the second half of the 1970s, however, two important processes began that contributed greatly to the growth of working-class identity and consciousness. The first was a structural process: the rapid growth of the number of factory workers and their spatial concentration in a few industrial centers, increasingly in heavy and chemical industries. The second was the active social and political movements that occurred outside the industrial arena but began to be articulated with the grassroots labor struggles from the late 1970s. These two processes greatly enhanced the structural and spatial capacity of the Korean working class, as well as their cultural and organizational resources for developing a new collective identity and class consciousness.

The dominant pattern of South Korea's industrialization—swift, compressed, and highly concentrated—has a lot to do with rapid class formation in South Korea. The export-led industrialization that began in the early 1960s accelerated its pace in the 1970s. Not only did the working class expand significantly during this period, its spatial concentration became more pronounced. Almost all the manufacturing factories were located in large urban areas and in a few industrial complexes or newly emerged industrial towns around Seoul and along coastal areas. Such an urban-centered industrial development necessarily entailed a large-scale rural exodus. In South Korea, the migrants were most likely to be permanent migrants with no intention of returning to rural areas. Thus, this concentrated pattern of industrialization helped create working-class communities around industrial belts, populated by full-time proletarians who realized that they were doomed to urban wage employment for the rest of their lives. The literature on working-class formation suggests that close-knit working-class communities provided important resources for the working-class struggle in most societies, West and East (Calhoun 1981; Hanagan 1989; Gutman 1977; Perry 1993). A somewhat similar process began in South Korea in the early 1980s as an outcome of the highly concentrated pattern of industrialization during the 1970s.

Another and probably more important process occurred outside the industrial arena. Beginning in the second half of the 1970s, the highly politicized intellectual community began to connect with the shop-floor resistance movement.

Two groups in society played a particularly important role in supporting grassroots labor struggles. The first was church organizations influenced by progressive theological orientations, such as Latin America's liberation theology. These Christian organizations took advantage of their international networks and their relatively secure political and ideological position in society to provide guidance and shelter for labor activists. They also ran workers' night schools and organized small-group activities where workers had opportunities to share their experiences and to develop a sense of identity and solidarity among themselves. Union consciousness in South Korea was first born through these activities, and so was the first group of grassroots union activists. Significantly, the majority of these union activists were women workers employed in the garment, textile, and electronics industries, and they led the grassroots labor movement from the late 1970s to the first half or the 1980s. Thus, one of the most interesting aspects of the South Korean labor movement is the unique role played by women workers in the light manufacturing industries. Why women played such an important role in the Korean labor movement is, therefore, an important question to be explored in this book.

From the early 1980s, students took over the role played by church groups. Korean students played a very active role in Korea's modern political history, and during the three-decade period of military rule since 1961, they were the most active and politicized element in South Korea.

Student political activism began to spill over into the industrial arena in the mid-1970s, and in the early 1980s a large number of students entered factories with the goal of raising class consciousness among workers and helping them to organize independent unions. The involvement of these students-turned-workers in many labor disputes helped to politicize labor conflicts and sharpen political consciousness among workers.

The South Korean working-class movement was also tremendously helped by the development of a social movement, called the *minjung* (people) movement, that began in the mid-1970s and became a dominant intellectual trend in the first part of the 1980s. This broad populist movement was led by dissident intellectuals and students and aimed to forge a broad class alliance among workers, peasants, poor urban dwellers, and progressive intellectuals against the authoritarian regime and economic injustices (Koo 1993; Abelmann 1996; Wells 1995). The movement was simultaneously a political, social, and cultural movement and advocated the populist ideas of democracy, distributive justice, national cultural identity, and the role of *minjung* in history. It introduced new political language and cultural activities by reinterpreting Korean history and reappropriating Korea's indigenous culture from the *minjung* perspective. The new language and cultural forms raised workers' political consciousness and contributed to a positive worker identity by helping them look at their role in society and history in a new light. Lacking internal cultural resources and facing the strong authoritarian state, Korean industrial workers drew ideological, political, and organizational support from the active social and political movements in civil society.

Thus, one of the most interesting aspects of the South Korean labor movement, in comparison with those of the other East Asian tigers, was the intimate linkages that developed between the workers' grassroots union movement and the political movements for democracy led by students, intellectuals, church leaders, and dissident politicians. What caused the two levels of struggle, the shop-floor level and the political level, to be interconnected so closely? The answer, I believe, lies in the role of the state as the major determinant of the economic, political, and social processes of South Korea's "late industrialization." South Korea's deeply intrusive state shaped labor relations and labor conflicts in several important ways. First, the development strategy of the South Korean state exerted a direct influence on industrial relations in Korean firms. The Park Chung Hee government adopted a strategy of accelerated, rather than balanced, economic growth and tried to claim the regime's legitimacy on the basis of economic performance. The political economy based on this growth-oriented strategy encouraged an expansionist accumulation strategy among Korean capitalists; their main concern was to identify and capture new lucrative investment opportunities and to get access to state-controlled financing. Consequently, developing a committed and productive workforce was of secondary concern to most Korean industrialists, especially because the labor supply was abundant until the mid-1980s.

The state had a more direct influence on labor relations on the shop floor. Throughout the 1970s and 1980s, the South Korean government approached industrial relations with a blatantly pro-capital and anti-labor attitude. Whereas the government ignored customary violations of labor practice laws by management, it was quick and ruthless in cracking down on any signs of labor unrest. Whereas workers' pleas for government protection against labor abuses were commonly ignored, employers' requests for intervention to block unionization efforts received a willing response. The natural consequence was a growing level of politicization among workers. The capitalist nature of state power was too easy to see, especially after workers had gained a rudimentary understanding of the importance of organizing themselves into independent unions.

Although the South Korean labor regime is usually described as a corporatist system, its actual operation was based on a crude repressive form of control rather than a sophisticated corporatist system. Unlike the situation in most corporatist labor regimes, in which officially sanctioned unions are allowed to channel worker representation, the South Korean government was primarily interested in keeping workers unorganized and controlling them through security forces rather than through labor branches of the government. In centrast to Taiwan, for example, where local unions were deeply penetrated by the ruling party and where various preemptive measures were adopted to ensure labor passivity, the South Korean government relied primarily on threats and punishment, using security ideology to control labor agitation (Shin Kwang-Yeong 1994). This exclusionary approach produced a cadre of hard-core unionists by driving them out of the industrial arena—many union activists were fired and blacklisted from future employment—and by pushing them, inadvertently, to develop close ties with political activists and student radicals.

Thus, culture and politics have played critical roles in the formation of the South Korean working class, not in the usual roles ascribed to them in the literature on East Asian development—as factors of labor docility and quiescence—but as sources of labor resistance and growing consciousness. My discussion of the Korean working-class movement demonstrates that culture and political power in South Korea have simultaneously suppressed and promoted worker identity and consciousness. Whereas the preindustrial elements of Korean culture bolstered the patriarchal authority of managers and discouraged collective identity among workers, reconstructed historical memories of the past and the *minjung* culture became an essential cultural tool for forging a resistant identity of *nodongja* (workers).[4] Whereas the oppressive state policies limited the political space and organizational resources of social movements, they played a critical role in politicizing labor conflicts and promoting close linkages between labor struggles and political movements for democracy. It is these contradictory effects of culture and politics, both on the shop floor and in civil society, that promoted the rapid growth of labor militancy and class consciousness. In this way, the dialectics of class conflict has intimately intertwined with the dialectics of culture and politics in the course of rapid industrialization in South Korea.

In the following chapters, I describe how Korean workers struggled to improve their situation in the factory and how they have developed a new sense of collective identity and class consciousness through these struggles. Chapter 2 describes the nature of industrial transformation that began in South Korea in the early 1960s and presents the structural conditions for the formation of the working class in South Korea. South Korea's export-oriented industrialization has been characterized by an exceptionally fast, compressed, and geographically concentrated pattern of development. This chapter examines the dominant pattern of proletarianization that accompanied this economic change and the social and demographic character of the newly emerged industrial proletariat in South Korea.

Chapter 3 moves closer to the lived experiences of the workers inside the factories. Based on workers' diaries and personal essays, this chapter describes how work was organized and how authority was exercised in a typical South Korean factory in the 1970s and 1980s, and the physical and psychological sacrifices the factory system exacted from the workers, especially from young women workers. Workers' essays and diaries are filled with resentment against the highly personalistic and arbitrary exercise of power carried out by their employers and against the constant symbolic assaults on their self-esteem and social identity. This chapter demonstrates that their constant cries for humane treatment were not simply a reaction to the poor material conditions of work, but also a reaction against the despotic authority relations that denied them basic human dignity.

South Korea launched its export-oriented industrialization in the early 1960s, but collective responses to this industrial experience began to emerge in the early 1970s. The main concern of chapter 4 is with the first phase of the grassroots union movement led by women workers employed in the textile, electronics, and other light manufacturing industries. The narrative focuses on two cases of unionization struggle, at Dongil Textile and Y. H. Company, which epitomized the amazing spirit of resistance

4. Abelmann (1996) describes the importance of historical memory and the *"minjung imaginary"* in the development of the South Korean farmers' movement in the 1980s.

demonstrated by women workers and the role of outside groups, especially church organizations, in supporting their struggles. This chapter also demonstrates how class and gender experiences are fused to allow the young women workers play a vanguard role in the working-class movement in South Korea.

Chapter 5 follows the events of the first half of the 1980s, during which intensive politicization of labor conflicts occurred. Students played a critical role during this period. The "worker-student alliance" became the dominant strategy of the student movement in the 1980s and thousands of college students dropped out of school and entered the industrial arena to raise political consciousness among workers. The chapter explores the reasons for this development and its implications.

Chapter 6 steps back from the chronological treatment of events and explores the distinctive pattern of Korean workers' reactions to their industrial experiences. The focus of the analysis is on how culture and power worked to suppress factory workers' awareness of a shared interest and collective identity, and how workers were nonetheless able to acquire a shared identity as workers (nodongja) and began to express their collective consciousness through their solidarity struggles and through cultural activities. This chapter also demonstrates how some unique Korean cultural concepts and historical memories served to foster worker identity and consciousness.

In 1987, cumulative changes that had occurred in workers' identity, consciousness, demographic composition, and social networks were expressed in a gigantic explosion of labor unrest, the Great Worker Struggle. Chapter 7 describes the development of this watershed event of the South Korean working-class movement and how it has affected the subsequent development of industrial relations. Significant changes occurred after the 1987 worker uprising, including a major shift in the main actors of the labor movement—from predominantly female workers in the light manufacturing industries to male workers in the heavy and chemical industries—and significant changes in the objectives and themes of worker struggles. Workers' collective identity and class consciousness greatly advanced, with a noticeable improvement in their market position and in their shop-floor influence thanks to the increasingly empowered unions.

Labor advances made in the late 1980s were, however, met by strong counteroffensives from capital and the state in the 1990s. Chapter 8 describes many interesting changes that have occurred in this era of democratization and globalization. Labor militancy was countered by sophisticated managerial techniques, and the labor movement gradually separated from the political and social movements and became predominantly an economic trade unionism. A new capitalist strategy of accumulation increased the fragmentation of the previously homogeneous working class, along industrial, sectoral, and occupational lines, diluting its class identity. At the same time, economic restructuring necessitated by globalization caused new struggles focused on protecting job security. Increasingly, labor struggles and the union movement in South Korea lost their distinct political and cultural patterns that had been associated with the previous authoritarian capitalism and gradually converged into the more universal pattern of trade unionist movements prevalent in other industrial societies. At the turn of a new century, the South Korean working class stands at the crossroads, to become either a class-conscious and politically organized class or a disaggregated group of workers preoccupied with narrow and particularistic economic interests.

2 Industrial Transformation

The Road to Seoul
I am going.
Do not cry;
I am going.
Over the white hills, the black, and the parched hills,
down the long and dusty road to Seoul
I am going to sell my body.
Without a sad promise to return,
to return some time blooming with a lovely smile,
to unbind my hair,
I am going.
Do not cry;
I am going.

(Kim Chi Ha 1980)

One major factor that facilitated export-oriented industrialization (EOI) in South Korea was the absence of strong organized labor. Labor weakness in Korea was not simply due to the Confucian cultural tradition. Korean labor had been mobilized during and immediately after Japanese colonial rule, and it was stronger and more politically oriented in the second half of the 1940s than it was in the 1960s and the 1970s. But a series of geopolitical events during the post-colonial period completely destroyed this strong leftist labor movement and paved the way for the labor-exclusive development trajectory in the later period. By the time the export-oriented industrialization strategy was launched in the early 1960s, organized labor

Figure 1. An image of a young girl leaving her rural home for a job in the city. (From Oh Yoon 1996, 96)

had been completely emasculated, leaving a new generation of workers to enter export industries as atomized laborers with no organizational or cultural resources to secure a decent position in the new industrial order.

South Korea's rapid economic growth is due, to a great extent, to this labor condition, as well as to favorable external economic conditions in the 1960s. South Korea experienced, since the early 1960s, a profound transformation of its economy and society, no less significant than the "great transformation" that Polanyi (1957) describes for nineteenth-century Europe. Rapid industrialization was accompanied by proletarianization on a massive scale, turning millions of farmers and their sons and daughters into wage workers in urban industry. It was one of the swiftest and most compressed processes of proletarianization the world has seen, producing in one generation the same magnitude of change that took a whole century in most European societies. The evolution of the Korean working-class movement is closely related to this swift and geographically concentrated pattern of proletarianization.

This chapter sketches the historical experience of the Korean labor movement and describes the development of the South Korean political economy and the proletarianization process. This provides us with a basic understanding of the historical background and the structural context in which the Korean working class emerged and struggled to carve out a positive identity in the rapidly changing society.

The Early Demobilization of Labor

The modern Korean labor movement began with rapid industrialization in the later period of Japanese colonial rule (1910–1945). Although Japanese colonial policy in Korea was primarily to maximize the extraction of agricultural surplus, Japan's military advance into Asia required an expanded industrial base in the Korean peninsula, and thus substantial investments in mining, chemical industries, railroad construction, and hydroelectric plants were made, all geared to Japan's war efforts. The number of Korean factory workers increased rapidly, from 49,000 in 1921 to 80,000 in 1925 to 102,000 in 1930 (Kim Yun-hwan 1978, 67; see also Chung Jin-Sung 1984). The majority of these workers were hired by Japanese employers (large industries were mostly owned by Japanese capitalists).

The labor movement began to emerge in the early 1920s and involved frequent labor conflicts directed against Japanese employers and managers (see Kim Yun-hwan and Kim Nak-jung 1970; Park Young-Ki 1979). The number of labor disputes occurring in the 1930s surpassed even those of the 1960s and the 1970s. In 1920, for example, there were 81 cases of labor disputes involving 4,599 participants. In 1930, the number increased to 160 cases involving 18,972 workers. The climax of the labor conflicts during this period was the Wonsan general strike of 1929, a three-month-long bitter struggle waged by some 2,000 workers. However, the labor movement during this colonial period was not simply an economic struggle but part of the independence movement against Japanese colonial rule. The colonial government, of course, did not allow such a politically oriented labor movement to continue to gain strength and began to crack down hard on it, beginning in the 1930s. As a result, the Korean labor movement during the last decades of colonialism remained underground, closely associated with the communist movement.

After Korea's liberation from colonial rule in August 1945, the labor movement resurfaced with stronger organization and leadership than before. Within three months of liberation, strong leftist unions were created under the umbrella organization, the National Council of Korean Trade Unions (Chŏnp'yŏng). Even before the formation of this national organization, Korean workers had become active at the plant level, taking over and managing many factories left behind by Japanese owners. With the formation of *Chŏnp'yŏng*, labor conflicts increased sharply, with frequent clashes with police and with the U.S. military occupation forces. Between August 1945 and March 1947, there were 2,388 labor demonstrations involving 600,000 participants. This was the most violent period in the pre-1987 history of the Korean labor movement (see Kim Yun-hwan and Kim Nak-jung 1970; Park Young-Ki 1979).

However, the strong labor movement did not last long. In March 1946, right-wing groups, backed by U.S. military forces, created a new labor organization, the Federation of Korean Trade Unions (FKTU or *Daehan Noch'ong*). The FKTU had no grassroots base and no genuine interest in promoting worker welfare. Rather, its sole objective was to compete with, and eventually destroy, the leftist labor unions. Many violent clashes occurred between the leftist and rightist unions, and gradually the *Chŏnp'yŏng* was destroyed by the combined forces of the police, rightist unions, and the U.S. military government. The fatal blow to the leftist labor movement came during a massive railroad strike in January 1947. This bloody confrontation between leftist and rightist labor groups ended with the decimation of the communist labor leaders; hundreds of them were killed or executed, and thousands were imprisoned. In March 1947, the U.S. military government outlawed the Korean Communist Party, which put an end to the already weakened communist labor organizations. Thus ended the first period of active labor mobilization in Korea.

The next twelve years after the establishment of the first Republic in South Korea (1948–1960) marked the lowest point in the Korean labor movement. A series of events—the division of the nation into two hostile states (1948) and the Korean War (1950–1953), followed by a hysterical anti-communist atmosphere—created a hostile environment for the independent labor movement. Under Syngman Rhee's regime, the FKTU quickly degenerated into a marketplace for corrupt labor leaders and was transformed into a political tool for consolidating Rhee's power base. It was officially incorporated into the Liberal Party in 1955 and became an auxiliary arm of the ruling party. Detached from its rank-and-file members, the FKTU was more active in organizing political rallies in support of Rhee than in promoting the welfare of workers.

The Rhee regime was toppled by the student uprising against the rigged election in April 1960. During the short-lived democratic government led by Chang Myon (1960–1961), the country saw a resurgence of labor unrest and of the union movement; the number of labor disputes in 1960 increased to 227 cases, from 45 in 1957 and 95 in 1959. Many of these labor disputes involved street demonstrations. Workers created 315 new unions and obtained 15–50 percent wage increases. The FKTU faced severe criticisms from its rank-and-file members and was challenged by the newly created independent union, the National Council of Trade Unions (NCTU or *Nohyŏp*).[1] In November 1960, a new configuration of labor leaders decided to merge the FKTU and the NCTU into a new national center, *Hankook Noryon* (with the same English name, FKTU). A particularly significant development during this period was the rise of the left-leaning white-collar unions, especially the Teachers' League, which challenged the state's ideological control over school curricula and stressed a liberal orientation toward unification issues. This period and especially the radical teachers' union movement represented a revival of the earlier leftist legacy in the Korean labor movement of *Chŏnp'yŏng*.

This brief period of labor activism ended with the military coup led by Park Chung Hee in June 1961. The Korean labor movement had to start all over again, under a newly powerful state and in a new economic context. The historical legacy bequeathed to the new labor movement was mainly negative; the authorities had an easy excuse for suppressing labor organizations on the grounds of security, sowing a deep fear of possible political persecution for involvement in labor activism in the minds of workers. Instead of a proud tradition, the post-war labor struggles became just a bad memory to be forgotten for the next generation of workers. In fact, the labor movement could exist only by denying and dissociating itself from the dangerous tradition of the post-liberation period.

Export-Oriented Industrialization and the Labor Regime

One of the first steps the military junta took after it seized power was to restructure the labor organization. It dissolved the FKTU, arrested labor activists, and banned labor strikes. Three months later, the newly created Korean Central Intelligence Agency (KCIA) selected a group of labor leaders and had them create a new Federation of Korean Trade Unions (with a slightly different Korean name, *Nochong*). The new union structure was organized along industry lines, and officially sanctioned unions were given exclusive representation rights in the manner of state corporatism. In practice, however, industrial unions were not allowed to function as effective labor organizations. Only tenuous horizontal linkages existed among local unions within industry, and virtually all collective bargaining was conducted by the individual enterprise unions. Legally, these enterprise unions were organized as union shops, although compulsory membership was never enforced or even encouraged in practice (Choi Jang Jip 1989).

---

1. The National Council of Trade Unions (*Nohyŏp*) was created in 1959 by a group of independent labor leaders in opposition to the FKTU. By the late 1950s, labor volatility was visibly on the rise, caused by extremely poor economic conditions and a rising level of job instability. The official union, however, was completely blind to these problems.

The military regime also introduced important revisions in the existing labor laws. The South Korean labor laws had been laid down in 1953 under the Rhee regime. Modeled after the U.S. Wagner Act of 1935, the first Korean labor union law had a rather liberal and pluralistic orientation toward organized labor. The labor union law and the South Korean constitution guaranteed the three basic rights of labor: freedom of association, collective bargaining, and collective action. Under these laws, workers were allowed to form unions and to engage in collective bargaining with minimal state interference. Unions were also allowed to engage in political activities. Of course, the actual behavior of the Rhee regime toward organized labor was contrary to the spirit of these laws. Given the dreadful economic and geopolitical conditions after the Korean War, these liberal labor laws did little to promote a strong labor movement.

However, the Park regime, coming to power after a period of active social mobilization and the increasingly politicized labor movement that followed the fall of Rhee, clearly saw the potential threat of organized labor and sought to restrain labor's legal rights and to prevent linkages between organized labor and political groups. A 1963 amendment to Article 12 of the Labor Union Law prescribed that labor unions could not collect political funds from their members or use union dues for political purposes. In addition, a number of restrictive clauses were added to the labor laws that made union organizing and collective action more difficult, while expanding the scope of state intervention in labor relations. Nevertheless, the three basic rights of workers were maintained along with other labor-protective measures. Compared to what followed, the labor laws of this period were generally liberal and democratic. The main motivation of the Park regime in restructuring the labor unions and the labor laws at this time was primarily political rather than economic, that is, to keep organized labor depoliticized and disconnected from political opposition groups. A new labor regime was thus established to facilitate outward-looking industrialization that would soon radically change the working lives of millions of Koreans. The Korean working-class movement started anew under this new labor regime and in the new context of world market–oriented industrialization (Cho Seung-hyok 1988; Chang Myung-kook 1985; Choi Jang Jip 1989; Shin Kwang-Yeong 1994).

After some unsuccessful policy efforts within the framework of an import-substitution industrialization strategy in the first two or three years, the Park government, under strong U.S. influence and after some stumbling, adopted outward-looking, export-oriented industrialization (EOI) as its major development strategy. This strategy shift turned out to be a wise choice. Exports jumped from a mere $87 million in 1963 to $835 million in 1970, with the gross national product (GNP) increasing approximately 10 percent annually during this period. The growth rate in the manufacturing sector was approximately 19 percent annually. Profound changes began to occur in the economy and in the ways people made a living. The number of urban wage workers began to increase rapidly, from 1.3 million in 1960 to 2.1 million in 1966 to 3.4 million in 1970 (Suh Kwan-mo 1987, 169). With this change in the economy, labor activism gradually shifted from the public service sectors to export manufacturing sectors, although the overall level of labor disputes remained very low.

After impressive growth in manufacturing production and exports, the South Korean economy ran into its first major crisis toward the end of the 1960s, caused by a serious balance-of-payment problem and widespread business failures by foreign-invested firms. Frequent labor conflicts occurred in response to layoffs, delayed payments, and plant closures. In response to this economic crisis, Park took several extraordinary measures to improve the investment climate for foreign capital and the financial structure of domestic firms. One critical element of these measures was a repressive labor policy. In 1969, the government proclaimed the Provisional Exceptional Law Concerning Labor Unions and the Settlement of Labor Disputes in Foreign Invested Firms. These new laws prohibited strikes in foreign-invested firms and instituted various restrictive measures to deal with labor disputes in other sectors as well. This action marked a major turning point in the Park regime's labor policies, dictated by the imperatives of the export-oriented industrialization strategy as well as by the political necessity of the authoritarian regime to curb the opposition forces.

Political opposition to the Park regime intensified with the economic crisis toward the end of the 1960s. In the 1971 presidential election, Park barely escaped defeat by the opposition candidate, Kim Dae Jung, despite all the organizational and financial resources he had mobilized. This was also a period of great change in geopolitics. Nixon's 1971 visit to China signaled the coming end of the Cold War in Asia, and the partial withdrawal of U.S. military forces from South Korea caused great concern for South Korean political leaders. Park's response to these economic and political challenges was harsh. In December 1971, Park declared a state of emergency and simultaneously proclaimed the Law Concerning Special Measures for Safeguarding National Security. These National Security Measures suspended two of the workers' three basic rights guaranteed by the constitution: the rights of collective bargaining and collective action. Workers were allowed to form unions, but only under many new administrative restrictions, and legally deprived of their only effective weapon in bargaining with employers—the right to undertake collective action. In March 1972, the government introduced another restrictive measure, the Measure Dealing with Collective Bargaining under National Emergency. This measure expanded the range of enterprises defined as belonging to the

public interest and that were thus barred from union actions; it also placed
further restrictions on the activities of industry-level unions. The culmi-
nation of all these extraordinary actions was the installation in October
1972 of a Korean version of bureaucratic authoritarianism, called the
yushin (revitalization) regime. The *yushin* constitution closed all the
political space and bestowed on Park a lifetime presidency with unchecked
executive power.

This enormously unpopular move aggravated Park's perennial problem
with political legitimacy and led to intensified political opposition,
although it temporarily banished dissident political activities on the surface. As before, Park tried to diffuse popular discontent and buy political
legitimacy with economic performance. In his January 1973 presidential
press conference, Park made a tantalizing promise to the nation that
he would deliver "$10 billion in exports, a $1,000 per capita GNP, and a
'my-car' age" by the end of the decade (which he almost achieved just
before he was assassinated in 1979). Simultaneously, he announced a
new ambitious plan to promote heavy and chemical industrialization
(HCI). To carry out this industrial upgrading plan, the government selected
six strategic industries (steel, electronics, petrochemicals, shipbuilding,
machinery, and nonferrous metals) and channeled the bulk of heavily sub-
sidized policy loans to them. After some initial years of structural problems, the HCI industries began to perform well in the mid-1970s, largely
thanks to a favorable turn in the world economy after the first oil crisis
in 1973. South Korean firms benefited tremendously from the Middle
East boom, obtaining huge construction projects and easy access to loans
on favorable terms. The South Korean economy also profited greatly
from participation in the Vietnam War. In addition to a huge number of
remittances sent home each year by Korean soldiers serving in Vietnam,
Korean businessmen received many profitable contracts from the United
States, while enjoying preferential treatment for their exports to the U.S
market.

Between 1971 and 1980, the South Korean economy achieved a growth
rate of 7.8 percent per annum, and the manufacturing sector grew at an annual rate of 14.8 percent. The GNP per capita jumped from $289 in 1971 to
$1,592 in 1980 (Economic Planning Board 1990). With this rapid economic
growth, Korean business organizations also grew remarkably in scale, especially among *chaebol* (family-owned conglomerate) firms. By actively
participating in the HCI industries, by exercising their monopolistic rights
in exports and imports through their ownership of General Trading Companies, and by engaging in land speculation and other commercial investment, *chaebol* groups were able to accumulate enormous capital during
the second half of the 1970s. *Chaebol* firms had consolidated their dominant position in the South Korean economy by the late 1970s. Capital con-

centration among *chaebol* groups developed to the extent that in 1980 the largest thirty *chaebol* groups accounted for 36 percent of the total shipment of goods and 22.4 percent of employment in the nation (Lee Kyu-uck and Lee Sung-soon 1985, 97).

To understand the dominant character of capital accumulation and its impact on labor conditions in South Korea throughout the period of rapid industrialization, we must consider two crucial mechanisms of capital accumulation, both of which were controlled by the state. The first is the allocation of financial loans, from both domestic and international sources. As acknowledged by many students of South Korean development, credit allocation was the most important tool with which the government controlled business (Amsden 1989; Soon Cho 1994; Jones and Sakong 1980; Eun Mee Kim 1997; Byung-Nak Song 1990; Woo 1991). Throughout the period of the Park regime, domestic interest rates were far below market prices, often even negative after adjustment for inflation. Foreign loans tended to be even lower. Thus, obtaining domestic bank loans or foreign credits itself constituted a major source of profits. The second mechanism is the allocation of investment licenses, especially licenses to invest in state-selected priority projects (Kim Seok Ki 1987).

These two mechanisms were intimately related: those who obtained major investment licenses received cheap loans through government-controlled banks, whereas those who were in a position to obtain large loans were in an excellent position to obtain new profitable licenses. In the second half of the 1970s, more than half of all domestic loans were distributed as "policy loans" at preferential rates to those who were selected by the state to participate in the priority projects of the HCI plan. At the nexus of the two lies the most critical ingredient of Korean capital accumulation, access to state power. Unlike the previous Rhee regime, the Park regime stressed economic performance as a major criterion for the allocation of both loans and investment opportunities (Jones and Sakong 1980; Amsden 1989), but there is no question that it was political connection, not just economic capability, that determined who participated in profitable projects doled out by the government.

These state policies encouraged a double-edged strategy of accumulation among Korean capitalists—on the one side, in productive investments in manufacturing industries and, on the other, in speculative investments, especially in land ownership (Kim Seok Ki 1987; Jung Hee-Nam 1993; Han Do-Hyun 1993). Rent seeking in South Korea was extensive, especially in land speculation and private money-lending businesses, and it is a well-known secret among South Korean experts that large capital was most active in these areas. Land speculation by large businesses was serious enough that Park and his successors were forced to set limits on land ownership by *chaebol* groups and on occasion even to compel them to sell off lands they had purchased, but always in vain (Jung Hee-Nam 1993). This investment climate created very poor financial structures for most enterprises. Korean firms were heavily indebted, and *chaebol* firms were the most heavily indebted. An overriding business strategy among Korean firms throughout the 1970s and 1980s was to move quickly into profitable business ventures in a rapidly changing economy geared to export markets, and the state's industrial policies encouraged such a strategy.

This South Korean pattern of capital accumulation had a significant effect in shaping industrial relations in Korean manufacturing industries. Because the major focus of business owners was to discover new profitable niches in the market and move into them faster than their rivals by mobilizing external funds, they had a minimal interest in developing a stable and committed workforce or in cultivating workers' skills and productivity by offering higher wages or other incentive mechanisms. While they tried to maximize profits by exploiting cheap labor, Korean capitalists made minimum investments in developing company welfare until the late 1980s. Nor did they invest much in training of their workforce. Instead, the state took primary responsibility for providing training and upgrading skills for the entire labor force through state-run technical and vocational schools (Song Ho Keun 1991; You Jong-Il 1995).

Part of the reason that Korean industrialists could ignore manpower development was a relatively abundant supply of labor, which lasted well into the early 1980s. Although the well-known South Korean labor economist Bai Moo Ki (1982) argued that the unlimited supply of labor in Korea had ended by the mid-1970s, there is no sign that large firms experienced problems recruiting or maintaining their workforce up to the mid-1980s. A severe shortage in the supply of skilled workers did occur in the late 1970s, forcing many large firms to compete with one another in scouting skilled and technical workers from other firms, but as far as semi-skilled workers were concerned, a relatively large pool of untapped labor existed in the countryside and in the reserve army of female labor until the late 1970s. The ethnographic data I examined for this study indicate that a major concern for many workers employed in the textile and electronic industries, well into the early 1980s, was still job security; managers often threatened to fire workers who were involved in labor activism. Other sociologists who investigated labor-market conditions in the 1970s and 1980s also disagree with Bai's analysis and argue that the real labor shortage did not occur until the mid-1980s (Song Ho Keun 1991; Shin Kwang-Yeong 1999, 46).

In any event, while the state's developmental strategy and the conditions of the labor market in South Korea greatly facilitated rapid industrial expansion, these same conditions acted as serious obstacles to developing an advanced industrial-relations system and to improving working conditions for the majority of wage workers. In a sense, the Park era was a capitalist's heaven; not only was the international market condition favorable, but the developmental state was completely pro-capital. The state did practically everything for the capitalists as long as they carried out the state's development plans successfully. In short, the combination of the expansionist accumulation strategy dictated by the state's industrial policy and the state's strong pro-capital and anti-labor policies led to deepening problems in industrial relations and to the accumulation of resentment and anger among the helpless workers.

Proletarianization of the Labor Force

Rapid industrialization in South Korea brought about a radical change in the structure of its economy and in the ways people worked and made a living. At the end of the 1950s, before embarking on the EOI strategy, South Korea was predominantly an agrarian society, with an absolute majority of its population residing in rural areas and about half of its gross domestic product (GDP) derived from agricultural production. With the progress of EOI, agriculture declined precipitously in its share of the GDP, from 39.9 percent in 1960 to 14.6 percent in 1980 to 9.0 percent in 1990. Concomitantly, the share of manufacturing increased sharply from 18.6 percent in 1960 to 41.4 percent in 1980 to 44.7 percent in 1990, while the tertiary (service) sector grew at a moderate rate from 41.5 percent to 46.3 percent between 1960 and 1990 (see table 2.1).

This structural change in the Korean economy entailed a large-scale sectoral shift of labor. As shown in chart 1, four-fifths of the total Korean labor force in the late 1950s was composed of agricultural workers, most of

Table 2.1 Structure of Production (percentage distribution of GDP in current prices), 1960–1990

Sector	1960	1970	1980	1990
Agriculture	39.9	31.1	14.6	9.0
Industry	18.6	28.4	41.4	44.7
Mining	2.3	1.3	1.4	0.5
Manufacturing	12.1	19.1	29.6	28.9
Construction	3.5	6.4	8.2	13.2
Utilities	0.7	1.6	2.1	2.1
Services	41.5	40.5	44.0	46.3
Total (GDP)	100.0	100.0	100.0	100.0

Note: Sector classification is based on the World Bank method suggested in World Bank, *World Development Report*, 1995.

Sources: Bank of Korea, *Economic Statistics Yearbook*, 1978, 1995; *National Accounts*, 1994.

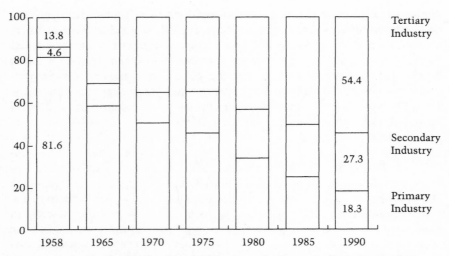

Source: Economic Planning Board, *Annual Report on the Economically Active Population*, 1972, 1985.

Chart 1. Sectoral Distribution of the Labor Force by Industry, 1958–1990 (percent)

whom were small owner-cultivators. By 1970 the agricultural labor force was reduced to one-half of the total labor force, and by the late 1980s only one out of five working people remained on a farm. Thus, after only three decades of industrial transformation, a nation of small cultivators became a nation of urban wage workers. The magnitude of industrial transformation that South Korea underwent in three decades of export-oriented industrialization is equivalent to a century of early European industrialization.[2]

This large-scale sectoral mobility from agriculture to secondary and tertiary industries necessarily involved a swift process of proletarianization of the Korean labor force (Koo 1990). Each year, thousands and thousands of farmers or their sons and daughters left rural areas and joined the proletarianized labor force in urban areas. The pace of proletarianization in South Korea was remarkable. At the inception of EOI in the early 1960s, there were a little more than two million wage workers in Korea, but by the mid-

2. Between 1841 and 1961, Great Britain's agricultural labor force declined from 26 percent to 7 percent, while the secondary-sector labor force increased only moderately from 41 percent to 44 percent. In France between 1840 and 1962, the agricultural labor force declined from 53 percent to 22 percent, while the secondary-sector labor force increased from 25 percent to 37 percent. In Germany, which experienced late industrialization at a faster pace than Great Britain, the primary sector declined from 50 percent to 16 percent between 1882 and 1961, while the secondary sector increased from 32 percent to 45 percent (see Bairoch et al. 1968).

1980s, the number had quadrupled to eight million; wage earners constituted 31.5 percent of the total labor force in 1963 but increased to 54.2 percent in 1985. In cities, two out of three working people were wage earners
in the mid-1980s. The growth rate of wage workers was much faster in the
manufacturing industry, where their numbers increased more than seven-
fold, from 417,000 to 3.1 million during the two-decade period from 1963
to 1985. Wage workers employed in the commercial and service sectors
more than tripled from 1.3 million to 4.5 million, while agricultural wage
laborers decreased from 725,000 to 437,000 (table 2.2).

The EOI strategy of industrialization in South Korea and elsewhere relied heavily on the female labor force. The female labor force in South Korea increased significantly, both in absolute and relative numbers, both in
the farm and nonfarm sectors. Between 1965 and 1980, the female-labor-
force participation rate increased from 30.9 percent to 36.1 percent in
nonfarm sector, and from 41 percent to 53 percent in farm sector. Female
workers' participation in industrial wage work increased dramatically during this same period. In fact, the rate of proletarianization among women
was even faster than among men. The number of women employed in the
manufacturing sector increased 7.4 times, from 182,000 in 1963 to
1,353,000 in 1985, while the number of men increased five times, from
428,000 to 2,147,000. The growth in the number of women workers was
most noticeable during the early period of EOI up to the mid-1970s, but began to taper off thereafter. In 1963, there were only 182,000 female workers in the manufacturing sector, but the number increased more than seven
times to 1.4 million in 1985. In comparison, the number of male manufacturing workers increased less than five times, from 428,000 to 2.1 million
during the same period (Economic Planning Board 1974, 1984). The number of female workers, which was 41 percent of all production workers in

Table 2.2 Growth of Wage Workers in Industrial Sector (in thousands)

	1963	1970	1975	1980	1985	Rate of Change 1985/1963
Agriculture	725	743	677	551	437	0.6
	(30.0)	(19.6)	(14.1)	(8.5)	(5.4)	
Manufacturing	417	995	1,782	2,475	3,146	7.5
	(17.3)	(26.3)	(37.1)	(38.2)	(38.9)	
Service &	1,272	2,049	2,344	3,459	4,507	3.5
Commerce	(52.7)	(54.1)	(48.8)	(53.3)	(55.7)	
Total	2,414	3,787	4,803	6,485	8,090	3.4
	(100)	(100)	(100)	(100)	(100)	

Note: Numbers in parentheses indicate percentage of labor force.
Source: National Statistical Office, Annual Report on the Economically Active Population,
1972, 1985.

Table 2.3 Proportion of Women Workers among Wage Employees, 1963–1985 (percent)

	1963	1973	1976	1978	1985
Of all the employed	37.9	46.7	48.5	45.5	42.0
Of production workers	41.0	50.7	53.0	49.6	46.3

Source: Suh Kwan-mo (1987, 105) (original source: Economic Planning Board, *Mining and Manufacturing Census Report*, each year).

1963, increased to 53 percent in 1976 and then declined to 46 percent in 1985 (see table 2.3).

Women workers were concentrated in a few light manufacturing industries. They constituted a large majority in industries such as the textile, garment, and electronics industries, and a small minority in heavy industries such as metal, tool making, and transportation equipment. In 1985, for example, women workers constituted 88 percent of garment workers, 77 percent of textile workers, and 68 percent of electronics workers (Suh Kwan-mo 1987, 171).

An absolute majority of female factory workers were single, semi-skilled workers in their late teens and early twenties. In 1966, almost 90 percent of female factory workers were under twenty-nine, and one-half were under twenty. In the 1980s, the number of teenage workers declined noticeably, but still two-thirds of women workers were under twenty-nine. Several factors discouraged women from remaining in factory employment after marriage. First, the intensity and long hours of work, plus overtime, made it extremely difficult for married women to work in a factory environment. A second, more important factor was the employers' discriminatory actions against married women. Because the typical factory work done by women required relatively simple skills and a high level of labor discipline, employers generally preferred to substitute fresh, young, malleable workers for older workers, with a substantial savings in wage bills.

Thus, female factory workers constituted a highly homogeneous group, characterized by their predominantly farm background, young age, single status, low educational attainment, and usually heavy burden of supporting their poor families. They were also highly homogeneous in terms of skills and the type of work they did. Furthermore, they were highly concentrated in a few light manufacturing industries and geographic locations. This demographic homogeneity and spatial concentration contributed greatly to Korean women workers' active involvement in the labor movement, as we see in later chapters.

A large proportion of both manufacturing activities and production workers were located in large-scale firms employing mass production technology. In 1985, almost two-thirds of Korean factory workers were employed in firms employing 100 or more workers, as compared with only one-third in 1959 (see table 2.4). Concomitantly, the percentage of workers in factories hiring fewer than 20 workers declined from 33 percent to 10 percent between 1959 and 1985. The growth of large factories continued throughout the 1960s and 1970s, although this trend began to slow down in the 1980s due to the decline of large firms in the textile, garment, and leather goods industries as well as to the increase in subcontracting firms linked to conglomerate corporations.

Capital concentration in South Korea created a dual structure in the Korean industrial organization. The core of the Korean economy was represented by some thirty *chaebol* groups. Since the mid-1970s, capital concentration in these *chaebol* groups occurred at a remarkable speed, so that by 1985 the top ten *chaebol* groups accounted for 30.2 percent of the nation's total sales and for 11.7 percent of total employment, and the top thirty *chaebol* groups accounted for 40.2 percent of total sales and 17.6 percent of total employment (table 2.5).

Now let us look at the changes in sectoral and demographic compositions of the Korean proletariat. First, notice that a significant change oc-

Table 2.4 Percentage Distribution of South Korean Factories and Factory Workers by Firm Size, 1959–1985

Firm Size	Factories				Factory Workers			
	1959	1968	1978	1985	1959	1968	1978	1985
5–19 workers	78.7	77.9	57.9	58.0	32.7	22.0	7.5	10.3
20–99 workers	18.8	17.7	29.6	32.7	34.1	22.2	18.4	25.5
100–499 workers	2.3	3.7	10.3	7.9	21.3	24.5	30.1	28.0
≥500 workers	0.2	0.8	2.2	1.4	11.9	31.3	43.9	36.3
Total	100.0	100.0	100.0	100.0	100.0	100.0	100.0	100.0

Source: Kim Hyung-ki (1988, 143) (original source: Economic Planning Board, *Mining and Manufacturing Census Report*, each year).

Table 2.5 Change in Business Groups' Share in Manufacturing Sales and Employment, 1977–1994

Chaebol Business Groups	Sales				Employment			
	1977	1980	1985	1994	1977	1980	1985	1994
Top 5	15.7	16.9	23.0	27.2	9.1	9.1	9.7	8.1
Top 10	21.2	23.8	30.2	34.1	12.5	12.8	11.7	10.3
Top 20	29.3	31.4	36.4	38.8	17.4	17.9	15.5	11.9
Top 30	34.1	36.0	40.2	41.5	20.5	22.4	17.6	12.8

Sources: Data for 1977 and 1980 from Lee Kyu-uk and Lee Sung-soon (1985). Data for 1985 from the Korea Development Institute. Data for 1994 from the Korea Economic Research Institute.

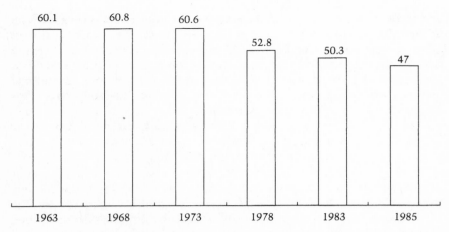

Source: Economic Planning Board, *Annual Report on the Economically Active Population*, 1972, 1985.

Chart 2. Sectoral Distribution of Manufacturing Workers in Light Industries, 1963–1985 (percent)

curred in the sectoral composition of the Korean industrial wage workers. As previously noted, the South Korean economy made a sectoral transition from labor-intensive light manufacturing to the heavy and chemical industries in the mid-1970s. This change was accompanied by a corresponding compositional change in the manufacturing labor force. Chart 2 demonstrates this sectoral change in the manufacturing labor force. The proportion of the manufacturing workforce employed in light manufacturing remained at approximately 60 percent from the mid-1960s through the mid-1970s, but declined to 47 percent by the mid-1980s. Concomitantly, those employed in the heavy and chemical industries increased from 39 percent in 1973 to 53 percent in 1985. In particular, the workforce engaged in machinery, fabricated metal, and other related industries doubled during this period from 20 percent to 31 percent. This sectoral change was accompanied by a relative decrease of female workers in manufacturing because the majority of the labor force engaged in heavy and chemical industries was male.

Another important change associated with industrial expansion in South Korea was a continuous upgrading of the educational levels of Korean industrial workers. The educational level of the Korean labor force has always been high by international standards.[3] In 1974, approximately

3. In 1982, 89 percent of school-age Koreans were enrolled in secondary schools. Comparable statistics for other countries are as follows: 32 percent for Brazil, 54 percent for Mexico, 59 percent for Argentina, 29 percent for Thailand, 64 percent for the Philippines, 92 percent for Japan, and 97 percent for the United States (see World Bank 1985).

47 percent of production workers had received a secondary education. The educational level among Korean workers continued to increase, so that in 1984 69 percent had received secondary education (Economic Planning Board 1974, 1984). Workers employed in the heavy industries, especially at large conglomerate firms, had a substantially higher level of educational attainment. In the machinery industry, for example, those who had completed high school constituted 59 percent of the semi-skilled workers and 90 percent of the skilled workers in 1984 (Kim Hyung-ki 1988, 355).

Changes in the Agricultural Sector

As in other societies, the early stage of industrialization in South Korea drew its labor force predominantly from surplus labor in rural areas. The pull of urban industries combined with the push of rural poverty triggered large-scale labor migration from rural to urban areas throughout the period of rapid industrial growth in South Korea. According to one estimate, approximately 5.1 million people migrated to cities from rural areas between 1966 and 1975, and another 5.9 million between 1975 and 1984 (Lee Young-ki 1988).[4] Altogether, some 11 million people left farms for the cities during the first two decades of export-oriented industrialization, an annual outflow rate of 4.7 percent from rural areas.

As a consequence, the number of farming households decreased precipitously, as shown in table 2.6. Between 1967 and 1987, the total number of households decreased by 28 percent, from 2,587,000 to 1,871,000. The reduction in farm population might actually be even larger than these household data indicate because a large proportion of rural migrants were individuals whose families remained in rural areas. During the ten-year period from 1975 and 1985, for example, the farm population declined by 36 percent, while the number of farm households decreased by only 19 percent (Lee Young-ki 1988). During this period, the average size of farm household was reduced from 5.6 to 4.4 people.

The majority of individual migrants were young people, and two-thirds of the rural migrants were under the age of 30. Consequently, the agricultural labor force became aged noticeably over time; the proportion of agricultural workers age 50 and over was 18 percent in 1965 but increased to 40 percent by 1985 (Chang Sang-hwan 1988). Therefore, by the mid-1980s many South Korean farming households were composed of one or two elderly people whose children lived and worked in the city and occasionally visited them. In the late 1980s, it became rare to see children in most rural villages, except on national holidays when city children accompanied their

4. Another study presents a slightly lower estimate of the size of off-farm migration (Chang Sang-hwan 1988, 152).

Table 2.6 Decline in Farm Households and Farm Population, 1966–1990

	Farm Households (1,000s)	Percentage of Total Households	Farm Population (1,000s)	Percentage of Total Population
1966	2,540	48.9	15,781	53.6
1970	2,483	42.4	14,422	44.7
1975	2,379	35.8	13,244	37.5
1980	2,155	27.0	10,827	28.4
1985	1,926	20.1	8,521	20.9
1990	1,745	15.4	6,459	15.1

Source: National Statistical Office, *Major Statistics of Korean Economy*, 1985, 1991.

parents to visit their grandparents. One by one, elementary schools in rural areas closed or continued with only a handful of pupils.

As the burden of farming increasingly fell on the elderly, women's agricultural work increased significantly. Although labor statistics are somewhat dubious when it comes to agricultural work, especially in accounting for women's work, they show that the female-labor-force participation rate in agriculture increased from 38 percent to 45 percent between 1965 and 1985 (Chang Sang-hwan 1988). Thus, the evidence is clear that South Korean economic development depended heavily on female labor—not only to meet the huge demand for industrial labor in urban areas but also to carry out farming in labor-depleted rural areas.

The crucial mechanism of this large-scale, rural-to-urban migration was the government's agricultural policy. The direction of this policy changed over time. Park Chung Hee, the son of a farmer, held a strong pro-agriculture orientation in his early years and implemented several bold measures to improve the conditions of farmers, such as reducing farmers' debts and stabilizing farm prices (Park Jin-do 1988). Also, in the 1970s, the Park government implemented the *Saemaul* (New Village) Movement to improve the infrastructural and environmental conditions of rural areas and to promote agricultural productivity through "diligence, self-reliance, and cooperation." The basic thrust of the Park government's agricultural policies, however, was maintaining low grain prices in order to feed urban wage workers relatively cheaply. Except for a few years in the early 1970s, farmers were forced to sell their grain at prices substantially below market prices—at approximately 85 percent of market prices throughout the 1960s and 1970s (Chung Young-Il 1984).

Statistics on the economic conditions in the South Korean agricultural sector demonstrates that there was a continuously deteriorating situation for Korean farmers during the process of industrialization. Since the mid-1970s, farming families increasingly found themselves in debt, partly due to rising production costs (purchasing fertilizers, machinery, and the like) and partly due to increasing costs for consumer goods and children's edu-

Table 2.7 Extent of Agricultural Income Covering Household Living Expenditures by Amount of Cultivated Land, 1965–1985

	<0.5 Hectare	0.5–1.0 Hectares	1.0–1.5 Hectares	1.5–2.0 Hectares	>2.0 Hectares	Average
1965	58.6	83.8	96.8	103.3	112.5	88.4
1974	78.4	114.8	135.4	159.1	159.3	124.4
1977	50.1	95.5	120.8	134.0	149.0	106.1
1981	41.9	84.7	105.7	114.8	130.7	92.5
1985	35.6	59.8	82.9	103.1	115.2	78.9

Source: Ministry of Agriculture and Fishery, *Nongka Kyŏngje chosa kyŏlkwa poko* [Survey Report on the Agricultural Household Economics], each year.

cation.[5] The extent to which agricultural incomes covered household expenses continuously declined since the early 1970s, as shown in table 2.7. In 1974, agricultural income for average farm household met 124 percent of family expenses, but in 1981 it declined to 93 percent and then in 1985 to 79 percent. Among rural households cultivating less than 1 hectare of land, the agricultural income met less than one-half of the households' living expenses and production costs in the 1980s; only households cultivating 2 hectares or more earned enough income from agriculture for self-sufficiency.

One important reason for the lagging income of South Korean farm households was the lack of nonagricultural income opportunities in rural areas—Korean industries were almost exclusively located in urban areas. In 1970, approximately one-quarter of farm household income was drawn from nonagricultural sources (Chung Young-il 1984, 63). Nonagricultural income increased to one-third of total farm household income in 1983, but a large proportion of the nonfarm income (approximately one-half in 1983) was transfer income, mostly remittances from family members who had migrated to the city. Nonagricultural employment provided only a tiny proportion of total farm household income in the 1980s (14 percent in 1983). Thus, it is obvious that the rural industrialization that successive South Korean governments identified as a major policy goal remained largely on paper and did little to improve the economic conditions of rural households.

Spatial Concentration of Industrial Workers

The continuing decline of agriculture and the absence of nonfarm income opportunities in rural areas determined the nature of off-farm labor migration. Young people who migrated to the city were highly unlikely to

5. Between 1975 and 1986, agricultural income increased 6.3 times, while agricultural production costs increased 11 times. See Lee Young-ki (1988, 197).

return to their rural hometowns after a short period of urban employment, a rather common pattern in other developing countries. Nor did they receive much economic support from their parents in rural areas. Whether they liked it or not, when young people left their rural villages, it was most likely a permanent migration to the city with no intention or the likelihood of return.

Therefore, Korean factory workers in the city, be they from rural or urban areas, represented a fully committed industrial workforce. Few of them may be characterized as "semi-proletariat" or "part-time proletariat," as frequently found in developing countries and referring to those only partially committed to factory employment, maintaining close ties with their rural households (Wallerstein 1983; Gates 1979; Shieh 1992; Sen and Koo 1992).

In this regard, the South Korean pattern of proletarianization diverges significantly from that of Taiwan, where geographically decentralized industrialization created greater opportunities for rural nonfarm sources of income and thereby produced a relatively large part-time proletariat. Furthermore, Taiwan's highly decentralized industrial structure, embracing a plethora of small familistic enterprises, made it relatively easy for workers to move from wage employment to self-employment, thereby weakening workers' commitment to proletarian work.

Also, in South Korea geographical origin of migrant workers did not produce significant internal division within the urban proletariat. Unlike in China, for example, native-place identity or the "politics of place" was largely insignificant in Korean labor activism (Perry 1993).

The geographic concentration of South Korean manufacturing industries is quite remarkable. Industrial development missed not only rural areas but also most of the smaller cities; and it bypassed some regions entirely, such as the southwestern (Cholla) and northeastern (Kangwon) regions. The majority of manufacturing industries were located in large urban areas around the major axis connecting Seoul and Pusan (see map). In 1984, approximately one-half of all manufacturing workers were found in the Seoul-Kyungin area (Seoul, Inchon, and the surrounding areas in Kyungki province), and another 40 percent were in the Yŏngnam (southeastern) region, which includes two major cities, Pusan and Taegu. The development of heavy industry in the 1970s created several new industrial cities, such as Ulsan, Masan, Changwon, Kumi, and Okpo, all of which are in the Yŏngnam region. In these and other areas, factories were mostly concentrated in a few areas, designated industrial estates or industrial parks. In the Seoul-Kyungin area, for example, there were twelve industrial parks, employing 192,000 workers, in the mid-1980s (Choi Chang-woo 1987).

Kuro industrial park in Seoul is a prime example of industrial concentration. This is a relatively small area located in the southwestern part of

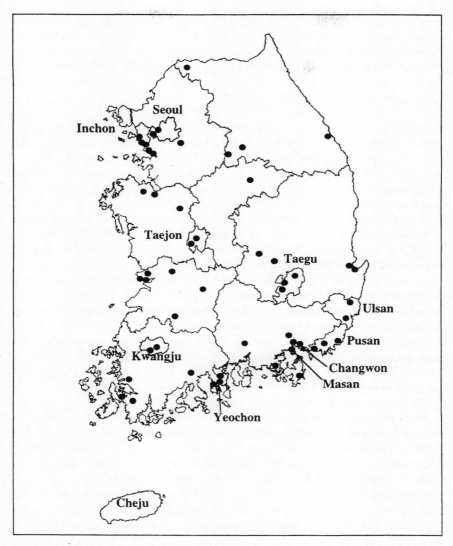

Map 1. Industrial Estates in South Korea (1980s)

metropolitan Seoul. It was developed as one of the major industrial centers in the early 1970s. In 1984, about seventy thousand workers, or one-third of Seoul's manufacturing workers, were employed in some 216 factories, all located in close proximity. Naturally, such a dense concentration of factories facilitated workers' interfirm job mobility and social contacts with fellow workers in neighboring factories. The majority of workers lived in tiny rooming houses in the surrounding areas, whereas others lived in dormitories in factory compounds. It was the close social networks that developed among workers employed in the Kuro industrial area that played a critical role in forging the solidarity struggles that began in the early 1980s.

Conclusion

South Korea's rapid economic growth based on the export-oriented industrialization strategy owes a great deal to two aspects of labor situation. The first was the abundant supply of high-quality labor, and the second was the weakness of organized labor. Both historical and geopolitical events played important roles in providing these conditions. Korean labor had been mobilized during and immediately following Japanese colonial rule, and it was stronger and more politically oriented in the second half of the 1940s than it was in the 1960s and the 1970s. But the destruction of this strong leftist labor movement paved the way for the labor-exclusive development trajectory in the subsequent period.

In the course of export-oriented industrialization, the state played a dominant role in controlling labor, both at the political level and at the workshop level. Capitalists depended on the state for both labor control and manpower training and made little effort to develop a mature system of industrial relations. Although the South Korean system of labor control during the industrialization era may be regarded as a form of state corporatism, in actual practice it departed from the pattern found in Europe and Latin America and instead relied heavily on a security-oriented, repressive, and anti-organizational approach to unionism.

The state's developmental strategy also shaped the pattern of industrial development and the spatial and organizational pattern of the Korean industries. There are several important features of the Korean industrial transformation that had great implications for the working-class movement in South Korea. The first is the swiftness of the industrial transformation. The speed and intensity of South Korea's industrialization was truly remarkable, involving migration from rural to urban areas on a massive scale and turning millions of sons and daughters of farmers into industrial wage workers.

The second is the predominantly urban nature of South Korean industrialization at the expense of rural sectors. This urban-biased pattern of industrialization accelerated the flow of labor from rural to urban areas and made it a permanent migration with the workers having little intention or likelihood of returning to rural areas. The newly emerged industrial proletariat thus represented a fully committed industrial labor force, composed of people who were more or less destined to live the rest of their working lives in industrial wage employment.

The third feature is the highly concentrated pattern of South Korean industrialization within the urban areas. Korean manufacturing activities
were concentrated in a few major industrial cities and, within them, in a
few densely populated industrial parks or estates. At the same time, the
majority of Korean industrial workers were hired by large firms rather than
small family-run enterprises. This geographically and organizationally
concentrated pattern of proletarianization facilitated the development of
working-class communities and close interfirm social networks among
workers. It also made the development of working-class identity and solidarity among industrial workers easier.

Finally, the Korean working class that emerged from this full-scale
proletarianization was characterized by a high degree of homogeneity, in
terms of demographic character, social background, and skill level. This
was particularly the case among workers employed in the labor-intensive,
light manufacturing industries. A majority of these workers were young
women from poor farming families. Male workers were also predominantly young and from rural backgrounds. The Fordist form of mass factory production in Korean export industries also required semi-skilled
workers with similar levels of education and training. The homogeneity
of the Korean industrial labor force continued until the mid-1980s, when
industrial upgrading of the Korean economy produced increasing internal
differentiation in the labor force.

These features of South Korean industrial development provided structural conditions highly conducive to the formation of a working class as a
cohesive class. Although class formation is certainly not a simple product
of structural conditions, the relatively rapid development of collective
identity and class consciousness among Korean workers is attributable, to
a large extent, to this accelerated and highly concentrated pattern of industrial transformation, that began in the 1960s.

3 Work and Authority in Korean Industry

> Boss, please, our work is too hard. It's too cold in our
> workplace. The machine is running too fast and I'm afraid
> of getting hurt. Please treat us like human beings rather
> than always trying to watch over us. Our rice gets cold and
> stuck. I'd like to have some sleep. I'd like to rest on
> Sunday. I'd like to attend church regularly. I'd like to read
> books. It's too dusty. Dark murky blood comes out of my
> throat. My arms ache so painfully as if they are being cut
> off from my body. The smell of poisonous gas gives me a
> headache. My feet are swollen. I cannot endure it
> anymore. I'd like to rest. I'd like to rest.
>
> (Kim Kyŏng-sook et al. 1986, 183–84)

Easy Adaptation

The transition from a preindustrial to an industrial work setting requires more than a change of worksite. As Thompson writes, it "entails a severe restructuring of working habits—new disciplines, new incentives, and a new human nature upon which these incentives could bite effectively" (1967, 57; see also Bendix 1956). Although early industrialists in Europe and America, as well as in Japan, had great difficulty inculcating their first generation of factory workers with new working habits, Korean industrialists in the post-war era experienced very few problems. (For excellent studies of adaptation problems among the first generation of American and Japanese factory workers, see Gutman 1977; Gordon 1985; Tsurumi 1990.) By the late 1950s, a significant proportion of the Korean population had

had some exposure to or direct experience with urban wage employment. Also, the high level of geographical mobility and social dislocation that occurred during and after the Korean War drastically altered the social orientation of the Korean population. Thus, although the South Korean labor force had been predominantly agrarian as late as the 1950s, the workers were far from a simple preindustrial labor force steeped deeply in traditional culture. They were instead a highly adaptive and mobility-oriented labor force with substantial exposure to urban lifestyles.

In addition, two modern institutions played an important role in preparing South Korea's modern industrial labor force. The first was the educational system. Thanks to the Confucian cultural legacy, with its great emphasis on education, and a substantial public investment in education during Syngman Rhee's rule, the general educational level of the South Korean population was high by international standards. Thus, by the early 1960s, practically every new recruit to Korean manufacturing industry had received a primary school education or higher. Undoubtedly, the modern Western educational system is the most powerful and effective agency for preparing industrial workers, where workers acquire the essential behavioral orientation for work in a bureaucratic setting, including subjection to formal authority, time orientation, regimented work schedule, and constant evaluation.

A second important institution was the military, in which every Korean man is required to serve by law. For many men raised in rural areas, military service provided the first sustained contact with modern lifestyles. Three years of military experience effectively socialize men into a highly regimented organizational life. Timed work routines, subjection to formal authority, punishments for failing to comply with the orders of superiors, and severely restricted personal freedom are common features of military life. Furthermore, the Korean military before the 1980s was characterized by extra doses of regimentation, authoritarianism, and violence. Thus, a long period of military service at a formative age provided Korean men with effective socialization for their later work in an equally regimented and hierarchical industrial organization.

But probably even more important than these two modern institutions in preparing the industrial labor force in Korea was the family. Family is, of course, not a modern institution. Nor is it just a traditional one. Family structure and modern work organization do not necessarily contradict each other. In fact, the authority structure and industrial relations in the factory often reflected and reproduced patriarchal family structure. In South Korea, as in many other newly industrializing societies, capitalists consciously sought to reproduce patriarchal authority relations in their enterprises and to ensure worker submission and loyalty by appealing to familial values (Salaff 1981; Kung 1983; Heyzer, 1988; Wolf 1992; Ching

Kwan Lee 1998). Patriarchal ideology played a particularly important role
in socializing women into the type of the labor force most desired in the
low-wage, labor-intensive export industries—one that was docile, submissive, diligent, persevering, and oblivious to workers' citizenship rights.
Thus, rather than being an obstacle, the traditional family system func-
tioned as a crucial mechanism through which a desirable labor force was
produced and reproduced for the export industries.

With the help of these historical and institutional conditions, Korean industrialists had no trouble recruiting a large number of young people from
rural areas and turning them into a highly productive industrial labor force.
Each year, thousands and thousands of the sons and daughters of farmers
entered the factory directly from the farm, and they adapted to the industrial world of work rather smoothly, showing no particular problems of
resistance or maladaptation to the new industrial system of work. Unlike
their counterparts in the West, Korean employers hardly ever complained
about their employees' disciplinary problems or preindustrial work habits.
Similarly, Korean workers wrote very little about the difficulty of adjust-
ing to the organizational structure of their work, although they wrote
volumes about their long hours of work and extremely poor working
conditions.[1] By and large, South Korean proletarianization was an
exceptionally smooth and peaceful process.

Long Hours and Hard Work at the Factory

If Korean workers made a smooth transition to the industrial setting,
the working life they found in the factory was still very hard and de-
humanizing. Even for those to whom hard work was nothing new, the
intensity and long hours of factory work were far more than they had
expected and too painful to endure. The working conditions were extremely poor and hazardous, and work relations were highly authoritarian
and hierarchical.

Working hours in Korean manufacturing industries were extremely long
and unregulated. According to the labor statistics compiled by the International Labour Office, South Korea had the longest workweek in the
world throughout the 1980s. In 1980, for example, the average workweek
for Korean manufacturing workers was 53.1 hours, compared with 39.7
hours for the United States, 38.8 for Japan, and 51 for Taiwan (see chart
3). Economic development in South Korea did not bring a reduction
of working hours, but actually caused a steady increase until the late
1980s. The average workweek for Korean manufacturing workers

1. Song Hyo-soon describes the first day of her factory life as follows: "I worked hard as
I was told to, because everything was novel to me. It was actually quite interesting. It
seemed that 6 o'clock, the end of the work day, came quickly as I worked diligently" (1982,
36). Other workers wrote similar stories; see Chun Chum-suk (1985, 94).

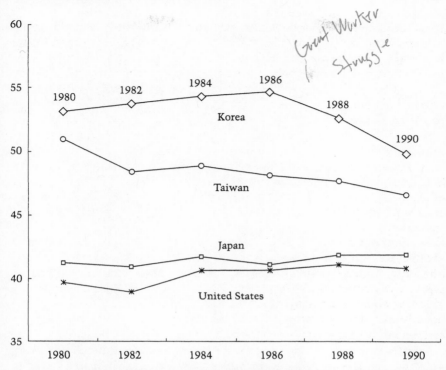

Source: Kim Hyung-ki (1988, 316) (original source: Ministry of Labor, *Maewol nodong tongkye chosa pokosŏ* [Report on Monthly Labor Statistics], each year).

Chart 3. Comparison of Working Hours per Week for Manufacturing Workers in Four Countries, 1980–1990

increased from 52.5 hours in 1970 to 53.1 hours in 1980, and to 54.5 hours in 1986. Working hours began to decrease only after the Great Worker Struggle of 1987.

Long working hours were not restricted to particular industries, but were common to all industries, although light manufacturing had slightly, but only slightly, longer hours than heavy capital-intensive industries (see Kim Hyung-ki 1988, 316). Nor were long hours prevalent only in small-scale enterprises. As the data in table 3.1 demonstrate, work hours were uniformly high across different sizes of enterprises, and if anything, large firms had a slightly longer workweek than small ones. For example, the normal work schedule for semi-skilled workers at a Hyundai automobile plant in 1983 was a 12-hour shift, Monday through Saturday, with frequent overtime on Sunday (Bae 1987, 23). There was no significant variation in the length of workweek for men and women. The average workweek in the manufacturing sector in 1978 was 53.2 hours for men and 52.7 for women, but in 1980 it was 52.8 hours for men and 53.5 for women (Korean Statistical

Table 3.1 Manufacturing Working Hours per Month, by
Size of Firms and Sex, 1977–1984

Size of Firm	Sex	1977	1980	1984
10–29	Total	230.3	225.6	226.2
	Male	226.7	222.7	226.3
	Female	237.1	231.3	225.9
30–99	Total	235.4	236.8	244.5
	Male	233.5	235.7	241.4
	Female	237.7	238.0	248.4
100–299	Total	233.7	239.4	255.2
	Male	234.3	241.0	255.5
	Female	233.2	238.2	255.0
300–499	Total	—	233.6	253.1
	Male	—	232.7	258.1
	Female	—	234.5	249.1
≥500	Total	231.9	237.9	246.8
	Male	240.0	242.8	250.4
	Female	226.7	233.9	243.5

Source: Kim Hyung-ki (1988, 316) (original source: Ministry
of Labor, *Maewol nodong tongkye chosa pokosŏ* [Report on
Monthly Labor Statistics], each year).

Association 1991, 124–25). Long work hours were the common lot of every
category of Korean worker, regardless of sex, age, industry, type of
employer, or occupational status. In fact, these labor statistics tend to
underrepresent the actual working hours among Korean factory workers,
especially among those employed in the labor-intensive sectors of the
manufacturing industries. In labor-intensive sectors, such as the garment,
textile, and food-processing industries, factory workers routinely worked
12-hour shifts in the 1970s and, on top of that, they were frequently forced
to work overtime to meet deadlines for rush deliveries.

The brutality of the labor exploitation in Korean factories is vividly described in many of workers' personal essays, written in diary form from the
late 1970s to the mid-1980s. These essays were most frequently written as
part of writing exercises at workers' night schools or as part of small-group
activities at church organizations.[2] The protest statements or petition let-

2. I make extensive use of workers' essays in this study. This could introduce some
methodological problems because these essays may not represent the level of consciousness of ordinary workers during the 1970s and early 1980s. To a certain extent, the workers who participated in night schools or in church-sponsored small-group activities might
be expected to have greater educational aspirations and to be more socially conscious than
the average worker (most probably as a consequence of participation in these activities, and
possibly even before). Therefore, their essays may reflect a somewhat higher level of class
awareness and sensitivity than those of the ordinary workers. For this reason, I try not to
use workers' essays to make generalizations about the state of class identity or conscious-

Figure 2. Female workers in a garment factory. (Provided by *JoongAng Daily*)

ters that workers wrote during this period also provide extremely useful sources of information. Recall the protest statement issued by Haitai workers regarding the dreadful working conditions in the food-producing industry, cited in chapter 1. The working hours in the export manufacturing industries were similar, if not worse. For example, here is a description of the working conditions at Kukje Sangsa,[3] a well-known export manufacturer of shoes under the brand name Prospex, in the words of its own workers:

> The working hours at Kukje Sangsa are from 7:50 am to 6:30 pm, but this is only a formal rule, and frequently, whenever we fall short of the production target, we have to come to work earlier in the morning and stay longer in the evening. We have to do overnight work two to five times a week, and during the peak season from fall to spring we have to do as many

ness in the working class as a whole. But there is little bias, I believe, in these workers' descriptions of their daily routines and work conditions and their feelings about the ways they were treated by management and by society. I use workers' writings primarily for the purpose of looking into their experiences, not to gauge the level of their class consciousness. When I cite their expressions of class feeling, my interest is in revealing the pattern of discourse rather than the extent or intensity of class antagonism.

3. Kukje Sangsa, a large employer of some 25,000 workers, was part of the Kukje conglomerate group.

as 15 overnight shifts. The managers' abusive and violent language is incredible. They gather us two to six times a week, and each time we are subjected to their severe reprimands and swearing. If we are to be absent from
work one day for illness, we are called into the office and receive a stiff
reprimand, and even corporal punishment. (*Minju nodong*[4] 1984, in Lee
Tae-ho 1986b, 125)

The main tool that Korean manufacturers used to make their factory
workers work such long hours was overtime (*chanŏp*). The base pay for regular work hours (8–10 hours) was so low in many factories that workers
were compelled to work overtime in order to increase their paychecks. In
the 1970s and through the mid-1980s, blue-collar workers in manufacturing earned approximately one-fifth of their wages from overtime (Kim
Hyung-ki 1988). Most likely, however, these statistics underestimate the
actual amount of overtime because overtime was not always accurately
calculated or properly paid. In fact, this was one of the major causes of
labor protests during the 1970s and 1980s, as illustrated in the protest by
workers at Kyŏngsŏng Textile Company, one of the oldest and largest textile and garment firms in Korea. These workers organized themselves in
1973 to demand payment for the extra hours they had been forced to work
for several years. Their letter of petition to the president of the company
states:

> For a long time, we have been forced to report to work 30 minutes before
> the regular shift and also to work an extra 30 minutes after regular work-
> ing hours. On Sunday, we start work one hour and a half to two hours ear-
> lier. On Saturday, we are supposed to work from 10 pm to 6 am, but we are
> forced to work until 7 am.
>   Despite all these extra hours we had to work beyond our regular work
> schedule, we have never been paid for that (extra work). (Han'guk ki-
> dokkyo kyohoe hyŏpŭihoe 1984, 379)

Strictly speaking, overtime was both voluntary and compulsory. From
the workers' point of view, especially for those employed in low-wage industries, overtime provided them with a means of increasing their paychecks. In many factories, workers even competed among themselves for
overtime assignments, especially during slack seasons. Needless to say,
such situations gave power to the foremen, who used overtime assignments as a tool for controlling and dividing the helpless workers. Workers
welcomed overtime when it was adequately paid and when it was within
their physical tolerance. Some workers even preferred a factory where
more opportunities for overtime were available.

---

4. *Minju nodong* was the union newsletter of the Korean Council of Labor Welfare
Organizations.

Very frequently, however, overtime was not voluntary; workers were simply expected to work overtime whenever the company needed them to do so. In the labor-intensive sectors, the boundary between the regular shift and overtime was blurred, and the assignment of and payment for overtime often depended on arbitrary decisions by the foremen. In most export-manufacturing firms, the amount of overtime was determined simply by the amount of orders from overseas buyers or from parent firms (in the cases of subcontractors), regardless of the personal wishes or physical condition of the workers. The way overtime was used in most factories is well described by one worker:

> The managers do not usually plan ahead and they act very casually in reducing or increasing (the number of) workers. They lay off workers (in a slack period) on some company pretext, but when a rush of orders comes in, they take all the orders with no consideration of how much burden it will be on the workers. In the end, the excessive orders becomes a whip to the workers. It is a natural inclination among workers who live on low wages to increase their income by working extra hours to a certain extent. However, since we are not machines, there is a limit to how much our bodies can endure. (Han'guk kidokkyo kyohoe hyŏpŭihoe 1984, 301)

A rush of orders and the greed of the employer operated as a whip rather than as an opportunity for the workers to earn more income. Overtime in many small-scale Korean factories in the 1970s and early 1980s meant not just working a couple of additional hours, but often meant working through the night, that is, working for twenty-four hours straight. As one worker reported, "when the delivery deadline approaches, we were frequently forced to do all-night work for three or four days in a row in the summer weather of 30–40 degrees, so when it was over, several of us collapsed and had to stay in bed" (Lee Mi-hyŏn 1984, reprinted in Lee Tae-ho 1986b, 94). In many small-scale factories, workers had to work continuously from Saturday morning through Sunday morning, so they had to spend all day Sunday sleeping; there was no weekly day off. In order to work such grueling schedules, it was a common practice among garment workers to take anti-sleeping pills, called "timing." One garment factory worker reported, "There is hardly anyone who does not take the [anti-sleeping] pills" (Lee and Kim 1985, 77). Workers paid for these pills out of their own pockets; sometimes they were provided by their employers. Another worker at Pangrim Textile Co., which was regarded as a model company in the 1970s, complained, "Three years ago when I entered this company, one tablet of timing was sufficient to prevent drowsiness, but now even two tablets are insufficient" (Han'guk kidokkyo kyohoe hyŏpŭihoe 1984, 552).

Problems of Reproduction

Long hours of exhausting work, frequent overnight assignments, and no
regular day off, even on Sunday, left no time for leisure or for keeping up
with families or friends. Factory work meant devoting practically one's
whole life to a wretched factory floor in exchange for less than a subsistence wage; it meant sacrificing the worker's "humanlike life" (*inkandaun
sarm*) and effectively being turned into a machine or a farm animal. Factory workers often considered themselves even worse off than machines or
cows because as they said, cows can at least sleep at night and machines
can rest during repair times.

> ... at night even cattle sleep, but we have to work through the night. As
> everybody knows, we work 10–12 hours a day, and quite frequently even
> throughout the whole night. In the morning I barely manage to lift my
> tired body and carry it to the dusty, noisy, and curse-filled factory. And
> when I return home at night I am simply too tired even to wash and eat.
> Repeating this life day after day, I cannot help telling myself, "Oh, I am
> worse than a machine." I am afraid that I may pass out one day living like
> this. (Kim kyŏng-sook et al. 1986, 154)

Devoting ten to twelve hours a day to the factory, spending extra time
commuting in a crowded bus, and often being forced to work extra night
shifts simply did not leave adequate time for anything other than minimum basic sustenance. Another worker writes:

> Of twenty-four hours a day, I must spend most of my nonsleeping hours in
> the factory, and in the remaining time, all the things I do, such as eating,
> washing socks, and even sleeping, are just a preparation for going back to
> the factory the next day. . . . Just like a pig who eats and gets fat to give his
> body to the owner, we eat to work, and we sleep to work. (Kim kyŏng-sook
> et al. 1986, 43–44)

Not only did factory employment deprive workers of leisure time, it also
did not allow adequate time for rest or for minimum self-maintenance.
The grueling work on the factory floor inflicted so much physical pain and
damage on workers' bodies that the damage never had enough time to heal.
Thus, the greatest cruelty of factory work in South Korea in the pre-1987
period was the rapid wear and tear on workers' bodies; the conditions in the
Korean factories failed to ensure even the minimum conditions for the reproduction of labor.

As notorious as its long hours of factory work was the high rate of
industrial accidents, at least in the early stages of South Korean export-

Table 3.2 Industrial Accidents Rates, 1970–1990

Year	Number of Injured People	Number of Deaths	Accident Cases	Frequency Rate*	Death Rate (per 10,000)
1970	37,752	639	35,389	15.5	8.2
1975	80,570	1,006	79,819	16.8	5.5
1980	113,375	1,273	112,111	11.1	3.4
1985	141,809	1,718	140,218	11.6	3.8
1990	132,896	2,236	126,966	6.7	3.0

* Frequency rate equals total number of accidents divided by (Yearly working hours × Total number of workers), multiplied by 10,000.
Source: The Korean Statistical Office (1991, 146).

oriented industrialization. As indicated by the data in table 3.2, Korean industrial accident rates were very high from the early period of industrialization up to the middle of the 1980s. During the period 1978–1980, for example, 126,250 accidents occurred each year involving 127,641 workers. During this period, 1,402 workers died each year from workplace accidents. These rates were comparatively very high. South Korea's industrial accident rate in 1976, for example, was five times that of the United States and England, and 15 times that of Japan (International Labour Organization, 1977, 829–30, in Han'guk yŏsung yukwonja yŏnmaeng 1980, 58). The majority of these industrial accidents resulted from forcing workers to work in unsafe conditions and not from careless work habits on the part of workers. Korean manufacturers made minimal investments in safety measures in their factories. Probably the most notorious case was the Hyundai shipyard in Ulsan. In the first three years of its operation (1972–1975), the plant had more than two thousand accidents, in which as many as eighty-three shipyard workers were killed (Donga Ilbo, May 3, 1975, in Han'guk kidokkyo kyohoe hyŏpŭihoe 1984, 443). Many of these tragedies could have been avoided had the company installed adequate safety measures.

Furthermore, the factory work itself in the labor-intensive industries had a serious long-term effect on workers' health. A large proportion of factory workers suffered from many occupational diseases caused by an intolerable degree of noise, dust, heat, and gas. One survey of work conditions conducted in 1975 by a Korea University research team found that over half (53.6 percent) of the 250 industrial projects at forty-one manufacturing plants in Ulsan violated minimum safety standards (Donga Ilbo, December 4, 1976, in Han'guk kidokkyo kyohoe hyŏpŭihoe 1984, 444). Another survey of female workers conducted in 1977 by the Federation of Korean Trade Unions (FKTU) (1978) revealed that health was their most important concern; when asked about their "current major concerns," 31 percent of the respondents mentioned health-related problems. Other concerns, in decending order, were economic problems (30.6 percent) and job security (15.1 percent). A follow-up survey in 1983 confirmed again that health problems were a major concern of Korean women workers (29.6 percent), although this time economic problems topped the list (38.2 percent) (because of the economic recession that had occurred in the previous years), while job security (19.5 percent) remained in third place.

The fact that one-third of the Korean women workers surveyed mentioned health problems as their major concern demonstrates the seriousness of the poor work conditions in South Korea, especially because the absolute majority of the respondents were ages 17 to 24. These should be ages of prime health, yet the majority of the women suffered from health problems, such as chest pains, digestion problems, hearing difficulties, loss of eyesight, frostbite, and skin problems. Whether due to such job-related illnesses or simply due to lack of rest and adequate nutrition, workers' health tended to deteriorate quickly after a few years of factory work. In a self-reflective essay, one factory old-timer writes about her feeling when she met a very young apprentice, whom her mother brought to the factory on the first day:

> I asked about her age and she said she was fifteen. It's exactly the same age when I started working. Sixteen years have gone! I feel sad when I think of what is left of me now. Her mother told me with deep concern on her face that it was because of her illness that she decided to make her daughter start to work. Will this young girl starting to work for the first time be able to stand the factory life here? I am afraid it will be too hard for her. On the other hand, since she's been reared healthily at home until now, she should have more nutrition left in her body and so she would be able to endure better than us. (*Wonpoong hoebo*, no. 18, reprinted in Kim Kyŏng-sook et al. 1986, 90–91)

In this worker's sad comment, we read the immense cruelty of South Korea's factory life in the 1960s through the 1980s. Workers brought their healthy bodies to the factory, but several years of the gruelling work in harsh and hazardous conditions quickly caused the wear and tear of their bodies. Not only were their bodies gradually worn out, they often acquired occupational diseases or fell victim to industrial accidents. By the time they left the factory, their youth had long gone, leaving behind prematurely aged bodies with many nagging diseases acquired from factory work. As workers often lamented, "when all the oil is squeezed out of our bodies, we are thrown out just like a trash." It is clear that factory conditions in the low-wage, labor-intensive sectors in the 1970s and into the 1980s simply did not provide adequate conditions for the reproduction of workers.

Job Market and Wages

Why did Korean workers work so hard under such inhumane conditions, suffering so much physical pain and damage to their health? Why did they comply with employers' unreasonable demands for long hours of overtime? Could they not refuse to work overnight or on Sunday? Logically, they could, because they were, after all, freely contracted wage workers and they could simply vote with their feet. Many did just that—the job-turnover rate in South Korean industry, especially in the light manufacturing sector, was very high (table 3.3). In 1980, for instance, the monthly job-separation rate in the Korean manufacturing sector was 5.6, compared with 1.2 in Japan, 3.4 in Taiwan, and 4.0 in the United States (Park Duk-je 1986). This means that the approximately two-thirds of the workforce in an average Korean factory was replaced each year. By and large, this high rate of job-changing in Korean industry was the product of poor wages and abusive labor practices.

However, the labor market in South Korea before the mid-1980s was not favorable to workers who wanted to improve their economic conditions by changing jobs frequently. The huge reserve of surplus labor in rural areas provided a continuous supply of new workers for the export manufacturing industries until the early part of the 1980s. There is some scholarly debate about the nature of the labor market in the first three decades of export-oriented industrialization. Some scholars argue that an unlimited supply of semi-skilled labor had ceased to exist by the mid-1970s, while others argue that South Korea did not really experience a labor shortage until the mid-1980s, except for technical and skilled workers (Bai Moo-ki 1982; Song Ho Keun 1991, 85). From the standpoint of the factory workers, however, the job market had been tight all along, from the 1960s through much of the 1980s. The writings of factory workers in the 1970s and early 1980s indicate that workers were most afraid of being fired and that the employers' favorite method of threatening workers was with dismissal. As

Table 3.3 Job Accession and Separation Rates, 1975–1993

Year	Total Nonagricultural		Manufacturing	
	Accession	Separation	Accession	Separation
1975	4.40	3.70	5.20	4.40
1980	4.40	4.80	4.90	5.60
1985	3.70	3.90	4.30	4.50
1990	2.99	3.20	3.32	3.78

Source: Korea Labor Institute 1994, *Quarterly Labor Review* 7:3 (original source: Ministry of Labor, *Maewol nodong t'ongye chosa pokosŏ* [Report on monthly labor statistics], each year).

Bando garment company workers wrote in their report in the mid-1970s, "Had the workers expressed their complaints or made demands which were up to their throats, the immediate consequence would be dismissal, which is like a death sentence to the workers. Nothing has changed in this respect. Had there been no danger of being fired, there would have occurred an explosive number of workers' demands and struggles for better working conditions" (Han'guk kidokkyo kyohoe hyŏpŭihoe 1984, 301). Arbitrary dismissal of workers was frequently used as a threat against workers who were involved in church-sponsored labor-organizing activities in the late 1970s and early 1980s. Hundreds of labor activists were fired and barred from factory employment during this period, and their reinstatement was a major focus of the grassroots labor struggles in the early 1980s.

Given a tight labor market for semi-skilled workers, employers were not forced to pay serious attention to motivating workers by improving conditions, while the helpless workers had no bargaining power to negotiate better relations with management. This power imbalance between capital and labor relates directly to the low wages of semi-skilled workers in the 1970s and 1980s. Despite the rosy picture of income distribution in South Korea painted in the economic literature—uniformly presented as a model case of equitable distribution combined with rapid growth—and despite the fact that the average rate of wage increase was indeed very fast after the 1980s, it remains an important fact that a large proportion of South Korean manufacturing workers were paid wages below subsistence levels throughout the 1970s and even into the first half of the 1980s. In 1982, for example, the average monthly expenditure of Korean urban households was 248,977 won, each household having an average of 1.3 income earners (Korean Statistical Association 1991, 90). In that year, approximately one-quarter of all manufacturing workers received 100,000 or less. Approximately 8 percent of male workers and 46 percent of female workers were in this category. One-half of all manufacturing workers earned 140,000 won or less, including 22 percent of male workers and 87 percent of female workers. According to the calculations of the FKTU, the average manufacturing wages from the 1970s through the mid-1980s met only 50–60 percent of subsistence requirements (Iltŏ ŭi sori 1985, 53).

Part of the reason for such wide discrepancies between the overall favorable picture of Korean income distribution and the large number of low-wage workers in South Korea were the wide income gaps that existed between manual and nonmanual workers, between male and female workers, and between workers of different educational levels. In 1983, for example, the average monthly incomes for manual and nonmanual workers in the manufacturing sectors were 176,905 won and 339,889 won, respectively—thus manual worker earned 52 percent of the average income of nonmanual workers (Iltŏ ŭi sori 1985, 175). Gender inequality in income was even more marked. In 1980, the average female factory worker earned

42.9 percent of her male counterpart's income (95,692 *won* vs. 222,956 *won*) (174). This ratio improved to 46.7 percent in 1985 and to 53.4 percent in 1990 (see chart 4). Undoubtedly, South Korea was one of the most sex-biased societies in the world in terms of its wage structure. No less serious were the large income gaps that existed between educational levels (chart 5). In 1980, those who received a middle school education or less earned

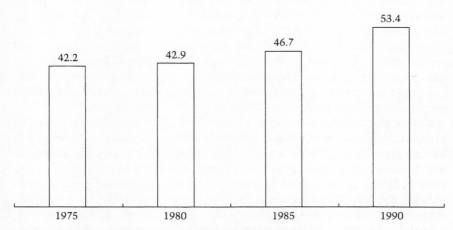

Chart 4. Women's Wages as a Percentage of Men's, 1975–1990

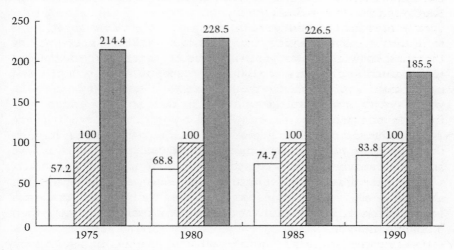

Chart 5. Income Differentials by Educational Level, 1975–1990

only 30 percent, and those who graduated from high school 44 percent, of the average income of college graduates (Korean Statistical Association 1991, 134).

Thus, notwithstanding the impressive growth in average wage rates for the Korean working population in the 1970s and 1980s, there was a sufficient basis for Korean workers to feel deeply discontent about their wages and income distribution. A large majority of below-subsistence-wage earners were women employed in the garment, textile, shoe, leather goods, and food-processing industries. But there were also many men employed in these and other low-wage industries who suffered from poverty-level wages. And it was largely the low wages and the fear of losing their jobs that kept Korean factory workers powerless in the face of abusive managerial practices and the imposition of long hours of overtime that drove workers into early physical exhaustion.

Given the unfavorable labor market and poor wages, the common strategy of Korean workers was to change jobs frequently. The job market in the 1970s and 1980s was highly fluid and dynamic, as new jobs were continuously created by rapid economic growth. The high rate of job turnover during this period indicated not only the lack of commitment to the company on the part of the workers, but also the lack of commitment to the workforce on the part of the employers. This was in turn a product of the tight labor market condition that had prevailed until the mid-1980s. It is thus clear that the long hours of hard work for which South Korean workers were perfunctorily praised did not reflect their deep commitment to work or to the company. Robert Cole (1979), in his study of the Japanese work ethic, suggests a useful distinction among three forms of work commitment: that related to the company, that related to the work itself, and that related to economic betterment. He and other researchers characterize the Japanese work ethic as related to the workers' commitment to the company, to their sense of belonging to the "community of fate" (see also Abegglen 1958; Lincoln and Kalleberg 1990). If this is so, the Korean work ethic, at least the one that has predominated in most small- and medium-scale industries, seems to have been qualitatively different from that of the Japanese. Korean workers worked as hard as, if not harder than, their Japanese counterparts, but they did so not because of their strong commitment to their employers or to their work, but primarily because of their desire to improve their economic situation.

It is important to realize, however, that it was for the sake of their families, not just for themselves, that Korean workers were willing to put up with an incredible amount of hardship and abuse at work. Family was the crucial mechanism that ensured workers' devotion to their hard work schedule as well as their submission to the authority structure in the factory. Workers' diaries and essays demonstrate that young workers brought a strong family ethic to the factory, especially the women workers. All from poor families, many of them had sick parents and younger siblings to support. Workers' essays frequently express the thick emotional bond that tied workers to their family members in rural areas. As one worker wrote, "Because overnight work is so hard and painful I hesitate to take it, but thinking of my mother and younger siblings in our rural hometown, I realize I must bear with it however hard it is to me" (Song 1982, 46). Family was also an important source of strength and perseverance in their work: "when I get sleepy I think of my father who is sick in bed, and when my body gets too tired and my hands become numb, I crunch my hands thinking of my younger bothers and sisters. (Then) my eyes begin to sparkle" (Lee Kyu-hyun, in Kim Kyŏng-sook et al. 1986, 97). Here we find the real secret of Korean workers' pattern of hard work—not necessarily a strong work ethic or a strong commitment to one's job or to the company, but a deeply ingrained ethic of self-sacrifice for the family.

Patriarchal and Despotic Authority

A 1977 survey of a nationwide sample of women factory workers conducted by the FKTU revealed an interesting finding. It confirmed that the primary motivation for factory workers to change jobs was wages: among those who changed job, 46 percent said that they left their previous jobs because the wages were too low. Other major reasons included *inhumane treatment (pi'inkanchŏk taeu)* by management (12 percent), factory closings (10 percent) and the nature of work being too hard (9 percent) (FKTU 1978, 162). While clearly motivated by economic factors, workers were just as concerned about the quality of industrial relations at their workplaces. When asked to describe their ideal workplace, the respondents stressed noneconomic factors above economic ones: 48 percent mentioned places where they would receive *humane treatment,* while 15 percent mentioned jobs that would allow them to continue their education; only 14 percent identified jobs with higher pay, and 11 percent mentioned jobs with better prospects for a future career.

The fact that Korean women workers regarded humane treatment as such an important aspect of their ideal workplaces speaks volumes about the state of industrial relations in Korean industry in the 1970s. Cries for humane treatment were not restricted to female-dominated industries or to small-scale firms. Nor was it a short-lived phenomenon in the early stages of South Korea's industrialization.

What then is meant by "humane treatment"? Of course, this means being treated like a human being, not like a machine or an animal. Being treated like a human being, in turn, means being respected as a person who requires a minimum amount of rest and leisure time. It also means being treated as a free and autonomous human being, as a self-respecting person who is entitled to a minimum degree of human dignity and respect from others. Yet the reality of Korean factory life was a constant series of violations of this basic demand to be treated as a free, self-respecting human being.

An important feature of industrial relations in Korean firms is the sharp separation of manual and nonmanual work. Although this separation exists in any society, in Korea the status distinction between physical laborers and office workers has been much sharper than in most other industrial societies, even in comparison with other East Asian societies that have the same Confucian tradition. In 1985, for example, the ratio of manual-nonmanual wages was 55.6 for Korea, 67.4 for Japan, and 64.0 for Taiwan.[5]

Such large discrimination in wages against blue-collar workers in Korea reflected deeper societal attitudes toward manual and nonmanual work. Korean cultural tradition carries a deeply contemptuous attitude toward physical labor, partly due to the use of slaves to perform many forms of nonagrarian physical labor in pre-modern Korea and partly due to the absence of a well-established craft tradition, which in other societies secured a more respectable position for the working class.[6] Throughout the first two to three decades of South Korea's export-led industrialization, factory work was widely regarded as low status, dirty, and unrespectable. In the 1970s and early 1980s, factory workers were called *kongsuni* (factory girl) or *kongdoli* (factory boy). Both labels reveal the society's contemptuous attitude, ascribing the workers the same low status associated with the servants of earlier times.

This extremely contemptuous attitude toward and demeaning status of physical labor, coupled with the logic of capitalist production, was the basis of the inhumane treatment that caused so much agony and anger to the workers. In their workplaces, factory workers were constantly subjected to shouts, name calling, reprimands, and vulgar swear words, thrown at them by their superiors. They were most frequently called "the ignorant lot" and were addressed in condescending forms of speech even by much younger technical and white-collar workers. Before entering the

5. The manual-nonmanual wage gaps were large in South Korea until the mid-1980s, but after that the gaps began to close up fast, so that in the mid-1990s the manual-nonmanual wage gaps were smaller in South Korea than in Japan and Taiwan (see Lee Kyŏng-hee 1994).

6. In late Chosun society (1392–1910), many craft workers were ex-slaves, and they were hired by the government for the production of luxury goods to be consumed by the court and the nobility (Song 1973). In contrast, Perry's study (1993) shows that artisans played a far more important role in the early labor movement in China.

factory gate, workers said that they must "deposit self respect outside" until they left the damned factory compound.

Again, the best way we can look at the dominant pattern of authority relations in Korean industry is through the many perceptive writings that Korean workers have left us. Naturally, the dominant themes of their essays are the long hours of hard work and the poor industrial relations they experienced in their daily work lives. Workers' descriptions of their daily routines vividly reveal the patriarchal power exercised by the employers and managers, and their own sense of helplessness and resentment toward the power structure.

One worker wrote about her workday in a small factory, in what was probably a typical situation in many small South Korean factories in the 1970s and the 1980s:

> Can we get off from work a little early today? I keep looking at my watch. Time passes by but there is no sign that our work will end. I guess we have to do overtime work again today. Lately we've been doing overnight work continuously for several days. Near the end of the workday, we hear our boss repeating the same words: I am making you work over night for the sake of both you and the company. So even if you may have some complaints, please work hard. You can live better in your old age by working harder when you are young. (in Kim Kyŏng-sook et al. 1986, 144)

No consent was required from the workers, and no special incentive or remuneration needed to be proffered. The employer simply assumed the right to put workers to work any time he needed them. And he expected workers to comply, regardless of their physical condition or personal situation. Like a traditional patriarch, he exercised absolute power over his subordinates and expected complete obedience and loyalty from them.

Frequently, managerial power in Korean firms, particularly in smaller ones, was more despotic than paternalistic. One woman described the authority pattern in her garment factory. The regular workday started at 8:30 in the morning and was supposed to end at 8:30 in the evening, yet workers living in the dormitory could rarely get off at 8:30 P.M. One day, one worker asked for special permission to leave at 8:30 to take care of some personal business, only to receive a cold rebuke from the employer: "Hey you, do you think you are the only one who has personal business to do? They (other workers) must all have something to do. Can you see? So go back and finish your work, and then go to do your own thing or sleep as it pleases you. You understand?" (Kim Chum-sook 1984, in Lee Tae-ho 1986b, 98).

Despotic control over workers was not restricted to their work and working hours. Ultimately, it involved control over personal space and the workers' bodies. Foucault's (1979) notion of social control clearly operated in the South Korean factory system. Factory workers, whether they worked in small workshops or in large conglomerate firms, were minutely controlled in the private domains of life, including their clothes, hair styles, interpersonal relations, or even use of the bathroom. Here is another perceptive description of a worker's quite ordinary day in the factory. Workers at her garment factory had gathered for the regular morning meeting, where the assistant manager proclaimed, "You girls won't be allowed to take telephone calls from now on. Letters, you can receive them, but only after you first open the letter and read it in front of me. You must understand why I do so. [Don't you?]" Of course, the workers understood quite well why he did that—to make them work like machines with no interruptions. When workers grumbled here and there, the assistant manager snapped, "Hey you girls, why doesn't anyone stand up and say something as a representative?" But nobody dared to stand up (Kim Chum-sook in Lee Tae-ho 1986b, 100).

This kind of despotic authority was easier to see in small enterprises employing predominantly young women workers, but the essential nature of power relations in the larger, male-dominated industrial sectors did not deviate from this pattern very much—industrial authority there was equally authoritarian, patriarchal, and despotic. Just like female workers in the garment and textile industries, male workers in the heavy and chemical industries were treated with deep contempt by high-handed authoritarian managers. In most large-scale manufacturing plants, manual workers were sharply separated from white-collar workers in space and status. They had to use a different entrance, a different section of the cafeteria, and different utensils for dining. The privilege of commuting on a company bus was restricted to white-collar workers, and machine operators were expected to address the technical and managerial staff in a deferential manner, regardless of age differences. Control over the workers' personal space and bodies was even stricter in large conglomerate firms than in smaller ones. Accumulated worker resentment against many restrictions on supposedly private matters exploded in summer 1987, when political liberalization provided workers with a rare opportunity for open revolt. When angry workers finally stood up against managerial despotism at the Hyundai conglomerate in Ulsan, one of their top demands was the abolition of the company's restriction on hair length. Similar demands were part of labor protests at Daewoo and other large-scale firms.

It is important to note that Korean industrial firms were modeled on military organizations—this pervasive influence of military organization and military culture cannot be overestimated. Of course, this is very understandable in a society where the state rulers for three decades were ex-military generals and where many top-level managers in industrial firms had been recruited from the military. Also, practically all the foremen and supervisors had received a critical portion of their adult socialization in the military during their compulsory three years of service. In developing countries, the military represents one of the most modernized and rational organizations and thus often provides a model for other social organizations. Consciously or unconsciously, therefore, Korean industrialists adopted a military organizational structure and pattern of authority, making their organizations equally regimented, authoritarian, and hierarchical.

In fact, the similarities between industrial and military organizations were so striking that researchers, regardless of nationality and which conglomerate firm was studied, easily recognize them. Kyuhan Bae, a Korean sociologist who conducted research at the Hyundai factory in Ulsan in 1983, remarks, "When I visited the factory, many things reminded me of my experiences in the military service" (1987, 37). As he describes it:

> Everyday life of employees was tied to factory work. Workers spent most of the day in the factory, wearing the gray Hyundai uniform. They were required to obey the strict regulations of the factory. For example, their hair had to be cut short. Their rank was revealed by the shape of their name tags which were pinned on the left breast pocket. They came to the factory before 8:00 A.M. accompanied by marching music blared from loud speakers. At the factory gates, guardhouses controlled the entrance and exit of workers and guests. The workers took a ten minute rest after two hours work. They had a noon lunch in the company cafeteria which was divided into sections for different ranks of employees. (37)

Roger Janelli, a U.S. ethnologist, makes the same observation ten years later in describing another conglomerate firm. Like Bae, Janelli remarks that "In many ways my military experience served as a better guide to behavior in the office than my understanding of American bureaucracies or South Korean villages and universities" (1993, 226). Based on his participant observation in this firm, he provides an excellent description of the organizational features that resemble those found in the military:

> A duty roster was kept on the bulletin board of each division showing the daily assignment of responsibility for locking up the division's office door and reopening it the next morning. Posted on bulletin boards in hallways was a sketch of the proper length for men's hair. Summer dress codes went into effect on a given date regardless of that day's weather. At the monthly meetings of Taesong's headquarters staff, just before the president spoke, everyone sat up, bowed their heads, and relaxed in unison as a voice barked out crisp commands. In saluting the flag, all were ordered in similar fashion to sit erect, place hands over hearts, and return them in unison. During a presentation of computer systems, one man held a large pointer

at right shoulder arms and stood at attention when not pointing. The company song was in 4/4 time. Sections in many divisions were referred to by number instead of function or product line (cf. 2nd squad, 3rd platoon). (225–26)

Another U.S. observer, Robert Kearney, also stresses the militaristic management style in Korean firms and finds nothing surprising in this phenomenon: "In a society where so many other aspects of life have been contingent on military considerations (or on leaders who have been, for the most part, military men), why should economics, labor relations, and corporate life stand apart?" (1991, 8). As he suggests, the pervasive influence of the military on Korean industrial organizations did not stop at the level of outward forms but penetrated more deeply to shape the dominant pattern of authority relations and organizational culture.

We must also note that although the organization of the South Korean military was modeled on that of the U.S. military, its corporate culture has been shaped by two other powerful historical factors: the legacy of the Japanese military, in which many South Korean military leaders had served during the colonial period; and the impact of the Korean War, during which the Korean military took its final shape. These two historical factors, in my view, molded the Korean military into a distinctly authoritarian, disciplinarian, and violence-prone organization, far more so than its U.S. counterpart. A routine disregard for individual constitutional rights, the imposition of unreasonable demands and harsh discipline, the expectation of unconditional obedience to orders from superiors, and constant verbal and physical punishment, all seem to be distinct features of Korean military organization. To a large extent, these same features have been replicated in many Korean firms. "Do as you are told to do," with no questions and no excuses allowed, is the dominant organizational norm that pervaded both military organizations and industrial firms.

Thus, the dominant character of industrial authority in South Korea was more despotic and personalistic than technical or bureaucratic. Rather than exercising authority on the basis of well-established rules and rational procedures, Korean managers were apt to use their power in an arbitrary personalistic manner, with the frequent exercise of verbal and physical violence.[7] This authority structure was facilitated by the fact that practically all Korean enterprises were owned and controlled by individual

7. Chakrabarty (1989) makes a similar analysis with the Indian working class, stressing the absence of bourgeois culture of equality and individualism in early twentieth century India and the ways in which the persistence of precapitalist relationships shape the pattern of labor protests and labor organizations in India. In this regard, industrial authority in late developing non-Western societies is significantly different from what emerged in the early industrializers (see Bendix 1956).

families. As the founders and the owners of the enterprises, the modern industrial patriarchs were slow to develop modern bureaucratic forms of authority relations. It is instructive that, even in the largest Korean industrial firms, it was not until the early 1980s that a specialized personnel department was established to deal more systematically with personnel matters and industrial relations (Song Ho Keun 1991, 116). Clearly, Korean industrialists were very slow in developing a system of modern industrial relations commensurate with the impressive corporate growth they had achieved. In the meantime, Korean industrial workers suffered an incredible amount of physical and symbolic abuse on the shop floors.

Conclusion

Through the writings that many Korean factory workers have left us, we can see how much physical and psychological pain they endured during the early decades of export-oriented industrialization. Although the early stages of industrialization everywhere are associated with a high degree of labor exploitation, the degree of exploitation and oppression that Korean factory workers experienced during the 1970s and 1980s was truly enormous. In South Korea, labor exploitation and abusive practices on the shop floor were accentuated by a number of factors: the society's deep contempt for manual labor, a labor market with a relatively unlimited supply of semi-skilled workers for a long period of time, the power of patriarchal ideology, a militarized corporate culture that permeated Korean work organizations, and, above all, the very nature of the South Korean political economy, in which the strong capitalist state took a consistently pro-capital and anti-labor stance to promote rapid economic growth. These adverse historical, cultural, and political forces put Korean industrial workers in an extremely weak position vis-à-vis the capitalists and long hindered the development of a more advanced system of industrial relations in Korean firms.

The dominant form of authority found in South Korean firms, large and small, industrial and commercial, was authoritarian and patriarchal. Like the patriarchs in traditional society, Korean industrialists and managers exercised their authority not on the basis of legality or contractual relationships, but largely on the basis of cultural tradition. Workers were looked on not as the sellers of their labor with their own contractual rights, but as children or as traditional servants. Unlike traditional patriarchal authority, however, the power of the Korean industrial patriarchs was not rooted in a broad normative consent based on the culture of reciprocity. Whereas traditional patriarchs were expected to provide their household members with protection and care in exchange for obedience and loyalty, this element of reciprocity was largely absent in most Korean industrial

firms. Workers were expected to be completely obedient and respectful toward their managers, but managers were bound to no reciprocal obligation
to provide adequate care and personal concern for their workers. Thus, the
essential nature of patriarchal authority in Korean industry was more
despotic than paternalistic. Although paternalistic rhetoric has been used
constantly in Korean firms, there is little evidence that either the capitalists or the government made any serious effort to give substance to these
words.

The labor unrest that began in the early 1970s derived from the experiences of Korean workers in this highly exploitative and abusive system of
industrial production. While workers' frustration and anger kept growing,
they were denied legitimate outlets to air their grievances and seek remedies. Given the predominant role of the state in maintaining labor discipline, and given the long period of favorable labor market condition,
Korean employers felt no strong need to cultivate a satisfied and committed workforce. Under the façade of a "family-like factory system," a highly
despotic and abusive authority was exercised in Korean industry, producing the deeply resentful labor force. It is this bitter experience of labor in
Korean factories that provided a springboard for the later explosions of
labor militancy.

4 A Martyr, Women Workers, and Churches

> We fought in order to free ourselves from oppression. We struggled in order to live like human beings. Oh, where is the equality God has bestowed upon us? Oh, the world, do you see our pains?
>
> (A workers' song, in Suk Jung-nam 1984, 168)

On the afternoon of November 13, 1970, a small protest occurred in a garment district, known as Pyunghwa Market, located in the western section of Seoul. A dozen young workers shouted slogans demanding the improvement of working conditions for Pyunghwa garment workers. But shortly after they gathered, the police and market security rushed in and tried to break up their protest. The protesters refused to budge. They had been planning this protest for some time and were determined to make their voices heard. This was not their first attempt to demonstrate. Previous attempts had been aborted by false promises from the government that it would comply with their demands and force employers to improve working conditions. These protesters were the members of a small labor group, called *Samdonghoi*, composed of a dozen young tailors working in the sweatshop district of Pyunghwa Market. The man who organized the group and also the demonstration was a 22-year-old tailor named Chun Tae-Il.

Chun Tae-Il had been deeply concerned about the wretched working conditions in the garment district and had devoted a great deal of his time and effort to seeking ways to improve the working conditions for some 20,000 workers. He had written petition letters to the Bureau of Labor, to newspapers, and even to the president, pleading for their attention to the human suffering that was going on in the garment district. He even conducted a survey, with the help from the *Samdong* group members, to present to the authorities with hard evidence of the inhumane working conditions that existed in Pyunghwa Market, but all to no avail. His pleas were simply disregarded, ridiculed, or responded to with false promises. Finally, Chun Tae-Il came to the grim conclusion that there was no other recourse than an extreme act of protest. As he prepared for the demonstration on November 13, Chun secretly prepared to sacrifice himself for the cause of labor struggle.

While scuffles were going on between the protesters and the police and market security, Chun disappeared for a few minutes. When he returned, he was holding a can of gasoline in his hand. Suddenly he poured gasoline over his body and set himself on fire. His body was instantly wrapped in shooting flames. The stunned crowd heard Chun shouting from within the flames: "We are not machines!"; "Let us rest on Sunday!"; "Abide by the Labor Standard Laws!"; "Don't exploit workers!" People saw he was holding up a booklet of the Labor Standard Laws. This was the booklet he had been delighted to discover a couple of years earlier at a used book store because he found, to his surprise, that the nation's labor laws prescribed favorable working conditions and worker compensation. He had studied these labor laws diligently and had pinned his hopes on them. He had written many letters to government authorities, hoping they would make employers abide by these laws, and ultimately realized that neither the government nor employers paid any attention to these laws. When his fellow workers finally managed to extinguish the fire, his body had already been burned dark. Semi-conscious, he pleaded with them, "Please do not waste my life!" He was taken to hospital, where his final words were to his beloved mother, Lee So-sun: "Mom, please accomplish the work which I haven't succeeded in accomplishing." Then, breathing his last, he again told his mother, "Mom, I . . . am hungry" (Cho Young-rae 1991, 281–292).

In many ways, Chun's self-immolation marked the beginning of South Korea's working-class formation. It sowed the spirit of resistance and rebellion in the minds of millions of workers and provided a powerful symbol for the working class in a society that had thus far had no sacred symbol or venerable tradition to inspire and mobilize workers for a collective goal. This incident also indicated that the industrial problems generated by the rapid process of export-oriented industrialization (EOI) were not going to remain hidden in the industrial arena, but were going to be a volatile source of tension and social conflicts. Industrial workers had entered the stage of history as a critical force of social contention and social transformation in South Korea.

The Pyunghwa Market was a one-block-long, four-story-high maze of small garment factories interspersed with clothing shops, employing some twenty thousand young workers, about 90 percent of whom were women, between the ages of 14 and 20. They worked in small cubicles with no more than four- or five-foot-high ceilings, and with no sunshine and no ventilation. They were forced to work, on average, 14 hours a day and received less than $30 a month in wages (at the 1970 exchange rate). Apprentices constituted more than one-third of the workforce and they received one-fifth (3,000 won a month) of the regular stitchers' wages. The average age of the apprentices was 15 years, and with this low wage they could not even feed themselves adequately (Cho Young-rae 1991, 99–112).

Chun Tae-Il began his labor struggle out of his deep humanistic concern with the plight of these young women apprentices. One day, he wrote to a friend, "We usually start work at 8:30 in the morning and finish at 10 or 11:30 at night. What do you think about it? Don't you think it's too grueling? Fourteen hours a day! How can these young apprentices bear such long hours of work?" (Chun Tae-Il 1988, 122). He continued; "Although they are denied an affluent environment, aren't they also human beings with human frailty? Dear Won-sup, as a tailor I must spend a whole day with them. That's too painful for me. At the age of fourteen, they are only children, but they must toil the whole day doing such difficult work, and then they often get scolded by the tailor for not finishing their jobs on time, and during lunch time, they eat their tiny packed lunch box they brought from home, just like an elephant eating biscuits" (123). He was also deeply concerned about the inequality in society. His diary, letters to friends, and the draft of a novel he wrote, all demonstrate how much he was tormented by the sufferings of young factory girls and by all the social injustices surrounding him. "While employers spend 200 won on their lunch," he lamented, "young workers spend 50 won for their three meals—this is an inhumane thing. . . . Why must these pure and unspoiled young girls become manure for the dirty and greedy rich people? Is this the reality of society? The rule of the rich and the poor?" (Cho Young-rae 1991, 207).

The unabated labor exploitation and the enormous amount of human suffering Chun Tae-Il protested against were the prevailing conditions for a growing number of factory workers employed in the labor-intensive export manufacturing sector in the 1970s. Yet the groans of the suffering workers were not heard by the mainstream society. In the 1970s, the success of EOI strategy was visible, with booming export industries and rapid growth in GNP and living standards. The nation's leaders were content with the way the economy was going and were preoccupied with quickening the pace of economic growth. Workers' complaints or protests were treated simply as a temporary nuisance, something that could be solved only by the nation's economic pie growing bigger. Both political leaders and the majority of the middle class did not really have a sense of what was happening on the factory floor to produce this economic growth.

Chun Tae-Il's self-immolation sent a shock wave across society. In particular, it awakened the intellectual community to the dark side of export-oriented industrialization, to the problems of the millions of workers who were suffering under the façade of the economic miracle. Significantly, it provided the first critical moment in which students began to realize the serious dimensions of labor problems and that they must broaden their political struggles to encompass the issue of economic justice. Many students attended Chun Tae-Il's funeral, and students at several major colleges in Seoul staged demonstrations or held memorial services for Chun on campus. Chun Tae-Il's tragic death thus provided a critical interlinkage between labor struggles and the students' political struggles for democracy.

However, the 1970s was too early for the development of a well-organized labor movement. The number of factory workers employed in the export manufacturing sector increased rapidly, but these were predominantly neophyte industrial workers freshly recruited from the countryside. They were preoccupied with adapting to the new work environment and took the hardships of work more or less as normal. When the exploitation and abuse reached an extreme level, the accumulated pain and anger of the workers burst into violent acts of protest, many times in violent and emotional individualistic actions. After Chun Tae-Il's self-immolation, several other workers attempted suicide in protest against mistreatment at work. In fact, attempted self-immolation became a recurring theme in the Korean working-class struggles in the 1970s and the 1980s (Han' guk kidokkyo kyohoe hyŏpuihoe 1984, 85). Sometimes, a group of workers spontaneously got together to demand delayed or unpaid wages or to denounce physical or verbal abuse by managers. In some cases, protesting workers actually turned into an angry mob, as at the Hyundai shipyard in 1974, where three thousand angry workers, outraged by the company's introduction of a new subcontracting system, destroyed company buildings and set fire to managers' cars and other company property. These spontaneous and individualistic forms of protest had little effect in bringing the desired change to the industries. They generated only a short period of public sympathy, and usually ended in great individual sacrifice.

Struggle for Independent Unions

Gradually, however, another stream of labor activism began in the second half of the 1970s as workers began to realize the importance of more systematic and collective efforts to improve their lot. Union consciousness slowly crept into the minds of a small vanguard of workers employed in the light manufacturing industries and workers began to realize that representative unions were the most effective means of improving their situation. The majority of the workers in the export manufacturing sectors in the 1970s were unorganized, and where unions existed they were most likely to be controlled by the company (Choi Jang Jip 1989, 146–72; Cho Seunghyok 1988).

The unionization struggle that began in the 1970s was, therefore, aimed either at creating new independent unions or capturing control of company unions (ŏyong chohap) and transforming them into genuine representative unions. The first major attempt to organize an independent union occurred at none other than the place where Chun Tae-Il sacrificed himself for the cause of the working-class movement. Two days after Chun's funeral on November 18, 1970, his fellow workers in Pyunghwa Market organized a districtwide union, called the Chunggye Textile Union, representing more than 20,000 garment workers employed in the district.[1] The highly sympathetic atmosphere created by Chun's death made the establishment of this maverick, area-based union organization possible. At the time of its formation, it had an active membership of five hundred workers. Given the nature of this industrial district, the majority of its members were female workers employed in small garment factories, while the leadership was held by male tailors. Although its foundation was relatively smooth, the path of this union was thorny and tortuous. The union was under constant surveillance; its leaders were continuously harassed, beaten, and imprisoned; and ultimately the union was forcibly closed down in 1980. However, born from Chun Tae-Il's spirit, Chunggye union members never succumbed to pressure and intimidation, waging spirited battles to reopen the union in the 1980s. In many ways, the Chunggye union played a leadership role for the grassroots labor movement during the 1970s and through the mid-1980s. Lee So-sun, Chun Tae-Il's mother, in accordance with her son's last wish, played an important role throughout the Chunggye struggle as a symbolic leader, and as a "mother of all workers."

Following the lead of the Chunggye Textile Union, several major struggles to establish independent unions occurred in the 1970s. Interestingly, the clear majority of these unionization struggles were led by women. Two of the best-known cases during this period occurred in 1972 at two large textile companies, Wonpoong and Dongil. At both companies, women workers staged a coup to take control of the company union. Unionists at Wonpoong built the strongest union established in the 1970s, presenting an exemplary case of the independent union movement. After several

1. Chunggye is a broader area of garment factories encompassing Pyunghwa Market.

showdowns with the company and the male-dominated company union leadership, they succeeded in 1972 in electing their own (male) candidate to union presidentship and ousted the corrupt union officers. In the same year, women workers at Dongil Textiles staged an electoral revolt at the union election and elected the first woman union president along with a majority of women floor delegates. Similar unionization struggles occurred in the mid-1970s at several other light manufacturing firms where women workers were in the majority, including Bando Trading Co., Pangrim Textiles, Y. H. Trading Co., Tongkwang Textiles, Crown Electronics, Signetics, and Control Data.

Churches and the Grassroots Union Movement

The most distinctive feature of this early stage of union activism, apart from the fact that it was led by women workers, was the close association between union activists and church organizations. Almost without exception, the women union activists had been actively involved in small-circle activities or workers' night schools, organized under the auspices of progressive church leaders. Here they obtained an awareness of the importance of unions and received a basic education in how to organize and run unions. Furthermore, once the struggles began, invariably provoking tremendous retaliatory and repressive action from management, the core activists were those who had been involved in church-sponsored consciousness-raising activities. Even where the unionists had no prior linkages with progressive church organizations, their unionization struggles often led them to develop close relationships with them. The fact that the grassroots union movement in the 1970s, led by women employed in small to medium industries, occurred mainly in the Seoul-Inchon region, is closely related to the concentration of labor-oriented church activities in this region.

Two church organizations played critical roles in this 1970s democratic union movement: the Catholic organization Jeunesse Ouvnere Chretienne (JOC or Young Catholic Workers) and the Protestant group Urban Industrial Missions (UIM). Both were organized in the late 1950s, under the auspices of their international organizations, and began labor-oriented mission work in the early 1960s (see Han'guk kidokkyo kyohoe hyŏpuihoe 1984, 94–107; Cho Wha Soon 1988; Ogle 1990, 87). Inspired by the example of the worker-priests in Belgium and France during World War II, a small number of Catholic, Methodist, and Presbyterian clergy took up their ministry among the people who were toiling in the factories and dockyards. Some of them worked as laborers in factories and after a period of field experience they became "factory pastors." The UIM pastors set up their ministries in industrial towns and worked devotedly for workers or poor residents in the area.[2] The JOC recruited young people (workers, students, and other Catholics) to work at or near industrial sites to help improve the working conditions of the wage laborers. In the 1970s when both organizations were most active and received considerable social attention, their activities were more or less concentrated in the industrial areas surrounding Seoul and Inchon, although the JOC's activities were a little more widely distributed outside this region.[3]

Although the pastors were interested initially in preaching the Christian gospel among industrial workers and employers, their factory experiences opened their eyes to the hollowness of the individual spiritual approach and to the necessity of workers' collective struggle to improve their conditions in the factory. Thus, from the late 1960s, JOC and UIM leaders oriented their activities to assisting workers to organize unions. They conducted educational programs on labor laws and union organization, and sponsored a variety of cultural and social activities to promote social consciousness among industrial workers. The principal goal of these activities was to produce a small cadre of labor activists who would lead the grassroots independent union movement (Cho Wha Soon 1988; Ogle 1990; Han'guk kidokkyo kyohoe hyŏpuihoe 1984).

The most important vehicle for fostering worker solidarity and consciousness sponsored by these church organizations was the small-group (or small-circle) activities. An average of six to eight workers recruited from neighborhood factories formed small informal groups, giving the groups names such as "morning star," "pine tree," "young club," "victory," "diamond," or "cow birth-cohort." The members met regularly under the guidance of the pastors or their staff (many of whom were college students) to engage in a variety of recreational and cultural activities, as well as to discuss their daily lives and the problems they faced at work. Some of these small groups remained primarily friendship or recreational groups, but most of them eventually turned into loci where workers acquired a sharper class awareness and learned about the importance of unions. Much of the union consciousness that gave rise to the grassroots union movement in the 1970s was largely the product of these small-group activities. As Dongil Textile workers wrote, "The small-group movement and the educational programs that these organizations [UIM and JOC] conducted helped develop a sense of solidarity among workers laboring at the same plant and a new awareness that workers can improve their social and economic status through labor unions" (Dongil pangjik pokjik tujaeng

2. Ogle, who was himself a factory pastor during this period, reports that the total number of clergy who worked in the factories and at the docks did not exceed twenty-five in the 1960s (1990, p. 87).
3. In the mid-1970s, the JOC had several hundred members nationwide (see Han'guk kidokkyo kyohoe hyŏpuihoe 1984, 255).

wiwonhoe 1985, 33). Similarly, Wonpoong workers wrote, "Small group activity is a means of strengthening the union, and its goal was to teach the workers that unions are an essential organization for achieving a society where liberty and freedom are realized and where workers can live like human beings" (Wonpoong Mobang haeko nodongja 1988, 163).

The well-publicized union struggles at the Wonpoong and Dongil textile companies are most illustrative of the struggle for independent unions. Women workers at Wonpoong Textiles (located in Seoul) began their struggle in 1972 with the formation of the Committee for the Union Normalization Struggle at Han'guk Mobang (Wonpoong's previous name). Those who played a key role in organizing this rebellion were women workers who had been involved in small-group activities in close association with a Catholic church during the previous year. A few of them had taken a public oath to become "warriors" and provide leadership for the bitter struggle that was to follow. Their first challenge was to replace the present union leadership with their own members. Through well-organized planning, they achieved a surprising victory at the 1972 union election. Of the forty-two floor delegates elected, twenty-nine were women. They also succeeded in electing a male president (Chi Dong-jin), whom they supported in opposition to the pro-management candidate. The newly born independent union faced tremendous obstacles in the following years, but the highly committed and disciplined union officers, under the leadership of the second union president, Bang Yong-suk, one of the few men who had the courage to participate in the women-dominated 1970s union movement, developed probably the strongest and most well-organized grassroots union at Wonpoong Textile.[4] The assertive union at Wonpoong was destroyed in 1982 by the severe repression of the military government of Chun Doo Hwan and the divisive tactics of management of pitting male workers against female workers.

The democratic union movement at Dongil Textile (at its Inchon factory) was similarly led by a cadre of women workers who had been actively participating in small-group activities at the UIM Inchon office under the guidance of Reverend Cho Wha-soon, a dedicated woman worker-priest, who had briefly worked as a laborer at Dongil in 1966. The group skillfully maneuvered events to elect the first woman union president in South Korea, Chu Kil-ja, in 1972 and replace corrupt union officers with activist women representatives. Bitter struggles ensued between male and female unionists in the following years, but the women nevertheless succeeded in electing a woman president three times in the following years.

---

4. See Yu Dong-wu (1984) for another remarkable story of a male worker who initiated and led a struggle to organize a union in a women-dominated company, Samwon Textile, during the 1970s.

Whether or not union organizers had previous contact with church leaders, their struggles often led them to seek external help from church organizations or intellectual communities. For example, when workers at Crown Electronics organized a union and filed an application for union approval with the Office of Labor Affairs in 1972, the company exerted pressure on workers and forced many of them to withdraw their membership applications. The Office of Labor Affairs then disapproved the union application, citing these withdrawals. Not only was the workers' attempt at union organization blocked, the rejection letter included a stern insulting warning: "Under the national emergency, it is very regrettable that you violate laws and engage in activities that cause social instability, so please make sure that similar things do not happen again" (Han'guk kidokkyo kyohoe hyŏpuihoe 1984, 159). Faced with these obstacles, Crown workers decided to seek external help. They wrote a letter to the UIM:

> We would like to thank you, many ministers and priests who work for the realization of social justice and industrial peace and work so hard to protect the rights of the working people. Thousands of workers experience unfair treatment but out of fear we cannot even complain about it to anyone. In this miserable situation, we are asking for your help.
>
> We are helpless, we have no power or money. We have organized a workers' own organization, a union, but it was disapproved by the Office of Labor Affairs and by the company under the pretense that our action was illegal and would cause social instability. Please heed this absurd situation and help us to receive fair treatment under Korean law, since we after all are Korean citizens too. (159)

Why then did workers turn to church organizations for help? The answer is simply because they had nowhere else to turn (see Han'guk kidokkyo kyohoe hyŏpuihoe 1984, 453). The official unions within the FKTU had abandoned their ostensible role of representing workers and degenerated into nothing more than a vehicle of the state's corporatist control of labor under the dictatorial *yushin* regime.[5] Also, the government's Bureau of Labor, which was supposed to enforce the labor standard laws, was more interested in preventing labor unrest. On the other hand, Korean factory workers in the 1970s were too feeble to resist the extremely exploitative and abusive practices on the shop floor on their own. They needed outside help. Consequently, industrial workers, especially women who were employed in the many small, light manufacturing industries, sought external

5. Some industrial unions within the FKTU did work to protect workers in the 1960s and the early 1970s, and some independent unions were formed in the 1970s under the auspices of the Textile Union. But after the establishment of the *yushin* regime in 1972, the FKTU and industrial unions became no more than government puppet organizations (Cho Seung-hyok 1988).

help to stand up against management and found two groups sympathetic to their problems: intellectuals and Christian church organizations. (Students did not pay much attention to labor issues until near the end of the 1970s.)

Unlike the intellectuals who were highly sympathetic to workers' problems but organizationally weak, the church organizations were in a stronger position to render support to the workers because of their international networks and internal organizational structure. Furthermore, the Christian churches, thanks to the international standing of Christianity, were more secure than the intellectuals or political dissidents from the state's ideological persecution using red-baiting. Although Christian church leaders were not immune to ideological accusations by security forces—they were actually the main targets of ideological attacks, and many of the JOC and UIM leaders were arrested, tortured, and jailed during the 1970s—church organizations were nevertheless in a far stronger position to resist ideological persecution than other groups. The active involvement of progressive churches in the grassroots union movement necessarily caused animosity between the FKTU and church groups, the church groups severely criticizing the official union leadership for having sold out to the government.[6]

Union Struggle at Dongil Textile

Needless to say, the environment surrounding the new grassroots union movement in the 1970s was extremely hostile. Employers were not ready to accept independent unions, especially those suspected of being linked to outside organizations. They employed all possible means—harassment, threats, bribes, and help from the government-controlled industrial unions—to block attempts to organize independent unions or to reform the management-controlled unions. When they failed to block the formation of an independent union, their next strategy was to transform it into a company union. The favorite strategy to achieve this was to mobilize male workers to destroy the female-dominated independent union. The demo-

6. For example, the Protestant and Catholic Collaborative Council on Labor Issues, a group of progressive Christian leaders, issued a statement in 1974 denouncing the official union structure in severe language: "If they are not working to protect the basic rights of the workers, the FKTU and the National Textile Union must immediately dissolve themselves and apologize to the four million workers and to all citizens for having become a second organization that exploits the workers." In response, the FKTU issued its own strong denouncement of the church leaders: "We urge serious self-reflection among that small minority of religious leaders who penetrate our labor organizations and try to distort the right direction of the labor movement and cause organizational division and labor unrest by agitating innocent workers, and we warn them in the name of 600,000 organized workers that if they continue to behave in this way we will punish them by mobilizing all of our organizational power" (Wonpoong Mobang haeko nodongja 1988, 97–98).

Figure 3. Dongil Textile workers with a male supervisor in the late 1970s. (Provided by Suk Jung-nam)

cratic union movement in the 1970s was, therefore, characterized by bitter struggles between male and female workers. Among several important cases of union struggles in the 1970s, the most dramatic and illustrative was Dongil Textile factory located in Inchon. Women workers' struggles at other women-dominated factories in the labor-intensive export industries, such as at Wonpoong, Pangrim, Tongkwang, Samwon, Bando, Crown, Signetic, Control Data,[7] were equally significant, but due to space constraints, I focus here on the Dongil case. (This account is based primarily on Dongil pangjik pokjik tujaeng wiwonhoe 1985; Suk Jung-nam 1984; Cho Wha Soon 1988.)

As previously mentioned, the union leadership at Dongil Textile was won in 1972 by women who had participated in small-group activities at the UIM Inchon office. But the road to a democratic union was a tortuous path. Union activists had to overcome tremendous harassment, mistreat-

7. Union activists at all these companies published records of their unionization struggles, but the most useful and accessible sources are Han'guk kidokkyo kyohoe hyŏpuihoe (1984) and Lee Tae-ho (1986a).

ment, and attempts at bribery by management. They were given extra work, transferred to the most arduous and menial posts, subjected to sexual harassment, and reprimanded severely for every minor mistake. They were also tempted with promises of promotion and extra bonuses if they withdrew from union activities.

Harassment was only a preliminary method used by Dongil management to attempt to force workers to withdraw from union activities or from UIM small-group activities. Faced with stubborn resistance from the female workers, the company introduced a more vicious tactic: male workers were mobilized to break up the female-dominated union leadership and to turn the union back into a company union. In July 1976, when a new union election was scheduled, a group of male workers, with the full financial and organizational backing from the company, bribed other male workers and attempted to scare the more passive female workers in order to oust the incumbent union leadership. Ko Doo-young, the leader of this group, used a legal maneuver, having the then president (Lee Young-sook) and secretary of the union arrested on charges of misconduct and instigating workers to strike. On July 23, in the absence of the top union leaders and excluding the twenty-three women floor delegates, twenty-four pro-management delegates met hastily to elect Ko as the new union president. While this fraudulent election was going on, the company had locked their women workers inside the dormitory and nailed the doors shut from the outside. But the enraged workers broke the doors open and jumped out of broken windows to pour into the union hall. Some two hundred workers participated in a sit-in strike on the first day. The number of participants increased to eight hundred the next day, and three hundred more participated in the strike outside the factory gate because they had been barred from entering. The company cut off electricity and water, locked the toilets, and allowed no food to be brought in. Despite this, the workers did not waver, continuing their strike and demanding the release of their union leaders and the nullification of the illegal election.

On the third day, July 25, Dongil workers staged an extremely surprising and dramatic form of resistance, probably unique in world labor history. That afternoon, a few hundred riot police were brought into the factory. The appearance of these policemen in dark blue uniforms and with fully equipped combat gear was frightening (fig. 4). Some women cried out in fear. As the combat police began to approach the workers, the striking women began to undress and stood half-naked in front of the armed police. Later, workers reported that they took this action at the suggestion of a worker who had whispered in that panicky moment, "Men cannot touch undressed women, even if they are police" (Suk Jung-nam 1984, 49). Some 500–800 naked women held each other tightly and sang union songs, surrounded by stunned police and male workers. One worker, Suk Jung-nam

Figure 4. The dreadful riot police. (From Sahoe sajin yŏnguso [social photography institute] 1989, 153)

later described the scene beautifully: "In the face of such an enormous threat of violence, it was our ultimate resistance, an action spontaneously taken, with no shame or fear. Under siege by the armed police and male workers, we hung tightly together in our nakedness. Can steel be stronger and harder than this? Who dares to touch these people? That was like one huge rock. It was like a time bomb ready to explode at the slightest touch" (1984, 49). Faced with this incredible scene, the police were momentarily dumbfounded, but not for long. They moved in and began to break up the protesters, hitting the women with bats, pulling screaming women by their hair, throwing them onto the ground, and dumping them into police vans. While battling with the police, many women were completely exposed, but, as they wrote later, they felt no shame, but had only resentful tears, anger, and strong feelings of comradeship. The police arrested seventy-two women, but two hundred other women tried to block the cars with their naked bodies and some followed the cars on foot to the police station. Several women were hospitalized with severe bruises, and two women later developed mental disorders.

The enormous sacrifice by these workers did not bring immediate victory, but it at least prevented the coopted male workers from taking over the union. The management continued its divisive tactics of separating union activists from the rank-and-file and tried to drive the union into a state of paralysis. In order to fight this, the workers requested help from the national union, the National Textile Union. To the dismay of women workers, the Textile Union turned out to be a fox: the representative of the Textile Union (a man) made a secret deal with management behind the women's backs, recommending that the union include nonmanual workers in its membership. This was ostensibly to allow the conciliation of the two opposing groups of manual workers, but in reality it was a clever tactic to bring in male supervisors to control the union.

The union leaders then realized that they were powerless by themselves to fight against the allied forces of the government and management. Their strategy, commonly adopted by Korean workers in the 1970s, was to publicize the injustices they had suffered, in the hope of bringing pressure to bear on management. In February 1977, the Dongil workers organized a public disclosure meeting to be held at the Cultural Center of Myung-dong Cathedral in downtown Seoul. They called their plan the Surgery Performance of the Dongil Incident, and sent invitations to the mass media and to civic organizations. Listed as sponsors on the invitations were twelve Christian organizations, including the UIM, JOC, Christian Women's Organization, National Council of Churches (KNCC), and Commission for Justice and Peace. In their attached statement, the workers wrote:

> Please listen to the desperate cry of our poor workers, who are struggling to live like (respectable) human beings despite society's cold treatment and neglect and under the employers' whippings. . . . We want to live like human beings, and although we are poor and uneducated, we have learned about justice and democracy through our union. Are we wrong to engage in our desperate struggle in order to keep our conscience alive and not to surrender to injustices? We want to hear your honorable judgment. Please give us your generous encouragement. (Dongil pangjik pokjik tujaeng wiwonhoe 1985, 73–74)

This time, the workers won. Two days before the scheduled Surgery Performance, the police released the arrested union leaders, and the Office of Labor Affairs told the company to allow a new election. In the new election on March 31, 1977, Lee Chong-kak, a woman, was elected president. It was a sweet victory for the women workers who had fought so hard to defend their representative union. However, they were not allowed to enjoy their victory for long. Their opponents stepped up their attacks to destroy the new union leadership. The management used all means to force workers to withdraw from union membership, while continually harassing union activists. And when these tactics proved ineffective, they used a more vicious method—painting the activist union leaders as acting as the puppets of pro-communist organizations. In February 1978 the company distributed a booklet to workers, entitled "What Is the UIM Looking For?" The book alleged that the UIM, under the façade of a religious organization, was actually run with funds from international communist organizations and that the UIM's typical forms of activity clearly mirrored those of communist organizations. As labor conflicts grew steadily after the mid-1970s, the state intensified its attacks on labor-oriented religious and intellectual organizations. In addition to indoctrinating workers with anti-UIM messages, security agencies arrested several UIM officers, including Reverend Cho Wha-soon, on charges of pro-communist activities. The KCIA also broke into the offices of the Christian Academy and the Labor Institute of Korea University, both of which played important roles in training unionists and sponsoring pro-labor research, and arrested several researchers on charges of propagating communist ideology.

This ideological campaign provided a convenient vehicle for management to attack union leaders and to divide the workers. The coopted workers, predominantly men but also joined by a couple of women, claimed they were the saviors of the company's union and that their goal was to create a genuine independent union. "At the present time when an autonomous, independent, and practical labor movement is greatly called for," a flyer distributed by a woman who ran for the presidency on behalf of pro-management male workers in 1978 asked, "why don't we solve our problems on our own . . . [instead of being] manipulated by impure outside forces?" The flyer criticized the UIM for sowing mistrust among workers and inciting them to create instability in the workplace. "We are born into poor families, and so we have received little education and must work at the factory to earn money from an age when other people are attending school" (Dongil pangjik pokjik tujaeng wiwonhoe 1985, 97). Her flyer continues, "But I believe that we possess as pure and beautiful a mind as anyone can have. Why, then, does our mind turn into that of a hungry wolf whenever we listen to the preaching of the UIM? . . . They taught us many songs. They are lots of fun, but let's examine the lyrics of these songs carefully. They are all agitating and impure contents. What are they really aiming at?" Clearly, red-baiting was not simply a mechanism of the state to maintain ideological control of civil society but also a handy weapon of management in their attack on the independent union movement.

However, these vicious ideological attacks had no visible effect in alienating Dongil's rank-and-file workers from the activist union leadership or in severing the ties of the union leadership from outside dissident communities. Union membership remained high and worker solidarity was strong. When slander did not work, the self-appointed protectors of the independent union attempted to destroy the union by force.

On December 21, an election was to be held to select new members of
the union's executive committee. Before election day, an anti-union group
had attempted to postpone the election date and to change certain procedures for their own advantage. When they failed in this, they physically
attacked the voters. In the early morning of February 21, as night-shift
workers finished their work and entered the election booths, several men
sprang out of the toilet area carrying buckets filled with human excrement.
These men, assisted by two women, threw the human excrement at the
women and rubbed it on their faces and even inside their brassieres. The
shocked women tried to run away, screaming for help. But no one came to
their aid. Later, women workers reported that some policemen and election watchers sent by the National Textile Union were present but that
they did not bother to intervene.[8]

As soon as this shocking story came out, several hundred angry female
workers gathered in front of the union hall, which was now occupied by
several dozen male workers. The women tried to reoccupy the office, but
they were no match for the physical power of their male opponents. The
men were reinforced by several "action men" sent by the Textile Union,
all highly trained in the martial arts. The women later said that they feared
these men the most, more than the police or the hostile male workers. The
men inside the union office put up placards: "Drove out UIM!"; "Step
Down Lee Chong-kak!"; "Slaughter Cho Wha-soon!" (Reverend Cho was
regarded as the chief sponsor and agitator behind the UIM-linked women
activists.)

Why did the male workers behave in this way? Suk Jung-nam writes:

> Those so-called opponent male workers must have some reasons to be-
> come opponents. Either because the incumbent executive board is not per-
> forming its duty adequately or the current president is incompetent . . . but
> they don't seem to have any particular reason or justification. They don't
> have any dream, ideal, or a sense of right or wrong. They must behave that
> way simply because it's a lot easier than working, and because the com-
> pany lets them loaf, treats them with good drink and food, and compli-
> ments them for their behavior. (1984, 98)

But, of course, there were deeper reasons than just being bribed by the
company. As one man who was sympathetic to the women unionists confessed, it was because of "male pride" that men were unwilling to support
the women-dominated union leadership (Dongil pangjik pokjik tujaeng
wiwonhoe 1985, 102). The few men who were supportive of women union-

---

8. According to the workers' report, one policeman rebuffed the women's cries for help,
saying, "You, f— women, shut up! I will do something later" (Dongil pangjik pokjik tujaeng
wiwonhoe 1985, 100).

ists were ostracized by their male coworkers and had to withdraw from union activities or eventually betray the trust of the women workers. A deep-seated gender ideology was clearly the main obstacle.[9]

At this time, the Textile Union, led by Kim Young-tae, a notorious anti-labor president, stepped in. In the name of a "smooth solution," it rubbed salt in the wounds of the worker activists by proposing that the union be considered temporarily defunct for allegedly causing too much trouble and be put into receivership. When Lee Young-sook, the president of the union, and other women representatives refused to accept this proposal, the national union dismissed Lee and three other officers from their positions, charging them with committing an "anti-organization act." The workers protested vehemently, but they could not save their leaders from being dismissed.

Externalization of the Workers' Struggle

The democratic union movement of the 1970s spearheaded by women workers, as we have seen in the case of the Dongil workers' struggle, was characterized by the amazing spirit of resistance among workers in the face of a formidable alliance between state and capital. In the 1970s, however, this spirited resistance occurred only in a very small number of factories located in the Seoul and Inchon areas. The majority of the manufacturing labor force during this period remained submissive and passive, and the level of labor consciousness was quite low even among active union members; in fact, union activists had little knowledge of how to run an independent union. (The Christian Academy and the Institute of Labor Studies at Korea University played a very important role in preparing the grass-roots union leaders by offering courses on unions.) At this inchoate stage of the democratic union movement, therefore, the workers required outside help, especially given the completely coopted nature of the official union structure during the *yushin* period.

Thus, as the grassroots union movement intensified in the second half of the 1970s, workers' resistance became increasingly externalized and politicized, which in turn invited further repression from the state. From the state's point of view, the main problem was the growing ties between labor

9. This gender ideology was strengthened by the gendered nature of work organization in South Korea. Typically, men were given more authority and responsibility and became more loyal to the company. At most light manufacturing industries where women constituted the majority of the workforce, men were more likely to be in the skilled and technical positions with a possibility of promotion to a supervisory position, whereas women were employed in the dead-end, semi-skilled jobs. Apparently, many men who were anxious to be promoted felt that the women activists were going to destroy their chances. Their gender-based bias against the women activists was thus often mixed with profound hostility (see Dongil pangjik pokjik tujaeng wiwonhoe 1985, 45).

and political dissident communities, but ironically it was the state's ultra-repressive labor policy that drove labor activists from the industrial arena, thereby forcing them to develop closer ties with dissident political communities. We can see this interesting development in the continuing saga of the Dongil workers' struggles.

Despite their tenacious struggles to protect their union, the Dongil workers saw their hard-built union paralyzed by the collaboration of management and the national union. Dongil union activists decided to continue their fight outside the factory. On the morning of March 10, 1978, seventy-six Dongil women workers sneaked into Changchoon Stadium where government leaders, including the prime minister and other dignitaries and national union leaders, had gathered to celebrate Labor Day.[10] The ceremony was being broadcast live on television. At the moment when the president of the Federation of Korean Trade Unions came up the podium to deliver his speech, the Dongil workers stood up and shouted: "Solve Dongil Company problems!"; "We cannot live on human excrement"; "Step down Kim Young-tae." Protesters quickly opened their placards and threw leaflets into the audience.

During the few minutes in which this took place, the live television coverage was halted and police and security rushed in to remove the intruders from the scene. The protesters were badly beaten, kicked, thrown onto the pavement, and taken to the police station. The protest sadly brought no positive outcome for the workers. At the Dongil factory, men continued to occupy the union office and stepped up their accusations against the "ignorant women" who had been hypnotized and manipulated by pro-communist organizations.

Union members had to devise another strategy. A few days later, forty-one workers traveled fifty miles from Inchon to Seoul and began a hunger strike at Myungdong Cathedral. Another hunger strike was simultaneously held in the basement of the UIM Inchon church, joined by Reverend Cho Wha-soon. Many other workers participated in the protest by being absent from work or by conducting a work slowdown at the plant.

There was clearly a strategic calculation behind the Dongil workers' decision to stage a hunger strike at Myungdong Cathedral. In addition to publicizing their problems, they hoped that national Christian leaders would intervene to defend the UIM and JOC organizations, and the workers themselves, from malicious ideological accusations. Now their demands were broader than in their previous protests: "Guarantee labor's three basic rights!"; "Step down, Kim Young-tae"; "Solve Dongil's problems!"; "Stop the oppression of religion." This strategy proved more effective than

10. The South Korean government purposely celebrated Labor Day on March 10, not on May 1, to dissociate itself from the international labor movement.

the previous ones. The Dongil workers' hunger strike generated broad support from the churches, intellectuals, and students. Prayers for the Suffering Dongil Workers were held at many churches, and a number of church leaders, professors, writers, and journalists joined together to organize the Committee to Solve the Problems at Dongil. But the public media turned a blind eye to this incident. Although this incident was covered in several foreign newspapers, none of South Korean newspapers, radio stations, or TV stations mentioned the strike.

The Dongil workers ended their 9-day hunger strike when three of the nation's top Christian leaders—Cardinal Kim Soo Hwan, Reverend Kang Won-yong (an influential Protestant leader and the founder of the Christian Academy), and Reverend Kim Kwan-suk (the secretary of the Korean NCC)—met with government authorities and obtained a verbal promise that everything at Dongil would be returned to the situation prior to February 21 (the human-excrement incident), that workers would be allowed to hold a new election, and that no protesters would be penalized by the company.

The protesters were exhilarated by their victory and came back to Inchon on a chartered bus provided by the church. Alas, what they found in Inchon the next day was exactly the opposite of what had been promised; both the workers and the nation's top Christian leaders had been completely fooled by the government. Not only were the protesters forbidden to return to their union, they were dismissed from their jobs. The company, with the approval of the Bureau of Labor, fired 126 workers who had participated in the hunger strike in Seoul and Inchon for being absent for more than three days without the company's permission and for having damaged the public image of the company.

The workers thus lost everything—their jobs, their hard-built union, many of their coworkers who had caved in, and their trust in their church leaders. What they did not lose was the strong bond they had developed with each other and their strong determination to fight back. The immediate goal of the Dongil workers' struggle was now no longer to revive the independent union, but to regain the strikers' lost jobs, and they had to wage this struggle outside the factory compound.

On March 26, 1978, another surprise workers' protest disrupted a grand public ceremony that was being telecast on television and radio. It was a huge Thanksgiving service, attended by one-half million Christians in Seoul's grand Yeouido Square. Suddenly in the middle of the service, a minister's prayer was halted as six women jumped onto the stage, snatched the microphone from him, and shouted: "Guarantee Laborers' three rights!"; "We cannot live on human excrement!"; "Solve Dongil Company Problem!"; "Pay Pangrim's (delayed) wages!" (Dongil pangjik pokjik tujaeng wiwonhoe 1985, 123). In less than five minutes they were quickly removed from the stage by security agents. These invaders of the solemn religious gathering were not all Dongil workers. The six protesters were from diverse textile companies where democratic union movements had developed and been severely suppressed, including Dongil, Wonpoong, Pangrim, Namyoung Nilon, and Samwon Textiles. These six women had met through a church-sponsored activity and decided to do something to shake up the placidity of mainstream Christians by exposing how the peace, love, and freedom preached at churches every week were so blatantly disregarded in the factory. They were equally angry at the media, which had given no attention to their struggle. Their surprise protest was, in a sense, a desperate attempt to capture a few minutes of media attention, to let the society know of the incredible injustice suffered by millions of workers who toiled day and night to produce the affluence the society was enjoying. Again, however, these protesters failed to capture the media's attention; the little that was reported by the media focused on the violent actions of the workers and insinuated that there was an external influence behind the protests.

This seemingly futile protest was significant in that it portended an emerging pattern of labor struggles in South Korea—interfirm solidarity struggles, which were to become a major trend in the 1980s. Growing workers' consciousness, the close linkage of the workers with democratic forces, and the government's repressive and exclusionary approach to labor control worked together to push the labor struggles outside the industrial arena and to facilitate close ties among labor activists. Interfirm linkages between labor activists began to occur more frequently toward the end of the 1970s as the independent union movement led by women workers intensified and became politicized, and as many of activists were dismissed from their jobs and continued the struggle from the outside their places of employment. The close proximity of the factories, concentrated mostly in industrial areas in the vicinity of Seoul, was of course the critical ecological factor facilitating the close interfirm linkages.

As time passed, Dongil's dismissed workers waged an increasingly isolated battle to return to work. Outside help was only temporary, while the repression became more vicious. Ten days after their dismissal, the president of the Textile Union sent out an official memorandum to all local unions and to the many textile and garment factories: "Attached is a list of the workers who were fired from Dongil Textiles because they had left their jobs and were engaged in violent behavior under the direction of external forces. So, please take proper precautions" (Dongil pangjik pokjik tujaeng wiwonhoe 1985, 126). This blacklist followed the workers wherever they went. Those who tried to obtain employment at other factories were usually detected during their job interviews and were denied employment. Those who avoided detection and obtained jobs were caught later on and forced to resign. The workers were often told by the managers that they were not personally against them, but that they could not help because of instructions from the government (Suk Jung-nam 1984, 155).

The Dongil workers continued their struggle for several years. In many ways, the Dongil workers' struggle was no less important in the workers' tenacious attempts to return to their jobs than in their initial union struggles. If their early struggle represented an effort to improve their work conditions by establishing a representative union, their post-dismissal actions contributed to the growing underground network of the democratic union movement because it occurred outside a single workplace. The Dongil worker struggle, therefore, contributed greatly to the growing ties between the labor movement and the democratization movement of students and dissident intellectuals. By expelling the labor activists from the industrial arena, the Park regime actually facilitated the process it had been so intent on preventing—the alliance of the anti-regime political movement with the growing labor movement.

The Y. H. Worker Protest

A major labor struggle of the late 1970s that best demonstrates this growing tendency of externalization and politicization is the Y. H. struggle. (This account is based primarily on Chǒn Y. H. nodong chohap and Han'guk nodongja pokjik hyǒpuihoe 1984.) The Y. H. Trading Company, established in 1966, was a major wig exporter to the United States. Its founder, Y. H. Chang, emigrated to the United States in 1970 and established another trading company, leaving the management of the Korean wig factory in the hands of his brother-in-law. Instead of concentrating on the wig business, the new manager diverted profits from the Y. H. Company to buy a new shipping company. A third manager also made side investments in electronics and film production companies. This continuous outflow of capital drained the Y. H. Company, because, in addition, the world wig market was declining in the 1970s. The total number of employees decreased from 4,000 to 1,800 in the late 1970s. In March 1979, the management announced a plan to close the plant, which triggered a strong reaction from the union, one of the new breed of independent unions formed in 1975.

A series of sit-in demonstrations followed in protest. As the conflict between management and the union escalated, several outside organizations became involved. The Y. H. union meetings were attended not only by religious leaders and intellectuals, but by representatives from the democratic unions at Wonpoong, Dongil, Control Data, Bando Trading, and Tongkwang Textile companies. The Y. H. workers' strike intensified as the announced date of plant closure approached. The police was called in and was ready to break the strike by force. Facing an imminent police attack, the strikers decided to move to a safer place to continue their struggle. The place they chose was, surprisingly, the headquarters of the opposition party, the New Democratic Party (NDP) in downtown Seoul. The decision to stage a protest at the opposition party headquarters was made at the advice of several Christian dissident intellectuals. According to Y. H. workers' own report later, they maintained close contact with these out-side supporters during the strike, although they had had no prior links with the UIM or JOC. On the evening of August 9, several "young Christian men" met secretly and discussed another site for the Y. H. workers' protest. They reportedly considered Choheung Bank, the U.S. Embassy, and the NDP headquarters, but concluded that "the NDP is the place where workers can escalate their economic struggle to a political struggle, and therefore, regardless of the success or failure of the struggle, it will make a great impact on the entire society." At dawn on August 9, these men visited the dormitory and reported the result of their discussion. "Having heard of their report, union members sensed the urgency of the situation, and after some discussion over a second location for their strike, they decided on the NDP headquarters, considering the likely impact it would make both inside and outside the country and the relative easiness of entering the place." In the meantime, three well-known dissident Chris-tian intellectuals (Ko Un, a poet; Reverend Moon Dong-hwan; and Profes-sor Yi Moon-young) met with Kim Young Sam, the NDP president (and later the South Korean president), and asked for his help (see Chŏn Y. H. nodong chohap and Han'guk nodongja pokjik hyŏpuihoe 1984, 186–87).

On the morning of August 9, 1979, 187 Y. H. workers stormed into the NDP building and occupied the fourth floor of the building as their new site of demonstration. The NDP headquarters was immediately surrounded by police and tension arose as Kim Young Sam declared his sup-port for the striking workers. This highly emotional, tense confrontation between strikers and police lasted through the next day. But at dawn on the third day (August 11), some one thousand riot policemen broke into the building. They smashed windows, overturned furniture, and violently at-tacked NDP party members, opposition congressmen, and newspaper re-porters, as well as the desperately resisting Y. H. workers, indiscriminantly. In the midst of this police violence, one worker, Kim Kyŏng-sook, fell from the fourth floor and died.[11] Kim Young Sam was taken away by force.

The Y. H. workers' struggle thus ended in the same way as the Dongil workers' struggle—the battle was lost due to state repression. Four union leaders went to prison, and 233 workers were sent home to rural areas by

11. The cause of the death is still uncertain. Police claimed that it was a suicide, whereas workers argued that she was killed by the police. Several protesters, including Kim, did in fact attempt to commit suicide with broken glass when the police poured into the building.

Figure 5. Y. H. protesters carried away by police from the NDP headquarters. (Provided by *JoongAng Daily*)

the police. Several Christian leaders were arrested and interrogated. But, again, the Y. H. workers' struggle also made a tremendous contribution to laying the foundation for the ever-expanding working-class movement. In particular, the Y. H. struggle contributed to externalizing and politicizing labor struggles and to the fusion of labor struggles and pro-democracy political struggles.

In fact, the Y. H. incident had a greater impact on the political movement than on the labor movement. The NDP, which had been more or less aloof from the labor movement thus far, suddenly became accidentally involved. Party politics plunged into a crisis when the ruling party ousted Kim Young Sam from his congressional seat, charging him with inciting violence and social instability. Mass demonstrations occurred in Pusan, Kim's congressional district, and spread to the neighboring industrial city of Masan. Participants in the street demonstrations included not just students but also workers, the unemployed, and ordinary citizens who had become deeply disaffected with the Park government's authoritarian practices. The recessionary state of the Korean economy during this period helped escalate the political unrest. As political protests intensified and spread across country, a crack began to occur within the ruling group and serious rivalries developed among Park's aids, which eventually led to Park Chung Hee's assassination by his own CIA chief on October 26, 1979. With his sudden death, one phase of South Korean authoritarianism came to an end, and so did the formative stage of the Korean democratic labor movement.

Sources of Female Workers' Union Activism

Labor struggles at Wonpoong, Dongil, Y. H. Company, and several other textile and electronics factories during the 1970s demonstrated the amazing spirit of resistance among Korean female workers against oppression, despite all the odds against them. To a great extent, it is the pioneering role of these courageous women workers that provided the basis for the democratic union movement and formation of the working class in South Korea. Of course, the role of the male workers in the 1970s must not be ignored. After all, it was Chun Tae-Il, a male tailor, who initiated the strong labor resistance by burning himself to death, and it was his colleagues, the male tailors at Pyunghwa Market, who organized the first independent union and showed the way toward the grassroots independent union movement. Other male workers, such as Yu Dong-wu (at Samwon Textile) and Bang Yong-suk (at Wonpoong Textile), played a leading role in the grassroots union movement in the 1970s. It was, however, the female workers who carried the torch of the democratic union movement during this time. The absolute majority of labor disputes involving unionization struggles in the 1970s were led by female workers in the textile, garment, electronics, and other female-dominated export industries. Even where the independent union movement was led by male workers, female workers were the main participants in the struggle, demonstrating stronger resistance, determination, solidarity, and resilience than male workers (see Yu Dong-woo 1984, 126–30).

The Korean case of women workers' activism is, therefore, at odds with the usual characterization of female workers in export industries. The literature on female workers in export-processing zones stresses the extent to which they are (super-)exploited by international capital and suffer from low wages, market vulnerability, and sexual oppression (Elson and Pearson 1981; Fernandez-Kelly 1983; Kung 1976; Linda Lim 1978; Safa 1981). The dominant image of Asian female factory workers is one of docility, passivity, transitory commitment to industrial work, and lack of interest in union activism. Dubbed "factory daughters" or "filial workers," these young female workers in the export sector are described as being controlled not only by the capitalist system but also by the patriarchal traditional culture that had been reproduced in the industrial organization (Salaff 1981; Wolf 1992). Similarly, the women-dominated light manufacturing sector in developing countries is characterized as having a high rate of job turnover, weak unionism, and largely timid and ineffective labor actions (Deyo 1989, 187–96).

Recently, a new perspective has emerged to counter this image of docile female workers in the internationalized production system. It has been recognized that female workers are not merely victims of capitalism and patriarchy—they also resist and protest against the oppressive structure as active agents (Ong 1987, 1991; Milkman 1993; Chhachhi and Pittin 1996). As Amrita Chhacchi and Renee Pittin argue, "women workers have organised to defend and extend their rights and improve their situation, even in the unorganized sector and free trade zones often seen as unorganisable" (1996, 24). It is thus necessary to understand, as Jeong-lim Nam argues, "the dual nature of Asian women's experience at workplaces: both oppression and resistance" (1996, 328). The new literature on female workers thus seeks to move away from "the 'victimology' which has too often coloured studies on women workers" (Chhacchi and Pittin 1996, 24).

What we have seen in this chapter definitely supports a shift of focus from the victimization of female workers to their resistance and organizational activities. Korean female workers were far more active and aggressive in the union movement than female workers in other developing countries. They did not only resist in sporadic protests or in subtle everyday forms of resistance, but participated in and led the grassroots union movement in direct confrontation with harsh authoritarianism.

What caused them to become a leading force in the early stage of the South Korean labor movement? In one of a few studies that considers this question directly, Nam suggests three reasons for the Korean female workers' union activism in the 1970s. The first concerns the structural conditions: "The concentration of women in a few industries and their constant exposure to gender discrimination provided a basis for raising collective consciousness among the workers. Young women from the same school or region, living closely together in dormitories, could develop shared understandings and a sense of sisterhood" (Nam 1996, 331). The second reason is "the relatively low cost of participation in labor struggles," because "under these conditions, young, single women did not have much to lose from participation in labor struggles." The third reason is the availability of "few opportunities to serve their (female workers') economic interests through individual effort." In contrast, Nam argues, "Korean male workers were given opportunities for promotion and raises through individual effort, which offered incentives for cooperation with management" (332).

While helpful in understanding why women participated in labor protests, these three reasons are insufficient in explaining why Korean fe-

male workers played the unique role of leading the grassroots union movement in the 1970s because all these factors could equally apply to female
workers in other developing countries. Also problematic is that some of
Nam's factors could work in the opposite way. For example, the fact that
women retired from the workforce at an early age (i.e., did not have much
to lose) was just as likely to make them less interested in the long-term
improvement of their conditions through collective action, especially
when it involved much personal risk. (In addition, female workers had
quite a bit to lose in terms of personal and family security.) As for the third
factor, it must be recognized that opportunities for promotion in the Korean factory were extremely limited not only for female workers but also
for male workers. It is also questionable whether women were less likely
to pursue individualist means of upward mobility than men because of
their position in the job market. In fact, a more common view is that
women sought upward mobility through marriage (although reality most
often belies this view).

What then is the critical factor that accounts for the Korean female
workers' exceptional role in the labor movement in the 1970s and early
1980s? I believe that the answer lies in the close linkages that developed
between female workers in light manufacturing industries and the progressive church organizations. As we have seen, almost all union struggles
in the 1970s were linked to and assisted by church organizations. Even
when unionists were not directly linked to these organizations initially, as
was the case with Y. H. workers,[12] protesters sought assistance from intellectual and religious communities in the course of their struggles. UIM and
JOC activities were concentrated in the women-dominated light manufacturing industries in the Seoul and Inchon areas, and female union activists
of the 1970s were closely associated with their industrial missions. The
fact that the 1970s union movement was concentrated in Seoul-Inchon
area coincided with the industrial mission by church organizations being
concentrated in this area. Whether women would have played such an important role in the Korean labor movement had the church organizations
not been involved in the labor arena is an interesting question to ask. My
guess is probably not.

Union activists of the 1970s, whom I interviewed, agree with this view.
Suk Jung-nam, who wrote a beautiful documentary of Dongil workers'
struggle, said: "The outsiders' [church leaders' and intellectuals'] role was
essential. Our struggle was not really spontaneous or made by ourselves.
Without their help, downtrodden workers would not have entered the

12. The history of the Y. H. union written by the previous Y. H. workers states that the
"Y. H. union, as reported in this book, had no relationship with the UIM whatsoever, and
none of our union members belonged to the UIM" (Chŏn Y.H. nodong chohap and Han'guk
nodongja pokjik hyŏpuihoe 1984, 255).

labor movement on their own. It was because they showed deep human concern toward us and gave us encouragement that we could have done that. They provided an outlet for us" (interview, March 29, 2000). Another 1970s unionist, Kim Ji-sun,[13] who staged the 1978 surprise protest at the national Thanksgiving service at Yeouido Square with five other workers, also acknowledged the crucial role of church groups and intellectuals at the early stage of their struggle: "When nobody in society looked at us as deserving human beings, they showed us genuine concern and treated us as respectable human beings. That meant a tremendous thing to us. We had deep trust and appreciation toward the people who genuinely cared about us and helped us with affection. We had a feeling that everything would be fine if we followed them" (interview, June 2000).

Both Suk's and Kim's comments provide a hint of why female workers, not male workers, developed a special relationship with church organizations. First of all, church groups showed more interest in the female workers because they were the most exploited and oppressed. As Reverend Cho Wha Soon stated, female factory workers were "the most alienated and oppressed of all" (1988, 135). It was natural that the industrial mission be targeted at the workers who were most severely exploited and most helpless. Intellectuals also had, to a certain degree, this paternalistic attitude toward young women workers, as people who were fragile and vulnerable and therefore must be protected. A second relevant factor is that the light manufacturing sector was relatively easier for the industrial mission to enter; it was far more difficult to gain access to the large-scale heavy industrial plants. For these reasons, a majority of the labor-oriented missionary activity was concentrated in the industrial sectors where women workers constituted the majority of the workforce.

More important, however, may be the difference in openness to church-group activities by female and male workers. First of all, female workers were more likely to attend church than male workers. More important, female workers were more interested in participating in small-group activities organized by church leaders—the main vehicle of the church-labor linkage was the small-group activities rather than regular church attendance. Why were women more interested in participating in these activities? We can think of several reasons: compared to men, women workers suffered greater psychological and emotional hardship in the factories and therefore had a greater psychological need for spiritual comfort; they had a greater desire for educational and cultural experiences to compensate for their damaged self-identity as factory workers; and they enjoyed less freedom to engage in diverse leisure-time activities. But Kim Ji-sun has

13. Kim Ji-sun used to be called Kim Bok-ja because she used a relative's name when she was first hired at Samwon Textile to hide that she was under the legal age of employment.

pointed out to me yet another factor—that women are generally more open and flexible in human relationships than men, so that they had fewer inhibitions about participating in unfamiliar social activities with strangers at the church, especially if they were not Christians. In contrast, male workers, in her view, were "more rigid and hierarchical" in human relationships and were more uncomfortable in participating in small-group activities or in any activities organized by church unless they themselves are Christians (interview, June 2000).

Whatever the reasons, the fact is that a good number of female workers in Seoul-Inchon area participated in small-groups activities organized by church groups and students, and, through these activities, they developed a strong solidarity among themselves and a sharper awareness of the injustices in their workplace. Gradually, this new awareness developed into union consciousness and a collective resolve to solve their problems by their own effort by establishing an independent union.

Gender Issues in the 1970s Labor Movement

Given that women workers were the main actors in the South Korean labor movement in the 1970s and the early 1980s, it is interesting to see how important feminist issues were in their struggles. Various sources suggest that they were not important at that time; in fact, feminist issues had been mute in virtually all labor disputes until the mid-1980s. Even in several well-organized and rather militant labor strikes led by women workers, such as at Wonpoong, Dongil, and Y. H. Trading companies, women strikers did not raise any gender-related issues as a major point of labor dispute. A minor exception was at Control Data, where women workers fought to obtain maternity leave and fairer promotion opportunities for women from their foreign employer in the late 1970s (Shin In-ryung 1988, 322–34). In virtually all labor conflicts of the 1970s, the main contention was over humane conditions for the entire working class, men and women, and over organizing independent unions to secure such a condition.

This was, of course, not because women workers were not concerned about the tremendous sexual inequality and oppression they experienced in their everyday life. We have seen in this and previous chapters that Korean women workers suffered an incredible amount of labor exploitation and patriarchal domination as well as sexual violence. Yet in the 1970s and until the second part of the 1980s, the majority of Korean women workers did not possess a proper interpretive framework or language to understand their experiences in terms of dominant gender relations. As Kim Ji-sun told me, "Of course, there were so many unfair things we, women workers, had to suffer. But at that time, we did not think that those were gender issues because the problems we faced at that time, both men and women, were so overwhelming that we thought only in terms of one whole working class. Now we can see that there were serious feminist issues" (interview, March 2000). My interviews with other early female activists also confirmed that until the mid-1980s women labor activists did not have a high level of feminist consciousness. Kim Ji-sun, Han Myung-hee (at Control Data), and Suk Jung-nam all told me that what bothered them the most at that time was the fact that women unionists had to leave the labor movement when they married; this handicap, they said, made them aware of patriarchy and gender inequality as a serious problem apart from class inequality.

But, as in other societies, gender consciousness deeply embedded in patriarchy was the slowest to change among Korean women. Based on her analysis of women workers' essays, Chung Hyun-baek observed, "What changed the slowest in their overall consciousness was gender consciousness. Especially difficult to overcome was their traditional conception about marriage. Nowhere in their essays can we find a statement that participation in the labor movement and contribution to society through these activities were as important as marriage for women" (1985, 156). It was, however, not just workers; the intellectuals who assisted women's labor movement revealed a similarly low level of feminist consciousness. Reverend Cho Wha Soon, in her recollection of her activities in the late 1970s, wrote, "In retrospect, I recall numerous experiences of sexism. However, then I was not conscious. When the awareness is raised, the same reality takes on a different face. Now I have crossed the bridge of no return" (1988, 138).

Furthermore, the movement circles in the 1970s and into the first half of the 1980s actively discouraged stressing gender issues apart from class issues; the two issues were regarded separate and potentially competing rather than interconnected. As Shin In-ryung, a highly respected female labor expert and professor of law, argues, "It is very important not to confuse a primary objective with a secondary one. Selecting a wrong 'primary objective' involves a serious mistake of obscuring the essential contradictions [in society] and stressing secondary problems. To caution against taking women's issues as a 'primary objective' also means to warn against a reformist feminist movement" (1988, 333–34).

Slighting gender issues in favor of class issues continued in the 1980s even among student labor activists. As Seung-kyung Kim observed in the late 1980s, "Despite their daily experiences with discrimination based on gender, women student activists saw gender issues as of secondary importance compared to class. They complained among themselves about the hierarchical and patriarchal structure of the student movement, but they rarely discussed their grievances with men, and women who did bring up gender problems were generally dismissed by male students as not taking class issues seriously enough. In spite of sharing experiences of sexual subordination with the workers they organized, these commonalities were seldom noted by female labor activists" (1997, 141).

Conclusion

Both the Korean government and employers continuously claimed that labor unrest in the 1970s and afterward was primarily due to agitation by "impure outside elements." There is some truth to their claims in that almost all union struggles in the 1970s were linked to and assisted by church organizations or dissident intellectuals. It seems sure that had there been no involvement by the religious and intellectual communities, the labor scene in the 1970s would have been quite different.

But this claim denies the real truth about the 1970s labor struggles. What caused the labor protests in the 1970s and the 1980s was not really outside agitation but the existential reality that Korean industrial workers experienced in their daily working lives. It was the dreadful conditions of work, poor wages, and, above all, unfair and unjust treatment by management, in short "inhumane conditions," that were unquestionably the real source of the labor struggle of the 1970s. As we have seen in chapter 3, production relations in Korean industries, especially in the women-dominated light manufacturing industries, exacted physical and emotional sacrifices beyond human endurance. Furthermore, the contemptuous attitude of management toward manual workers, and especially toward female workers, caused deep psychological wounds and resentment, providing a volatile source of labor protest.

Labor exploitation combined with gender-based oppression made the conditions of women workers much worse than those of men. Young inexperienced women workers, recruited fresh from the countryside, were prime objects of labor exploitation in the labor-intensive export industries. It was, however, not just the exploitative work conditions that encouraged women to become involved in labor struggles; probably more important was the rampant symbolic and physical abuse they experienced at work. They were constantly shouted at or beaten if they refused to behave submissively, they frequently became objects of sexual harassment, and they were frequently called "ignorant girls" and treated as if they were unworthy human beings. It was natural that under such circumstances women workers cried out for humane treatment more desperately than did men.

Ultimately, these material and symbolic conditions in the workplace triggered collective actions among a new generation of the Korean proletariat in the 1970s. When these collective responses began to emerge, however, the Korean industrial system allowed no legitimate channels for airing these grievances and seeking remedies. As we have seen, the exclusionary state corporatist system of labor control in the 1970s forced workers to find outlets outside the official union structure. At that point, a small group of Christian leaders and dissident intellectuals were willing to render assistance despite the risk of repression from the state.

Church organizations made several distinct contributions to the development of the Korean the working-class movement in the 1970s. First of all, the progressive churches provided a shelter, a social space, where workers gathered and shared their problems and perspectives. In the 1970s, there was no other place where Korean workers could interact freely and discuss their common problems. Second, church organizations helped workers to direct their efforts at organizing independent unions rather than sporadic individualistic protests. Through small-group activities and night schools that the church groups sponsored, workers learned about the importance of unions as the only effective means of improving their conditions in the factory. Third, church leaders assumed the role of protecting workers against state oppression, although not always effectively, and of mobilizing democratic alliances to support the fledgling democratic union movement. All in all, progressive church organizations played a critical role in facilitating the Korean labor movement and shaping the pattern of its development.

But, again, we must be careful not to be confused about who were the real agents of these struggles—the women workers not the church organizations. It was their experiences of brutality at work and the strong emotional bond they developed based on their common work experiences and common social background that made the remarkable solidarity actions possible. The role of the church leaders and intellectuals can best be understood as that of a catalyst, helping transform a structurally determined potentiality into an actuality.

In any event, it is important to remember that it was the women workers in the labor-intensive export sectors who fought hard to lay the foundation for the democratic union movement in the 1980s. The women-led struggles in the 1970s made a tremendous contribution in promoting worker consciousness, class identity, and networks of solidarity. Based on this groundwork, the Korean working-class formation developed rapidly in the next decade. Ogle is absolutely right when he writes: "When in the mid-eighties the male workers began to take action of their own, they found that they were standing on the shoulders of women who had been struggling for justice for more than ten years" (1990, 86).

5 Workers and Students

These barbarous repression and revenge given to our
solidarity struggle taught truth in starkest clarity. What is
choking workers is not just wicked employers, not just
violent police, not just the labor department which
became a tool of the regime, but the present regime which
hides its vile face behind all these.

(Declaration of the Workers' Solidarity
Struggle, in Donga Ilbo 1990, 72)

Several months of political freedom and uncertainty followed Park
Chung Hee's death in October 1979. The Spring of Seoul in 1980 was the
spring of political activism and democratic hope after the two-decade winter of authoritarian rule. The military was lurking behind the scenes, seeking the right moment and the right excuse to step in, but the people
enjoyed a new sense of power and freedom to speak out without immediate fear of police repression. The civil society was suddenly resurrected.

Workers did not fail to take advantage of this political opening to press
their bottled-up demands, and thus a wave of labor unrest erupted in spring
1980. The number of reported labor disputes increased sharply from 105 in
1979 to 407 in 1980. The absolute majority of these conflicts were concerned with economic issues such as delayed payments, wage increases,
plant closings, and layoffs. So the labor unrest during this period was primarily a reflection of the workers' desperate economic situation in the
ailing economy at the end of the 1970s. But the labor unrest during this
period of liberalization was not simply a reaction to these economic

problems, but also a challenge to the oppressive labor regime. A major objective of many labor protests was to dismantle the company-controlled unions (ŏyong chohap) and to organize independent unions, a natural extension of grassroots unionization movement that had begun at the end of the 1970s.

Labor conflicts during this period were by and large spontaneous and unorganized. They were expressions of the workers' long-suppressed demands for the minimum condition of "humanlike living," and there were few organizations that could systematically organize and guide workers' impulsive actions. Two cases of labor conflict that attracted much attention in 1980 reflect the general character of the labor movement in this period very well.

The first is the violent labor strike that occurred in April 1980 in the mining town of Sabuk in Kangwon province. Some three thousand miners employed at Tongwon colliery had long been suffering incredibly poor and dangerous working conditions, which had become worse in previous years due to the general decline of the coal industry. Miners' wages were very low and their overtime pay was not adequate. On top of that, the miners bitterly hated the company union and especially their coopted union leader, who had long betrayed the workers, misusing his position for personal enrichment and being a puppet for management. The Tongwon miners went on a strike, demanding a substantial wage increase and the resignation of the union leader. During their confrontation with the police, however, an accident happened in which three protesters were hit by a police car. The number of protesters quickly increased to several hundred, turning into an angry mob. The protesters occupied the police station, set fire to the union office, and tore apart managers' houses, and, when the hated union president was not found, they held his wife in retaliation. The local police was unable to control the mob and withdrew from the area, leaving the town under the workers' control. But the absence of any form of leadership and a growing anxiety over the consequences of their illegal actions led them to surrender to the police after three days.

Another similarly violent strike occurred a week later, on April 28, at Tongkook Chekang, a steel mill located in Pusan. Here again, the labor protest occurred initially over low wages and poor working conditions, but the management's unresponsive attitude and unfriendly police intervention angered the workers and triggered violent actions. Workers broke into the company office and destroyed personnel files, set fire to the buildings, and beat up several managers and foremen. Later, they battled with riot police with stones, iron pipes, and wooden bars. But, again, this spontaneous protest lasted only two days, bringing hardly any gains for workers.

These incidents demonstrate the character of worker struggles during this period: highly emotional, violent, unorganized, and short-lived. Virtu-

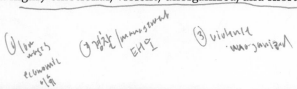

ally all labor conflicts and unionization struggles were confined to individual firms, and the labor activists of the time paid little attention to developing effective industry-level or regional-level labor organizations. The
dominant orientation among the unionists was economic unionism, concerned with improving the wages and working conditions of the workers
(Lim Ho 1992, 62–92; Kim Jin-ok 1984; Kim and Park 1989).

Repression and the Politicization of the Labor Struggle

The political activism that occurred in spring 1980 came to an abrupt
end when the military took over on May 17, 1980. A new military strong
man, Chun Doo Hwan, came to power after the bloody suppression of a
civil uprising in Kwangju, a provincial capital of the southwest region in
which more than two hundred citizens, students, and workers were mas-
sacred ruthlessly by a special military unit drawn from the demilitarized
zone (Clark 1988).

On assuming power, Chun Doo Hwan took extremely harsh measures to
demobilize the civil society and resume control of labor. Thousands of political activists were rounded up and, along with hoodlums and racketeers,
were sent to jails or purification camps. The regime cracked down especially hard on labor, abolishing the newly created independent unions one
by one and expelling labor activists from union leadership. The Chun regime was determined to wipe out "impure elements" from the industrial
arena. Employers took advantage of this anti-labor atmosphere and fired
thousands of workers who had actively participated in the democratic
union movement. These fired workers were then blacklisted by the security agency and barred from gainful employment. This fierce attack on the
democratic union movement continued until 1983. As a consequence of
these joint attacks on labor by the state and by employers, the number
of unions dropped drastically, from 6,011 in May 1980 to 2,618 by the end
of the year; the number of union members also decreased from 1,120,000
to 950,000. Again, workers were forced into silence and submission, and
the labor movement was virtually suspended, at least on the surface, for
the next three years (Kim Jang-han 1989).

Ironically, however, the Korean working-class movement grew stronger
and more mature during the first years of the Chun regime. Beneath a surface of political passivity, students, workers, and other dissident groups
were reflecting on their defeats in 1980, on the meaning of the Kwangju
massacre, and on their future strategy. As one prominent intellectual labor
activist, Kim Moon-soo remarked, "The 5.17 [military coup in 1980]—that
was a critical occasion that shook not only me but also our nation's labor
movement at its roots and forced us to search for a radical redirection"
(1986, 146). This was a period of much important theorizing about the

nature of South Korea's social formation, the historic mission of the *min-jung* movement, and U.S. involvement in the country's destiny. It was a period of Marxism and radical discourse; many students, intellectuals, and political activists were strongly influenced by Marxism, dependency perspective, or people's liberation theology and embraced the idea of radical social transformation through collective action. (For a review of the many political debates during this period, see Park Hyun-chae and Cho Hee-Yeon 1989; Hong Seung-tae 1994.)

In this period, church influence on the labor movement declined considerably as labor leaders gradually became disenchanted with the church leaders' mild approach to labor struggles. They realized that in the face of the determined efforts of the Chun regime to pulverize the democratic union movement, the church organizations were of little help and the church leaders' humanitarian orientation was too meek and passive in light of the workers' recent experiences with the repressive regime. By the early 1980s, there were a large number of unemployed blacklisted workers, such as the unionists at Wonpoong, Dongil, Y. H., and Control Data. The Chun regime's ferocious attack on democratic unions produced still more determined labor activists with years of union experience who had been expelled from their jobs. Blocked from gainful employment by the government, they had no choice but to become professional labor activists. These outside (*chaeya*) labor activists played an instrumental role in interconnecting unionists across firms and linking them to dissident political communities. They organized mass demonstrations demanding the revision of the labor laws and the abolition of the blacklist. The consequences of hardline labor repression during the Chun regime was, therefore, the ever enlarging circle of *sŏnjin nodongja* (workers with advanced consciousness), who had acquired years of experience in the democratic union movement and, from it, a high level of class consciousness. With the growth of the number of grassroots labor activists, both inside and outside the industrial arena, the labor movement gradually outgrew the need to depend on outside organizations, especially on church organizations.

The growth of class-conscious labor activists and grassroots organizations, however, did not lead the South Korean labor movement to develop autonomously. On the contrary, the working-class struggles became more intimately enmeshed in the larger political struggles against the authoritarian state. Increasingly, however, the workers' ties with outside agencies were not because of the workers' weakness or inability to defend themselves but because of their strength and strategic value, which other antigovernment opposition groups began to recognize. Despite their internal organizational weakness, and despite workplace conditions that stifled their interest articulation beyond immediate economic circumstances, the number of factory workers grew to three million by the early 1980s and constituted the largest occupational group possessing huge potential. The concentration of these workers in a few industrial centers, the slow improvement of their working conditions in a rapidly growing economy, and the rapidly growing class awareness among workers promised that the industrial proletariat was destined to become a major social force in the evolution of the new industrial society.

Those who recognized this potential most clearly were the student activists. Although students had been involved in labor affairs since the 1970s, their direct involvement in the labor movement was relatively insignificant until the early 1980s. However, the bitter experiences of struggle in 1980 and harsh political repression by the Chun regime led them to view labor mobilization as a new strategy of the anti-regime democratic movement. During the first three years of Chun's rule, when political opposition was not tolerated, the student movement adopted labor praxis (*hyŏnjangron*) as its major political strategy. Their methodology of labor praxis was to enter the industrial arena by becoming factory workers and try to promote class consciousness among the workers and help them organize unions. The ultimate goal was to lead the labor struggles toward the larger political goals of ending military rule and achieving the radical transformation of South Korean society. The development of the labor movement in the 1980s was intimately connected to the large number of students who dropped out of college and became students-turned-workers, whom the government labeled "disguised workers." Thus, it is important to examine the role of activist students during this period more closely.

Worker-Student Alliance

South Korean students' involvement in the labor movement began in the early 1970s. Chun Tae-Il's self-immolation in 1970 was an important trigger of this movement. On hearing of Chun's heroic protest by self-sacrifice, students from several colleges rushed to the hospital emergency room where he had died. They tried to carry out Chun's funeral, but the police forbade this. Students were particularly touched when they discovered that Chun Tae-Il had longed for acquaintance with intellectuals who could render some help in his lone struggle against the unsympathetic government. Chun was known to have said frequently, "How I wish I had a college student friend" (Cho Young-rae 1991, 168). He lamented his ignorance in legal matters and his lack of ties with influential people. Chun's death thus provided an awakening for students. They discovered one of the most serious problems in South Korean society hidden behind the glory of economic development, something to which they had paid little attention in their preoccupation with political issues. The students who had to become involved in labor issues in the 1970s, however, were primarily motivated by humanitarian concern for workers who suffered from inhumane conditions, and thus their orientation was not much different from that of church leaders. One of the earliest students-turned-workers, Kim Moon-soo (who became a factory worker in the early 1970s well before labor praxis became popular among student activists) explained his motivation for entering factory world: "the rudimentary realization that not only do industrial workers constitute a large group but also the labor movement constitutes the core force for societal development, that workers must also be able to live as respectable human beings, and that when Chun Tae-Il even committed self-immolation I must make at least a small contribution ... these are all the reasons why I decided to select the life of a factory worker at that time" (1986, 148).[1]

Entering the 1980s with bitter political experiences and a growing awareness of the need to build broad alliances with other democratic forces in their struggle against the immensely powerful state, students developed a new orientation toward labor. They no longer looked at industrial laborers as mere objects of humanitarian concern. They now looked on them as their most important political allies and as potentially a most powerful force for social transformation. They had seen how powerful and threatening mass labor mobilizations could be in the violent labor strikes of 1980, such as the Sabuk miners' strike. They realized, however, that the power of labor remained only a potential; it had yet to be tapped and mobilized. They defined their critical task as that of raising political consciousness among workers, helping them organize themselves into effective unions, and leading their collective actions toward larger political goals. During the early years of the 1980s, out of the intense student debates on appropriate ideologies and strategies, worker-student solidarity (nohak yŏndae) emerged as a dominant orientation among radical students (Song Jung-nam 1985; Hwang Ŭi-bong 1986; Ilsongjung 1988).

Thus, from the early 1980s the number of students who carried their political convictions into the factories increased dramatically. Some dropped out of college, some graduated, and some were expelled from their schools for being involved in illegal anti-government demonstrations. The greatest number, several hundred a year, entered factories between 1983 and 1986. Ogle (1990, 99) estimates that there were approximately three thousand or more students-turned-workers by the mid-1980s. My informants gave slightly higher estimates and told me that about a half of these students

1. This essay presents an excellent description of the experience of an intellectual who participated deeply in the democratic union movement. Kim Moon-soo was one of a few students-turned-workers, who was elected president of a local union and was able to lead the union movement with strong support from the rank-and-file members even after the company disclosed his identity and tried to discredit his true motives for union activity. In the 1990s, he entered politics, and he was elected to National Assembly in 1996.

were women (Chung Kwang-pil, Roh Hoe-chan, Sim Sang-jung, and Lee Sun-ju, interviews, summer 1996; see also Hwang 1985, 15). They were mostly employed in medium-size manufacturing firms located in major industrial centers around Seoul, Inchon and Pupyŏng (west of Seoul), and Anyang (south of Seoul). Very few of them went to the heavy industrial belts in the southern part of the country, such as Ulsan, Masan, and Changwon.

In the early 1980s, there were so many students-turned-workers in factory towns in Seoul-Inchon area that they unknowingly bumped to one another in their disguised identities. Kim Seung-kyung tells one student-turned-worker's interesting story, a story similar to those I have heard from my own informants: "I went to work [as a disguised worker] at a small electronics factory with 140 employees in Inchon. And guess what? Of those 140 workers, there were about 10 disguised workers. Immediately, I could tell who were activists (*hwaldongga*). That small factory was over-flowing with *hwaldongga*" (1997, 135).

Students-turned-workers went through a difficult period of adapting to hard factory life and establishing themselves as sincere and trustworthy people to fellow workers. Then they began to recruit workers to form small groups (*sogŭrup*), designed to cultivate class identity and consciousness among workers through study, discussions, and recreational activities. Composed of seven to twelve workers, these small groups met regularly to discuss labor-management issues and study labor history, labor laws, and the logistics of organizing a union. During the first half of the 1980s, an estimated two thousand factory workers in the Kyungin (Kyungki-Inchon) areas participated in these small-group activities and received a consciousness-raising education. Close social networks developed among these small groups across firms through the overlapping ties of the students-turned-workers and the outside (*chaeya*) labor activists who had been fired from their jobs for their union activities. Many of those who played a major role in the democratic union movement in the second half of the 1980s were those who had actively participated in these small-group activities.

As the students' labor praxis became a dominant trend in the student movement in the 1980s, controversies arose among the activists over the most appropriate strategy for labor mobilization. Broadly speaking, student labor strategists were divided into two opposing camps.[2] The first was the "small-group movement" approach, which stressed the importance of fostering class capacity in the industrial arena by raising class consciousness among the rank-and-file workers and producing a nucleus of advanced-

2. There were several other, more extreme views. For more details on the political and ideological debates about labor struggles and the worker-student solidarity movement during the 1980s, see Kim Yong-ki and Park Sŭng-ok (1989), and Kim Jang-han et al. (1989, 98–113).

consciousness labor activists (sŏnjin nodongja), who would lead the work-ing-class struggle in the future. The advocates of this approach believed that any large-scale political mobilization of workers at that time was pre-mature and unrealistic without this foundational work. They argued that clandestine small-group activities were the most practical approach, given the political circumstances under which even legitimate unions found little space to operate.

The opposing strategy was more politically oriented and ambitious. Proponents of this approach, called the "area-based labor movement," crit-icized the small-group approach as putting too much emphasis on educa-tion and preparatory work while neglecting the importance of actual polit-ical struggle. They insisted that a more effective strategy was to organize the "explosive energy of the masses of workers" at the level of industrial area, rather than at the level of individual firms, and to develop political organizations that could coordinate and guide worker struggles at the regional level. Whereas the small-group approach emphasized the importance of ground work at the level of individual enterprises, the area approach stressed the strategic significance of area-based interfirm politi-cal organizations that could promote workers' economic and political interests.

Proponents of these two approaches adopted divergent methods of labor involvement. Whereas the small-group-oriented activists chose to enter factories and work at the lowest level of the labor praxis, working dili-gently to raise consciousness among workers and building the founda-tional units of labor organization, the area-oriented group attempted to form labor organizations at the regional level and engage in political struggles in open defiance of the regime. They also, however, regarded ac-tual labor experience in the factory as a prerequisite for their regional labor movement. Thus, the divergence of the two camps was not really as great as each group of labor activists believed at the time. Regardless of their dif-ferences in political and strategic orientations, there is no question that both groups of student activists contributed greatly to the development of the Korean labor movement in the 1980s. Whereas the small-group ap-proach represented the mainstream of the worker-student (nohak yŏndae) movement in the first years of the Chun regime, when political repression was at its height, the regional labor movement became more popular among radical students with a gradual weakening of political control by the regime.

After the brutal repression of civil society in his first years of power, Chun Doo Hwan decided to introduce a partial liberalization of political activities in the hope of broadening the popular base of his regime in the second half of 1983. In spring 1984, the government released a number of political prisoners, allowed dissident professors and students to return to their schools, and partially relaxed its tight control over labor activities. Several factors contributed to this partial political liberalization. Chun was troubled by the continual lagging legitimacy of his regime and felt it necessary to broaden its social base of support in preparation for the upcoming general election in 1985 and for the two sets of Olympic Games to be staged in Seoul, the Asian Olympic Games in 1986 and the worldwide Olympic Games in 1988. Furthermore, the goals of economic liberalization and a welfare society, which the Chun government identified as the regime's principal project, called for a more liberal political approach. Also, the robust economic growth after a brief period of political instability in 1980 probably made Chun feel fairly confident about securing popular support, especially from the middle class.

In any event, Chun's gesture of political reapproachment allowed an upsurge of political activism and labor conflicts. Labor disputes increased in frequency from 98 cases in 1983 to 113 cases in 1984 to 265 cases in 1985. When the labor movement resurfaced in 1984, it demonstrated a greater organizational strength and a higher level of political consciousness among workers than ever before. Workers swiftly organized numerous independent unions (about two hundred independent unions were formed in 1984) and fought to revive those unions previously dissolved by the government. Of particular significance was the effort to revive the Chunggye districtwide labor union, which had been formed by Chun Tae-Il's fellow garment factory workers after his self-immolation and which had symbolized the democratic union movement in the 1970s. An alliance of workers, students, and other political activists staged several public rallies and reopened the union in defiance of the government ban.

The Chunggye district garment union received the harshest repression by the military junta in 1980 and its members fought against it most fiercely. The military government first arrested Lee So-sun—Chun Tae-Il's mother, who was regarded as the mother of all workers by Chunggye district workers—and the military court gave her a 1-year sentence for her involvement in the labor dispute in the spring 1980. Subsequently, the authority ordered the Chunggye union to disband, and when its members defied the order it sent the police to remove union files and other materials and lock up the office. Chunggye union members, however, never accepted the state action as legitimate and fought for the reinstatement of their union. At a protest in January 1981, union leaders clashed with the police violently and threatened to commit mass suicide in protest. When the Chun regime loosened its iron-fist control a little in 1983, the Chunggye union leaders were the first to organize a mass protest in defiance of the security laws. Claiming the illegality of the previous state action, they organized a preparatory committee for the reinstatement of Chunggye garment union in March 1984, headed by Min Jong-duk. Subsequently, they organized public forums, attended by many church leaders and representatives of pro-democracy organizations, and a series of public rallies and street demonstrations. In fall 1984, an alliance of Chunggye union leaders, students, and other labor activists organized two large-scale street demonstrations in downtown Seoul and clashed violently with riot police. Some two thousand students were estimated to have participated in these street protests (Hong Seung-tae 1994, 126). The Chunggye union struggle thus portended the emerging pattern of labor struggle based on the alliance between students and workers.

The character of labor conflicts had changed noticeably by the mid-1980s. Increasingly, the focus of workers' struggles was no longer isolated economic issues but organizing new independent unions, and their new tactics centered on promoting solidarity struggles among workers in several factories located within an industrial area. The concentration of factories in a few industrial parks and the close personal networks developed among the labor activists made this strategy feasible. The changed character of working-class struggles in the mid-1980s was demonstrated most clearly by two major worker struggles that occurred in 1985: the strike at a conglomerate firm, Daewoo Automobile Plant, and the solidarity struggle among workers employed at several factories located in Kuro Industrial Park. Both were, to a great extent, the products of student involvement in the labor movement.

Daewoo Auto Strike

On April 22–23, 1985, a very unusual wage negotiation was held at Daewoo Auto Company's Pupyong plant, located approximately twenty miles west of Seoul. (This account is based primarily on Daewoo Auto Union 1985.) Two men faced each other across the table in a temporary meeting room at the plant. One man was Kim Woo Jung, chairman of the Daewoo group, at the time the fourth largest conglomerate in South Korea, and the other man, wearing a red ribbon on his head, was Hong Young-pyo, a representative of the striking workers. Until two days before, wage negotiations had been held between the president of the Daewoo Auto Company, Choe Myung-kul, and a team of union representatives. But as the negotiations deteriorated and the six-day strike became violent, and as the media began to highlight the strike, the conglomerate's chairman decided to settle the matter himself.

Hong, the 28-year-old leader of the striking workers, was not a union leader, nor was he a typical worker. He was an ex-college student who had majored in philosophy for two years and then dropped out to become one of several students-turned-workers who entered the Pupyong plant in the early 1980s.

Daewoo Pupyong workers' highly organized and aggressive struggle, unprecedented at Daewoo or at any Korean conglomerate firm, had been initially organized and led by two other students-turned-workers, Song Kyung-pyung and Lee Yong-sun. In August 1984, Song led a protest against the company for treating unfairly those who returned from compulsory military service during their tenure with the company. The law prescribed that the length of service in the military be counted toward tenure at the company, but management refused. Workers had been extremely unhappy about unpaid bonuses in the past two years and with underpayments in their holiday and overtime wages. Workers' brewing resentment burst out in a spontaneous protest in early August 1984 over another unreasonable work assignment for workers who had just returned from three days of reserve army drill. The workers were angry not only with management but also with the company union, which had been collecting dues from them but had done nothing for them. During the course of the workers' protest, Song and Lee skillfully articulated the workers' resentment and channeled it to the larger issues of labor relations and union representativeness.

The company investigated the backgrounds of Song and Lee and discovered that they were students-turned-workers. Management then assigned Song to a clerical post and transferred Lee to an affiliate company in another locality. However, both of them refused to comply with these transfer orders and fought to retain their posts. Although they were eventually fired and physically forced to leave the factory, their spirited fight made a great impact on other workers. Workers came to acquire a strong sense of their rights in the face of the many unfair and arbitrary practices of management and showed a strong desire to transform their puppet union into a genuine representative union. They organized a special Committee for Normalization of the Union and prepared themselves for a major confrontation with management and the incumbent union leadership. With overwhelming support from rank-and-file members, the rebel committee quickly took over the functions of the official union.

Thus, when the annual wage-negotiation period arrived in spring 1985, Pupyong's Daewoo workers were fully charged for aggressive wage bargaining. Workers had a good reason for demanding a high wage hike that year: they had not received a wage increase for the previous two years due to the company's poor financial situation. Daewoo Auto, under a joint ventureship with General Motors, had not performed well in the early 1980s, but had begun to turn around in 1984. In April 1985, Daewoo workers demanded an 18.7 percent wage increase and a fair share of the profit from the increase in productivity. The workers had rejected a more modest proposal made by the official union. Workers further expressed their distrust of the current union leaders by selecting a new wage-negotiation team. In particular, they demanded that Hong Young-pyo, a student-turned-worker, be included in the negotiation team. After a few days of tense negotiations and sit-in demonstrations, workers went on strike on April 16. On the fourth day of the strike, some 350 workers forced their way into the third floor of the company's Technology Development Center and began a vigil protest. The Daewoo strike soon became a sensitive political issue, and the Daewoo company came under heavy pressure from the government to settle the matter quickly, lest it spread to other firms where wage negotiations were being conducted in April.

Thus, the Daewoo group chairman, Kim Woo Jung decided to intervene in the negotiations. Arriving at the Inchon plant, Kim first met with the official union representatives. After a few unsuccessful meetings with them, he realized that it would be necessary to negotiate with Hong Young-pyo, the bona fide leader of the striking workers. In a move uncharacteristic of a Korean big business owner, Kim proposed to have direct, one-to-one talks with Hong. After several marathon meetings that lasted through two midnights, the two men agreed on a wage package that included a 10 percent increase in basic wage rates, a new allowance of 4 percent, and the expansion of the company welfare facilities, including the construction of employee apartments. All in all, this agreement came very close to the workers' original demands.

The Daewoo Auto strike was significant in that it was the first well-organized strike that occurred at a conglomerate firm and in the male-dominated heavy industrial sector. This strike thus presaged the arrival of male workers as the major agents of the South Korean labor movement. It also signaled that labor activism in South Korea was no longer confined to the light manufacturing sector, but had begun to spread to heavy and chemical industries dominated by large firms. The Daewoo strike also demonstrated that students-turned-workers constituted a critical element in labor activism in the Seoul-Kyungin industrial areas, where they entered in large numbers.

Kuro Solidarity Struggle

Two months after the successful strike at Daewoo Auto, a more significant labor struggle occurred in Seoul. (This account is drawn primarily from Seoul nodong undong yŏnhap 1986. More in-depth information was gathered from my interviews in 1996 with several active participants in the struggle, including Kim Jun-yong, the union leader of Daewoo Apparel whose arrest triggered the Kuro struggle; and Lee Sun-ju and Shim Sang-jung, members of a secret regional organizing committee.) In the early morning of June 22, 1985, the police appeared at Daewoo Apparel, a medium-size garment factory located in the Kuro Industrial Park, and arrested three union leaders. Workers at the Daewoo Apparel factory were extremely surprised because there were no particular labor problems at the time and the union had not initiated any activity that conflicted with management. The spring wage negotiations had been settled already and they believed that management was relatively content with this year's wage settlement. Then suddenly, two months after their collective action on the wage negotiation, the police arrested the union leader, Kim Jun-yong and two other union officers, Kang Myung-ja and Chu Jae-sook, on charges of organizing overnight sit-ins during the wage-negotiation period.

The arrest was made on a Saturday, so workers had to wait until Monday morning to respond to this offensive action. But on Sunday, forty-four union representatives met at the arrested Kim's apartment and decided to go on a strike and fight for the release of their union leaders. This incident also angered union leaders at other firms in Kuro Industrial Park and many students-turned workers who were active in the area. There was a consensus among labor leaders that the arrest of the Daewoo Apparel union officers was not a simple isolated incident but a clear signal of the government's new offensive on the labor movement. Indeed, the Chun government had been concerned about the escalation of the opposition movement and labor conflicts since the end of 1983, in the wake of partial political liberalization. The April strike at the Daewoo Auto plant and the astonishing degree of solidarity and aggressiveness it demonstrated must have made a strong impression on both employers and the government. Labor leaders believed that the government was intent on stamping out the democratic union movement, starting with the removal of the radical leadership from Daewoo Apparel. They also believed that the government had deliberately delayed its attack on the unions until late June because the colleges were on summer vacation and the national assembly was not in session. June was normally a relatively quiet political season in South Korea.

Most of the unions at the factories in Kuro Industrial Park had been formed during the short liberalization period since the end of 1983. The Daewoo Apparel union was formed in June 1984 by a small group of workers after years of determined efforts. Kim Jun-yong, who had previously worked as a tailor in the Chunggye garment district, had played a critical role in forming the union at Daewoo Apparel and was elected union president. In the same month that the Daewoo Apparel union was formed, several other unions were established in the Kuro area, including unions at Karibong Electronics, Hyosŏng Mulsan, Sŏnil Textile, and Puhŭngsa Garment Factory, all located close to one another in the densely populated industrial district of Kuro. From the establishment of these unions and even before, union leaders collaborated closely, exchanging information and devising common strategies for union action. They often organized interfirm

Figure 6. Kuro solidarity strike in 1985. (Provided by *JoongAng Daily*)

activities and received leadership training together at the office of the
Metal Industry Union or elsewhere. Thus, on hearing that Daewoo Apparel
union officers had been arrested, union leaders representing Kuro's democratic unions gathered quickly and decided to go on a solidarity strike
(fig. 6).

On Monday morning, June 24, workers who reported to work at the
Daewoo Apparel Kuro plant heard the news of Kim Jun-yong's arrest.
They were shocked and outraged. As soon as the morning stretching exercises were over, some three hundred workers stormed into the second floor
of the factory building and blocked the entrances with sewing machines
and rolls of fabric. The workers' demands, unlike most previous labor
protests, were primarily political. The placards they hung from the second
floor read: "Release our Union Officers!"; "Guarantee the Three Basic Labor Laws!"; "Stop Repressing Democratic Unions!"; "Revise the Oppressive Labor Laws!"; "Step Down, Labor Minister!"; "Go Away, Violent

Police!" There were no placards making economic demands or demands addressed to the employers. All the demands were addressed to the government, the oppressive power. From the very beginning, this was a political struggle.

At 2 P.M., the Daewoo Apparel workers heard the loud sounds of gongs (*ching* and *kkwaengari*) from the opposite building where the Hyosŏng Textile factory was located. The gongs were a signal that the Hyosŏng workers had started their strike. Daewoo workers rushed to the windows facing the Hyosŏng factory and there was a big placard: "Daewoo Fighting!" They also saw Hyosŏng workers dancing the "liberation dance" (popular among students and workers in the 1980s) on the second-floor veranda. Both groups of workers shouted encouragement and waved at each other. At about the same time, workers at three other factories went on solidarity strikes—at two of the Karibong Electronics factories and at Sŏnil Textile. Thus, by the afternoon of June 24, four firms were involved in solidarity strikes, involving approximately 1,300 workers (three hundred at Daewoo Apparel, four hundred at Hyosŏng Textile, five hundred at the two Karibong Electronics plants, and seventy at Sŏnil Textile).

On the second day, workers at three more firms, Sejin Electronics, Namsung Electronics, and Rom-Korea, joined the solidarity struggle by engaging in sit-ins, work slowdowns, and refusals to have lunch. And two days later on June 27, union members at another firm, Samsung Pharmaceutical Company (at Sungsu-dong), also joined the solidarity struggle. All together, eight firms and a total of 2,500 workers participated in the Kuro solidarity struggle, which lasted six days. In addition, Chunggye Textile Union, although not located in the Kuro area, played a very important supportive role from the very beginning. Its midtown office was a major gathering place for labor activists, who provided strategic guidance for the striking workers in Kuro Industrial Park, while organizing aggressive anti-government campaigns and demonstrations.

The Kuro struggle in June 1985 was a solidarity struggle in two senses. First, it was an interfirm solidarity struggle, drawing participation from workers employed in several firms in Kuro industrial area and its vicinity. Second, this struggle represented an effort to forge solidarity among labor, students, and various dissident groups fighting together for justice and democracy. Students and pro-democracy opposition groups were actively involved in the solidarity strikes from the first day. Every day during the six-day struggle, the Kuro industrial area became a battleground, as many students and labor activists who had been fired from their previous workplaces congregated to express support for the Kuro workers. From the second day, a large number of anti-regime groups waged sit-ins at various places in Seoul and issued a joint protest announcement denouncing the dictatorial regime and its oppressive labor policies. Also, several religious groups, including Protestant, Catholic, and Buddhist groups, expressed their support for the Kuro workers' struggle.

Daewoo Apparel workers went on a hunger strike demanding the release of their union leaders. In reaction, the company blocked the delivery of food to protesters and turned off the electricity and water to the building. Managers also used the familiar tactic of sending telegrams to the striking workers' parents, telling them that their children had been "duped and taken hostage by communists," and that their children were destroying the company's property and the parents would be charged for the damage. Many scared parents came and tried to take their daughters home. Many of them, upset and angry at their daughters' participation in this kind of protest activity, called their daughters names in angry voices and some even threatened their daughters using phrases such as, "You communist-like girl, I'll kill you when we get home!" (Seoul nodong undong yŏnhap 1986, 57). Some agitated fathers broke into the room where strikers were and took their daughters away, pulling them by the hair. After the strike had ended, the workers recollected that, other than enduring hunger, their parents' reaction was the most difficult thing to endure during the strike (Seoul nodong undong yŏnhap 1986, 50–65).

The strike at Daewoo Apparel ended on June 29 with a violent attack by pro-management male workers and company-hired thugs. In the early morning of that day, striking workers received unexpected guests—twelve students entered the second floor of the Daewoo Apparel building by climbing up the wall of the next building. They brought food in their backpacks, and they told the workers that they had come to participate in their struggle. Soon after the students and workers had exchanged emotional greetings, however, they were attacked by hundreds of strike breakers who broke into the room. The intruders, composed largely of hired thugs, hit strikers ruthlessly with wooden bars and iron pipes; the students were beaten almost to death. Hungry and extremely exhausted, workers had little strength to resist the violence, and the police surrounding the factory compound did not bother to interfere. The strikes at other factories ended in more or less the same way.

Undoubtedly, Kuro workers suffered enormous sacrifices. Many union leaders were arrested and jailed, while others left the area. The unions at Daewoo Apparel, Karibong, Hyosŏng, Sŏnil, and Puhŭng disbanded after the loss of their dedicated members. All firms intensified their labor surveillance, and the government proclaimed that it would employ whatever means necessary to eradicate "impure elements" from the industrial arena. Thus, it seems that workers lost everything—their jobs, their leaders, their comrades, and their hard-won unions.

However, these were just the immediate consequences. As world history has shown many times, class struggles can produce remarkable results in

the long run, from defeats as well as from victories. Although the Kuro solidarity struggle seemed to have brought only devastating defeat to workers,
this collective experience contributed tremendously in raising the workers' political consciousness and promoting mutual solidarity among workers across firms. Given the political nature of the Kuro struggle, in terms
of both its objectives and its organizational form, this solidarity struggle
had a much greater impact on workers' political consciousness than most
previous struggles.[3]

After the Kuro solidarity struggle, labor activists became more interested
in establishing broader and more politically oriented labor organizations
beyond the confines of enterprise unions. In August 1985, labor activists
who had led the Kuro struggle (the majority of whom were students-
turned-workers) formed a regional class organization, the Seoul Council of
the Labor Movement (*Sŏnoryŏn*), by merging three Seoul-based labor organizations that had openly challenged the state's labor repression in the
previous years (the Committee to Fight Labor Repression, Association
of Democratic Union Movements in Kuro Area, and Chunggye Textile
Union). In the following year, a similar regional political organization was
formed in the Inchon area, the Inchon Council of the Labor Movement (*In-
oryŏn*). Both organizations were the products of the changing orientation
among labor activists, especially among ex-student labor leaders, toward
building class organizations at the regional level, overcoming economic
unionism at the enterprise level, and channeling labor protests toward
broader political goals. Those who organized the Seoul and Inchon regional
labor councils represented the most radical segment of the democratic
union movement at the time. The two organizations positioned themselves as vanguard political organizations in the workers' revolutionary
struggles against the "fascist state," but neither of them existed very long.
Plagued by internal disunity due to ideological controversies, external repression, and lack of resources, both organizations were dissolved within
two years.[4]

Social Bases of the Solidarity Struggle

We have already seen that students played an active role in supporting
workers during the Kuro solidarity struggle. They were ubiquitous on Kuro

3. Kim Moon-soo writes about the significance of the Kuro struggle: "The Kuro solidarity struggle was an extremely meaningful struggle that provided a critical juncture in the
Korean labor movement by breaking at once with the past negative trend, the economistic
and preparatory orientation, and the limitation of trade unionism" (1986, 154).

4. Critics of this regional political labor movement in 1985 and 1986 argued that they
"had no proper appreciation of developing unions which is the basic mass organization of
the working class and even showed a tendency to denigrate the union movement itself"
(Kim Jang-han, et al. 1989, 107).

streets, shouting slogans and throwing leaflets, and they organized street demonstrations with workers from other areas. But the students' role in the Kuro struggle was more significant than just what they did on the streets. The government claimed that the Kuro workers' strikes had been instigated by leftist students who had penetrated the industrial arena in order to agitate innocent workers and cause social instability. Managers also told their workers that they had been duped and used by pro-communist student radicals. To convince their skeptical workers, some companies detected the students-turned-workers among their union officers and displayed their names in a big sign in front of striking workers. The mass media also collaborated by making many direct and indirect references to the role of "disguised workers" in organizing this politically motivated worker struggle.

The majority of workers must have been skeptical of these accusations, but were nevertheless scared to participate in the strikes. However, there were many workers who were willing to bear the consequences of joining the strikes. Workers were upset by the way they were depicted in the media, as if they were "just ignorant people or puppets who are incapable of defending their own rights." In an angry tone, one worker claimed, "What has awakened us was not 'agitations' or 'steerings from the rear,' but the wretched condition of our lives. That's what taught us everything" (Um Hyun-young 1986, 153).

Korean analysts tend to agree with this view. Choi Chang-woo, who analyzed the context of the Kuro solidarity struggle argues, "At the time of the strike, students-turned-workers had shorter periods of labor involvement compared with the ordinary workers who constituted the core leadership of the democratic unions, and they also had an insufficient understanding of the ordinary workers' thinking and attitudes" (Choi Chang-woo 1987, 117). He quotes one union leader as saying that the solidarity strikes were the course of action that "the mass of the workers selected and what they decided to do" (118). Choi further argues that there is no evidence to believe that "the solidarity strikes of the Kuro workers, which were a 'political struggle,' were possible thanks to the 'correct guidance' by the outside organizations (of the intellectual labor activists)" (118).

Obviously, attributing the occurrence of the Kuro solidarity struggle solely to agitation by radical students distorts the true nature of this struggle. Workers were not simply duped into these collective actions by student agitators. As workers themselves said, the abject conditions of their lives and all the mistreatment they had undergone made them angry and volatile. And it was their realization of the significance of the independent unions as their only hope of bringing change that made the Kuro workers fight fiercely in defense of their unions. In addition, there were ecological factors that made the interfirm solidarity struggle possible. A high concentration of production workers in a fairly restricted industrial town, the relative homogeneity of the labor force in terms of demographic and social characteristics, and a high rate of job mobility within the geographical area all promoted social ties and communication among the different groups of workers in this area.

These structural and ecological conditions, however, were probably not sufficient to produce the Kuro solidarity struggle. The cultivation of worker solidarity across firms required the role of an agency and a common experience of struggles. In this very regard, we must not underestimate the role of the student activists, as well as that of other (professional) labor activists from the working-class background, in fostering worker solidarity across firms and also across regions. As we have seen, an area-based labor-student solidarity struggle was an important strategy among the student activists, and a number of students-turned-workers in the Kuro industrial area before 1985 had devoted their efforts toward this goal. Also active in this area were many previous union leaders, who were genuine workers but had been fired from their jobs because of their union activism. These two groups of labor activists (from a working-class background and from a student background), despite some differences in political orientation,[5] were intimately meshed together to form large networks of professional labor activists, inside and outside the industrial arena. They were both actively involved in small-group activities, which mushroomed in Kuro industrial area and which produced a large number of workers equipped with a growing class awareness and union consciousness in the early 1980s. As previously noted, the unions at Daewoo Apparel, Karibong, Hyosŏng, and Sŏnil companies were organized at the same time in 1984 and went through the same struggles to protect themselves against hostile actions to destroy them by the companies. From the time of union formation, unionists cooperated closely among themselves by exchanging information, seeking expert advice, and devising common strategies. Subsequently, they invited one another to a variety of union activities, such as

5. In general, labor leaders from working-class backgrounds, be they inside or outside employment, tended to take a more cautious approach in linking labor disputes to larger political issues for fear of inviting punitive state actions on their unions, whereas students-turned-workers were more politically oriented and were generally more willing to sacrifice individual unions if deemed necessary for a larger political cause. Bang Yong-suk (who was the president of Wonpoong Textile union) told me that "students sometimes do not appreciate how precious our unions are and how much sacrifices we had to make in order to establish these unions," and that students-turned-workers were apt to engage in a kind of "political adventurism" at the risk of destroying these hard-built unions (interview, June 1994). Kim Ji-sun made a similar remark: "Jobs and unions are the basis of our livelihood. When fired, students can leave [factory jobs] but we cannot" (interview, June 2000). But both of them stressed that these differences between them and student labor activists were minor and caused no problem in the close cooperation between the two groups—because they had a common and formidable enemy.

the celebration of the union anniversary, overnight training of union officers, and cultural or athletic events. All these efforts had produced a strong sense of comradeship and common destiny among the active members of the four unions prior to the 1985 solidarity struggles.

Two Students-Turned-Workers 이사주

Lee Sun-ju was born in 1960 into a comfortable middle-class family. She and her younger brother grew up in Taegu, the third largest city in South Korea. After graduating from an elite high school in Taegu, she entered Seoul Women's University in 1979, majoring in nutritional science. She was a typical student, with a relatively quiet and passive personality, but with a great intellectual curiosity.

In her first years in college, she participated in circle activities, as many students did at that time, and became acquainted with many leftist books. Because there were few such books available in Korean, her circle members learned Japanese to read these books. She felt that these books provided very clear and persuasive answers to many questions she and her friends had about current problems in Korean society and the world, questions never addressed in her college classes. Their circle members spent many hours reading the then-prohibited Marxist literature and debating heatedly the root causes of the tremendous injustices they witnessed in Korean society. In particular, she agonized over what to do in order to live her life in the most meaningful and just way (chŏngŭiropke) in a society full of injustices and human sufferings. The answer was not difficult to come by during that period of student radicalism, Lee said. She decided to "go to factory" near the end of her sophomore year and she spent the rest of her college life primarily for preparing to become a factory worker. She purposely refrained from participating in student protests so that she would have a clean police record when she entered the factory. In the student activist culture of the early 1980s, those who had declared a factory-bound career (kongjanghaeng) were excused from participating in street demonstrations.

As a preparatory step, Lee first worked for a month at a garment factory in Kuro Industrial Park during winter vacation in her junior year. From the first day, she was given a tremendous amount of work with hardly any training. Because she worked more slowly than other workers, she was scolded and ridiculed frequently. More difficult than that was, however, behaving like a middle school graduate, using a simpler form of language, wearing the same type of clothes outside of work, and even changing her walking style. She finished the month of factory work without having her identity revealed to the foremen or other workers. It was a great educational experience for her. She saw how miserable the factory conditions were and how tender-hearted and nice the young factory women workers were. Returning to school after her trial month of factory work, she told herself, "I must never betray these people."

After graduation, she got a job at another garment factory, using the fake name Kim Soon-young. She was twenty-four years old at that time, but reported her age as twenty. This was a small subcontractor factory with about fifteen workers producing children's clothes. Overtime until midnight or even 2 A.M. was very frequent. The daily wages were approximately 1,600 won (equivalent to the price of lunch at a medium-priced restaurant in Seoul) and even these low wages were not paid on a regular basis because the business was slow at the time. One day, the employer gave them an unexpected vacation with a small sum of money. When they returned to work a few days later, they were astonished to find that the employer had closed the plant and disappeared. It was her first experience with the treachery of the factory world. The workers filed a suit at the regional office of the Labor Bureau. After a while, a labor officer arranged to meet with worker representatives at a tea house. When they met him, he brought them 40,000 won as compensation from the employer and told them, in a highly authoritarian manner, to withdraw the suit.

After another short period of employment at a small sweatshop, Lee got a job as a sewing-machine stitcher at Puhŭngsa, a relatively large manufacturer of export clothing in Kuro Industrial Park. Two of her college classmates got jobs in the same area, one at a clothing factory and another at an electronics firm. When Lee was hired at Puhŭngsa, another student-turned-worker was already there, and during her employment three or four more "disguised workers" entered the firm. Lee said that it was relatively easy to identify other workers from student background (known as *hakchul*) from their eye movement, their low tone of voice, and their exaggerated efforts to make friends with workers. But until 1985, most managers seemed unaware of or unconcerned with the penetration by many *hakchul* into their factories.

The working life at Puhŭngsa was both hard and exhausting. Lee said that she was a rather clumsy manual worker and so had a particularly hard time mastering the skills of sewing. At first, she did not do anything other than try to get friendly with many of her coworkers and to understand their world and their ways of thinking. Like other *hakchul*, she invited her coworkers frequently over to her rooming house after work and cooked *ddŏkbboki* (pan-broiled rice cake) and other favorite dishes for them. At that time, the workers in this company routinely worked 10–12 hours a day and had only one day off every other Sunday. But she said that she did not feel that the work was too hard. Nor did she find the managers' high-handed and condescending attitude unbearable. Life was too busy to reflect on or to regret her decision to become a factory worker, she said.

Gradually, she began to engage in workers' consciousness-raising activities by organizing small groups and linking them to similar activities outside the firm. The workers, especially those with some high school education, were quick to acquire a critical class perspective on their situation as well as a strong sense of solidarity with workers in other factories. In 1984, she and other activists decided to take over the hitherto management-controlled union. Labor activists ran in the union election and were elected shop stewards in large numbers. Lee was also elected to assistant secretary of the union. Management first tried to bribe her to stop her union activism, and when that failed tried to isolate her from other workers and harassed her in every possible way. She did not succumb to these pressures and devoted herself not only to Puhŭngsa union but also to building the Kuro area interfirm labor movement. In 1984 she became a member of the clandestine network of Kuro labor activists, called among activists the Committee of fourteen Members. This secret committee was organized by another *hakchul* woman worker, Shim Sang-jung.

SHIM Sang-jung, born in 1959, had been a student leader at the School of Education, Seoul National University, and entered factory employment in Kuro with several friends with a clear objective of developing the area-based political union movement. They purposely chose different factories in Kuro area as part of their strategy. They used as their major vehicle of workers' consciousness raising the interfirm small groups, each composed of six workers from different factories. From 1980 to 1985, Shim said that about eight such small groups were in operation at any time, producing about forty-eight *sŏnjin nodongja* (workers with advanced consciousness). The Committee of fourteen Members was an informal group of area activists, all *hakchul* workers and predominantly women (there were only three men).[6] It operated as a core planning group for the area-based small-group activities and Shim played a leading role in it. In addition to coordinating the small groups, the committee also published a newsletter for the Kuro-area workers, printing as many as 30,000 copies of each issue.

Before entering factory work in 1980, Shim had worked as a teacher at a workers' night school for six months. She said that this experience helped her to better understand the situation of poor and alienated people. The first question she had in her mind after entering the factory was, "Can they really become the master of history?" To raise workers' consciousness, she thought that first she should become a person whom other workers respected. And in order to become a respected worker, she must work harder than the others. She said that she worked unbelievably hard. After work,

6. Kim Jun-yong, the president of Daewoo Apparel union, told me that he had been invited to attend this group's meeting only once; he came to know more about the group after he went to jail in June 1985.

she invited her coworkers to her place and cooked for them and talked with them until midnight. After that, she met with other activists, whom she called "professionals," for planning meetings until 2 A.M. Despite this schedule, she said, she went to work at 8 A.M. in a happy mood.

HOWEVER, not every student-turned-worker made a successful transition to factory life and to the role of activist. Both Lee and Shim told me that it was usually those who had relatively passive and speculative personalities or those who entered the factory with a predominantly humanistic orientation who became doubtful of their role and left the factory early. Shim said that many student labor activists became disappointed with the workers because they were too impatient, expecting a quick change in workers' consciousness, and did not try hard enough to understand the workers on their own terms.

The democratic union movement in the Kuro area began in 1983 and became very successful in organizing new independent unions or in transforming company unions into genuine representative ones by 1984. *Hakchul* labor leaders played a critical role in these union organizations, although not assuming formal leadership positions, and orchestrated several labor actions concerning wages in spring 1984. At Puhŭngsa, the first strike occurred in spring 1985 over the issue of overtime on Sunday. During this period, Lee's identity was revealed to other workers. One day at dawn, the president of her union, who was from a working-class background, came to see her and asked if she was really a "disguised worker." Lee confessed that she was a college graduate and explained why she had decided to become a factory worker. The union president thanked her for telling the truth and told her that she understood and appreciated Lee's motives. After that, however, Lee began to feel that their relationship became distant and she was not given a leadership role in the union. That was a very unhappy period for her. Then, with the arrest of the Daewoo Apparel union leader, Kim Jun-yong, in June 1985, she became active again in organizing the interfirm solidarity struggle. As a result of this activity, she was arrested and imprisoned for ten months. After being released from prison in 1986, she participated in the Seoul Council of the Labor Movement (*Sŏnoryŏn*), organized by radical labor activists who had participated in the Kuro solidarity struggle, but became somewhat disenchanted with its rash political radicalism. Later, she worked as a labor consultant at the Institute for Workers' Human Rights and also participated in a research project on labor relations at the Hyundai Group. In this research project, she met her present husband, an economist at the Korea Labor Institute, who had not been an activist himself.

At the time of Kim Jun-yong's arrest, Shim Sang-jung was the leader of the Kuro clandestine network of labor activists. On hearing the news of

Kim's arrest, Shim immediately gathered the labor leaders in the area and they decided within thirty minutes to go for a solidarity strike. She then went to see the president of Chunggye Textile Union and asked for his support in the solidarity struggle. He gladly agreed to provide the Chunggye union office as a center for mobilizing broad support from all the democratic forces on behalf of the Kuro solidarity strike. Shim proudly said that the Kuro solidarity struggle was "the first product of our project." Although she had been on the arrest list since the end of 1983, she managed not to be arrested during the 1985 Kuro struggle or when most of *Sŏnoryŏn* leaders, including Kim Moon-soo, were arrested. Subsequently, she worked as a key organizing member of the National Congress of Trade Unions (*Chŏnohyŏp*) and later the Korean Confederation of Trade Unions (KCTU), and was serving as an assistant secretary-general of the National Federation of Metal Unions under the KCTU in 1996 when I interviewed her. She married a labor activist from a similar background and has one son.

Looking back on those days in the mid-1980s, Lee and Shim said that they had no regrets about what they chose to do. They both said that those were days when they led their lives in the fullest and most meaningful way. Lee said that her only regret was that she had been still somewhat immature and a little too simplistic and dogmatic in her political convictions, so that she rejected many people who held different political views and isolated herself from many of her close friends and even from family members. Her parents had not known what she was doing until a year after she became a factory worker. She recalled that working at the factory was not only a hard life in a physical sense but also a lonely one because she had no real close friends or family members to associate with, only other workers with very different family backgrounds and interests. Both Lee and Shim told me that several of their friends who had become *hakchul* workers ended their factory life in considerable despair—some of them became ill on the job; some became disenchanted with labor activism after becoming acquainted with ordinary factory workers, who were mostly conservative and individualistic in their interests; and some were pressured by their families to return to their normal lives.

Conclusion

One of the most distinctive aspects of the South Korean labor movement is the intimate linkages that developed between labor struggles and the political movement for democracy. As I have argued, this close articulation of the two movements is the crucial factor explaining why the working-class movement in South Korea became stronger more quickly than in other industrializing societies in Asia and elsewhere. Although it is true that the labor movements in other societies also received support from the intelligentsia, the extent and the depth of intellectual involvement in South Korea seems to have been exceptional. As we have seen in this chapter, the student movement in Korea actively pursued a strategy of worker-student alliance in the 1980s and sent thousands of students into industrial arena with the specific aim of cultivating class consciousness among workers and mobilizing labor for political struggles. The resurgence of labor disputes and the increase of solidarity struggles in the mid-1980s owed a great deal to these students-turned-workers, as well as to many ordinary workers who were fired because of their involvement in union activism in the 1970s.

The close interconnections that developed between labor and students was to a great extent the product of the state's repressive control of labor. From Park's *yushin* period through Chun's era, the state's consistent policy was to forestall the emergence of an independent union movement outside the government-controlled union structure and to prevent the development of connections between the labor and the political opposition movements. Thus, any sign of organized resistance was ruthlessly suppressed, allowing no channel for the release of the mounting tensions and resentments on the shop floor. The mode of labor control in South Korea was more repressive than corporatist, more direct and physical than bureaucratic or ideological, and more blatantly anti-labor than subtle and disguised. Workers who participated in labor disputes did not fail to confront repressive state power and see the true nature of the relationship between capital and state power. The authoritarian state's attempt to remove "impure elements" from the labor arena by having activist workers fired and blacklisted from industrial employment had the ironic consequence of strengthening student-worker ties and fostering a wide clandestine network of labor activists, church leaders, and dissident intellectuals. Harsh state repression thus helped produce organizational, ideological, and personnel resources for the Korean labor movement.

The Kuro solidarity struggle was the most significant labor struggle that occurred in the first half of the 1980s. But we must be careful not to take this struggle as representative of the level of development of the South Korean labor movement at that time. The South Korean labor movement in the early 1980s as a whole was at a much lower level. Apart from the Seoul-Kyungin region, the rest of the country had seen very little labor unrest. In particular, the major industrial cities in the southern region, such as Ulsan, Masan, Changwon, and Kŏje, where the heavy and chemical industries were concentrated and where large conglomerate firms employed a primarily male labor force, were hardly affected by the union movement until 1987.

Several factors were responsible for this labor passivity in the southern industrial towns; among these were the superior ability of conglomerate capital to control and coopt the workers, the more intense political control by the state, and the relatively higher level of wages and welfare benefits enjoyed by the workers. But probably the most important reason for this regional unevenness in the development of the South Korean labor movement was that the professional labor activists and many labor-supportive dissident organizations were located primarily in Seoul and its surrounding region. This is the region where the church organizations had been active in helping workers organize independent unions, and this is the site chosen by student activists as a primary locus for practicing their strategy of worker-student solidarity struggles.[7] Equally important, the grassroots unionization movement in the late 1970s and early 1980s produced a large number of workers who had been fired and blacklisted. These grassroots labor leaders were also active in the Kuro, Anyang, and Inchon areas and collaborated closely with the student activists who came later.

The major significance of the 1985 Kuro strike was that it was the first interfirm solidarity struggle based on close social ties that had developed among union members located in an industrial area and that the strike was triggered not by economic grievances but by political repression applied to the democratic union movement.[8] In this sense, this solidarity struggle marked a major transition in the development of the South Korean labor movement, and it was a precursor of the working-class movement to come. The massive worker revolt in 1987 inherited this critical legacy.

7. Before 1987, very few students went beyond the Kyungin region. The students' strategy prior to 1987 was to produce a substantial vanguard of politically trained workers in this region and then to penetrate large industrial firms in other regions. Roh Hoe-chan, a prominent labor activist, however, told me that by 1986, Inchon-based labor organizations had begun to send *hakchul* workers, though small in number, to industrial towns in the southern coastal regions.

8. The *Sŏnbong'e sŏsŏ* report on the Kuro solidarity struggle defines this event as "an intense political struggle to protect the independent unions against political repression and a solidarity struggle among the mass of advanced (class conscious) workers that overcame the enterprise-oriented trade unionism" (Seoul nodong undong yŏnhap 1986, 176).

6 Worker Identity and Consciousness

> Previously I disliked myself for being a worker and was
> afraid to be disclosed to others as being a worker. But now
> I have confidence to tell others that "I am a worker." And
> now I have pride and a sense of satisfaction for being a
> respectable member of society as a worker.
>
> (in Kim Kyŏng-sook et al. 1986, 117)

A major theme of South Korean workers' protests in the 1970s and into the 1980s was humane treatment (*inkandaun taejŏp*); many of the spontaneous and violent protests that occurred during this period demanded it and workers changed jobs frequently seeking it. The humane treatment that workers were so concerned about seems to have meant two things. The first was the demand for minimal working conditions: physically endurable working hours, a safe work environment, no excessive overtime, at least one free day each week, and adequate pay. When Chun Tae-Il set himself on fire shouting, "We are not machines," he was speaking for the tens of thousands of workers groaning under the most intolerable conditions of physical labor. The second meaning concerned an improvement in industrial relations, the ways in which workers were treated by employers and managers. Working in the factory, as we have seen in chapter 3, meant that workers had to accept constant assaults on their human dignity and sense of self-worth. The factories were filled with not only dust and machine noise but also shouting, swear words, and disparaging language thrown at the manual workers by foremen and supervisors. Workers were also subjected continually to verbal and physical abuse and, for women workers, to sexual harassment. Factory work in South Korea meant that a worker did not just sell eight or ten hours of his or her labor but also sacrificed his or her pride and dignity for a modicum of income.

Korean workers' cry for humane treatment was, therefore, a reaction against both the material and symbolic forms of oppression that workers experienced in their daily lives. The rather passionate and violent manner in which Korean workers reacted to their work experience stemmed from these two sources. In studying the development of worker identity and class consciousness in South Korea, therefore, it seems essential that we pay close attention to the symbolic and cultural dimension of class relations in addition to the material conditions of proletarian existence.

This chapter explores the cultural dimension of working-class experience and examines how this aspect of the workers' lived experiences shaped the form of their struggles and the ways in which they developed worker identity and class consciousness. Of particular concern is the status in working-class experience because much of what workers experienced as inhumane treatment was related to society's disdainful attitude toward factory workers. Factory work had long been viewed as a low-status, menial, and contemptible occupation. The highly authoritarian and abusive practices of authority in Korean factories were, to a great extent, based on this status judgment of factory workers, while the despicable factory conditions seemed to further feed society's contempt for factory workers.

Status, therefore, was a prime concern among Korean workers, and their class experiences were inexorably intertwined with their status. Class and status are not to be understood here, as is often assumed in conventional social stratification theories, as two separate and competing orders of social stratification. Korean workers struggled with both class oppression and status inequality, and their struggles were simultaneously to improve their class situation and status. (Gender is an important element, but it can be understood as representing one dimension of status.) Recognizing the importance of their status experiences helps explain the highly emotional and explosive nature of Korean working-class protests and the particular way in which Korean workers developed worker identity and class consciousness.

Chŏnhan Nodongja

As factory workers became a major and rapidly growing occupational category in the 1960s, South Korean society reacted to this group in contradictory ways. Although people recognized the vital role factory workers played in the industrialization process, they looked on them with considerable contempt. Factory workers were regarded as occupying a low, menial, and unrespectable status, and this societal attitude was expressed in everyday language and in the ways factory workers were portrayed in the popular media. The language that expressed this societal attitude most clearly, and thus caused great psychological pain among workers during the 1960s and 1970s, and even well into the 1980s, were the condescending words people used to call factory workers, *kongsuni* (factory girl) and *kongdoli* (factory boy). Both terms bring up the image of a servant, a person with a menial, subservient status who happens to be working in a factory (*kong* means factory or industry, and *suni* and *doli* are old-fashioned names for girls and boys of the lower class). The words *kongsuni* and *kongdoli* thus represent a projection of the traditional Confucian status hierarchy onto the modern occupational structure, maintaining the same negative evaluation of physical labor.

The label *kongsuni*, in particular, troubled sensitive young women workers who had left their rural homes with high aspirations of upward social mobility. Their stories are replete with despair at the negative social image thrust on them as factory workers. One worker wrote a beautiful essay on her sad feeling about these labels:

> Women working in factories are *kongsuni*; men working in factories are *kongdoli*. *Kongsuni* and *kongdoli* are mean guys, nothing worth counting, just loose folks. They describe us in this way as a whole group. We must become *konguni* even if we hate it, simply because we work in the factory. If someone asks us where we are working, we simply say, "I work at a small company." But, *konguni* cannot really hide their true identity. They show it however hard they try to put makeup on and dress well. They pay more attention to clothes, hairdo, and makeup in order to hide it. People blame us for spending so much on our appearance when we don't make enough money, but the reason is because we want to remove the label of *kongsuni* they put on us. (in Kim Kyŏng-sook et al. 1986, 111)

Women workers were so afraid of being seen in their factory uniforms that they made a point of changing their clothes even when they went outside the plant to make a quick telephone call during breaks. Several ex-factory women workers whom I interviewed confessed to me that they used to hide in the alley when they saw their old classmates coming in their direction; one said that she always carried a poetry book or a magazine in her hand when she went downtown to do some shopping or to watch a movie on a holiday. The negative societal image of factory workers was apt to be internalized by the workers themselves. "When I started factory work," one worker recollected, "I did not understand the meaning of the *nodongja* [worker], but after a while I came to realize that I am a *chŏnhan nodongja* [dirty or low-status worker] that society often talks about" (in Kim Kyŏng-sook et al. 1986, 116). The label *chŏnhan nodongja* was part of the workers' vocabulary in the 1960s and 1970s. A woman factory worker who was attending a night school for workers could not understand why those who had graduated from elite colleges became teachers at these night schools; she wrote, "How come . . . they spend time here dealing with *chŏnhan nodongja* like us? Perhaps, they, too, couldn't find more decent jobs" (Suk 1984, 22).

Society's condescending attitude toward manual work was deeply institutionalized in the industrial system. As we have seen in chapter 3, South Korean industry maintained a sharp wage difference between blue-collar and white-collar workers. In addition, a whole battery of organizational rules and rituals, from different dress codes and hair styles to differential access to company facilities (such as restaurants and commuter buses), were all designed to reinforce the status differences between blue-collar and white-collar workers. It was also common for young engineers (who were college graduates) to talk to production workers in condescending terms of speech, despite the fact that age is the principal basis of status differentiation in traditional Confucian society.

It must be recognized that factory workers in other industrial societies also suffered contempt from the middle class in the early stages of industrialization. The societal image of the early proletarians was almost invariably that of dirty, crude, low-status workers. In part, this was due to the nature of their work and working environment. More important, however, was that the behavior pattern of the early generation of factory workers failed to meet middle-class standards. From the viewpoint of the middle class, the mass of factory hands from peasant origins lacked discipline and moral sensibilities, let alone educational and cultural sophistication. Even in Japan, as Thomas Smith notes, "they [factory workers] were tirelessly reminded by middle-class sympathizers that, until they curbed a notorious propensity for drinking, gambling, whoring, and domestic quarreling, they would never achieve higher regard, and many workers agreed" (1988, 245). The workers themselves also believed that they were deficient. Referring to the situation in early twentieth century, Kazuo Nimura remarks, "As leaders of these groups were demanding the recognition of blue-collar workers as full members of society, they simultaneously were calling on the workers to become worthy of social acceptance by self-cultivation, by improving their skills, and generally 'endeavoring to become human beings who deserved respect'" (1997, 227).

In Korea, however, the new generation of factory workers that emerged in the process of export-oriented industrialization did not reveal behavioral characteristics that indicated a lack of discipline or moral failings. As far as their public morality was concerned, Korean factory workers deserved no less, if not more, social respect than anyone else. In fact, no negative comments are found in the popular discourse of the 1960s and 1970s about the social behavior of the Korean working class. The main reasons why factory workers were regarded so scornfully by the society at large were the legacy of the status hierarchy based on traditional Confucianism and the low income they earned from physical labor.

It is important to recognize, however, that it is not because the traditional Korean status system had remained strong and intact. In fact, the *yangban* status system had been dismantled early in the twentieth century by the Japanese colonial government, and its material base had been completely destroyed by the post-war land reforms and the Korean War. But notwithstanding the complete breakdown of the traditional *yangban* status system and the great political and social turmoil the Korean people experienced during the post-World War II period, it is interesting that the old status hierarchy was frequently used as a framework for status ranking and social identity in today's Korean society. To a certain extent, this is because of the instability and uncertainties in the Korean status system; although the traditional status hierarchy had been destroyed, a new status system had not formed to replace it (Kim Kyong-Dong 1993). The Korean bourgeoisie failed, as Carter Eckert (1993) argues, to establish its ideological hegemony over society because of the peculiar historical and political context in which it arose. The period of rapid industrial growth in South Korea, from the 1960s to the 1980s, thus represents a transitional period during which class power and the status hierarchy tended to overlap loosely and during which the status order was continuously influenced by the traditional hierarchy.

Power of Educational Ideology

Strictly speaking, it was not the traditional feudalistic status hierarchy that was used to downgrade the factory workers. Rather, it was the value on education, the core of the Confucian status system, that survived great social changes to remain as the most crucial yardstick of status ranking. Of course, education is also a primary criterion of stratification in modern capitalist societies. But in a society such as Korean where people had experienced great political turmoil and had seen so much fluctuation in individual fortunes, education became a surer and more reliable vehicle for social mobility. Furthermore, given the political economy of South Korea, educational qualifications commanded a greater moral claim than wealth or political power. While a status hierarchy based on the traditional class system (*yangban* vs. *sangmin*) became delegitimized and the status order of occupational hierarchy became blurred and ambiguous, the social hierarchy based on educational credentials remained intact and actually became stronger. Now almost everything in status competition seems to fall on the legitimizing power of education and both the claimants of status superiority and the sufferers of status degradation refer to educational qualifications as their main criterion of status judgment.

Thus, the typical way that factory workers interpreted and grudgingly accepted, at least partially, societal disdain for them was by reference to the ideology of education. Being uneducated, they believed, was the cause of all the mistreatment they received at work and the scornful attitude people showed them in the community. The power of educational ideology in South Korean society and its impact on the workers' sense of their place in society are abundantly demonstrated by workers' constant references to their educational status. The fact that they were less educated seems to have preoccupied their minds, even while they were conscious of and protested against economic injustice at work. "Don't workers also deserve at least a minimum amount of rest?" workers protested, but their resistance was apt to be followed by a reference to education. "Even if we are employed in this hard factory work because we have not received education, we cannot stand this kind of mistreatment anymore" (in Kim Kyŏng-sook et al. 1986, 144). Workers' personal essays and public statements issued by the independent unions during the 1970s and 1980s amply demonstrate how painfully Korean workers felt about their lack of education. For example, one of the Dongil workers' leaflets reads: "Even though we are not educated and therefore do not know much, we cannot compromise with the injustices we face, and even though we are poor and hungry, we cannot live on human excrement" (Suk 1984, 161).

Korean workers' constant reference to their educational handicaps suggests that in the 1970s and into the early 1980s, they had not developed an egalitarian ideology or a strong equal-rights consciousness. The qualifying statement "even if we are uneducated" implies that they were willing to take a certain amount of unequal treatment (because they were "uneducated") as long as it did not violate their sense of justice. Justice in this case was not the same as equality; the overriding demand for humane treatment among Korean workers in the early period did not necessarily call for egalitarian relationships. The educational ideology implicitly dictated that those who are "uneducated" must be subordinate to those who are educated and must not expect too much from society.[1]

---

1. But, of course, workers did not always submit to the power of educational ideology. Their own daily life experiences, hard and humiliating as they were, taught them to see the falseness of this ideology and the unfairness of the society. A factory woman who had been supporting her brother's education wrote to her mother: "I do also want to have Shiki [her brother] well educated and let him wear that marvelous square college cap and the bright badge [on his college uniform]. But nowadays I came to think that college education is not necessarily the way to become a true human being. Through my eight years' life away from home, I've seen, so many times, the educated people look down upon the poor and abuse their advantages" (in Kim Kyŏng-sook et al. 1986, 52).

In an interesting parallel, Smith stresses the importance of status and education in his analysis of early Japanese labor relations and labor protests. He observes that worker protests in Japan during the pre-World War I period were characterized not so much by rights consciousness as by status consciousness:

> The idea of rights did not call forth the expressions of moral feeling that status did. The employment relation was seen as one between status unequals, similar to the relations between lord and vassal, master and servant, parent and child, calling for benevolence on one side and loyalty and obedience on the other. For ignoring the ethical code governing such relations, employers were denounced as unrighteous, cruel, barbarous, selfish, inhumane, and ignorant of the way of heaven and man (1988, 239).

Smith also points out that at the core of status relations was educational ideology: "Status was based on education, of which the overriding aim was moral instruction—duty, loyalty, filial piety, the obligations of man to man—and this had been the aim of education for three centuries. Individual exceptions apart, it was taken for granted that moral sensibility would vary with education, and consequently workers were routinely described as uneducated, unknowing, mindless, and immoral" (245). Given this social context, early Japanese workers' demands, Smith argues, were focused on "the improvement of status and treatment" rather than on workers' rights in an egalitarian sense (245). Nimura makes the same point: "the Japanese labor union movement was from the start marked by a concern to do more than maintain and improve working conditions. It was sensitive to the position of the worker in society and continually demanded 'the acceptance of blue-collar workers as human beings by society as a whole and by individual companies'" (1997, 227).

It would be inappropriate to equate the Korean workers' protests in the 1970s to those of early Japanese workers in terms of their demands and consciousness. Korean workers were influenced by, but had not been fully socialized into, the traditional status ideology, whereas the early twentieth-century Japanese workers had been. Korean workers used status language often, just as early Japanese workers did, but they also used rights language as much. In short, Korean workers' sensibilities were influenced by both status and rights consciousness. Recall that the Korean status system was fractured and became unstable and inconsistent under the onslaught of the drastic historical changes of the twentieth century. Consequently, Korean society is characterized, as Brandt (1971) correctly observes in his perceptive study of a fishing village, by the coexistence of contradictory tendencies: individualism and collectivism, egalitarian spirit and hierarchical values, and harmony and conflict.

Nevertheless, education-based status oppression constituted a critical dimension of class experience for Korean workers. Workers clearly saw the world as unequal and unfair, but the inequality they described in their diaries and personal essays was more frequently the inequality between the educated and the uneducated than between the rich and the poor, much less between the capitalists and the workers. "There is almost a heaven-and-earth difference," a worker wrote, "between the educated and the uneducated" (Han 1980, 58) and it was the educated who stood above and always looked down on the uneducated with contempt.

Not surprisingly, educational difference was frequently cited by managers as a justification for their unequal and highly authoritarian treatment of production workers. When Y. H. workers complained about the discriminatory bonus system between managerial and production workers, for example, the manager told them, "it did not cost much money to raise you because you only graduated from elementary school, but the managers are all at least high-school graduates. So does it make sense to demand the same treatment?" (Chŏn Y. H. nodong chohap 1984, 74).When workers made unhappy faces, he told them in an insulting tone, "If you are unhappy, why don't you also get hired in a managerial position?" (74). The Y. H. women workers were said not to know how to respond, but just burst into resentful tears. As one worker who used to work in Anyang industrial area told me, there was probably nothing that made workers more angry and upset than being called "uneducated" or "ignorant." They have been frequently called such things by the managers, labor officials, and the police; and it was also the general attitude they felt from the larger society. Resentment against this symbolic oppression was at the base of violent worker protests that exploded in the 1970s and 1980s.

A being labeled as uneducated status diff

Gender Oppression

In addition to this status degradation of factory workers in general, female factory workers suffered further from acute and pernicious attacks on their femininity. For a woman, to be employed as a factory hand, doing hard manual work in a rough factory environment, was considered tantamount to losing her feminine virtues, becoming unwomanly. Young women were constantly plagued by this fear. One worker lamented, "They say that a woman's voice must not be heard over the fence of the house and that women must be polite, talk in a refined manner, and behave quietly ... but what about us? We must be at the zero mark by this measuring yardstick. We cannot be heard unless we shout at each other, and our behavior naturally becomes rough as we must rush between machines in our work uniforms" (Chang 1984, 42–43).

Young female workers thus suffered from a double oppression: sexism and the cultural degradation of manual work. *Chŏnhan nodongja* represented an additional status loss for young female workers. The scornful attitude toward women working in the factory setting, full of dust, noise, and vulgar language, was not restricted to the managers or foremen but was also common among fellow male workers. The incredible degree of physical and verbal violence that male workers inflicted on female protesters at the Dongil, Wonpoong, and Y. H. factories was a reflection of their deep prejudice against female factory workers. It was not just sexism that they were expressing, I would argue, for most likely they would not have behaved in the same way toward middle-class women; it also involved status-based contempt. Sadly, male factory workers revealed the same degree of contempt for their fellow female workers as did the managers. But this is not unique to Korean male workers; in fact, as Paul Willis (1977) suggests, a certain degree of sexism and a double standard for certain classes of women seem to be an universal aspect of working-class culture. While male blue-collar workers may gain a false sense of superiority by glorifying manual work with masculine ideology, female factory workers fall victim to this male chauvinism prevalent among blue-collar male workers. Willis suggests that humiliating fellow female workers may be an important trait of the male working-class culture in general. Korean male workers' hostility to fellow female workers who were engaged in labor activism might have derived, in part, from this working-class culture.

Female factory workers were also subjected to symbolic violence in the contemptuous phrase *kongsuni chuje'e* (being a mere *kongsuni*) that male superiors used to spit at them whenever they showed any signs of resistance. Female union activists were routinely ridiculed by the management with the insulting remark, "What do you girls know about this matter . . . as mere *konguni*."

Sexism also appeared in a more explicit form in Korean industry. As is reported in many ethnographic studies of factory women in other societies, Korean factory women were also widely stigmatized as being loose and sexually wanton (see Ong 1991). Vicious rumors spread around factory towns that "there is no virgin inside the industrial complex" (Yu Dong-wu 1984, 44). This sexual stigmatization was one important reason why women factory workers detested being labeled *kongsuni* and tried to pass as students or white-collar workers in public places.

Consequently, female factory workers had a stronger desire to "exit," to borrow Hirschman's (1971) term, than male workers. Defining their factory employment as a temporary phase in their lives was their most typical exit orientation. Yet they realized that there was nothing much better waiting for them when they left their factory jobs.

Another, more positive response was their attempt to acquire an education while they worked in the factory. A large number of women workers attended night schools run by church organizations, commercial institutions, or sometimes by their company. "It would be rare," one worker said, "to find a worker who has not attended at least some *hakwon* (commercially run institutes offering evening classes)" (Song 1982, 99). Needless to say, it was extremely difficult for these workers to go to school after a long day of grueling labor, but many workers were determined to attend the schools despite all the difficulties. As one worker explained, "It was because I believed that the reason why I was treated like a sub-human was because I was not educated. I thought I must attend the school even if I was extremely exhausted after 10 hours of hard work and even if I did not find time to have an adequate dinner and thus suffered continuous weakening of my body, only if I be treated as a human being after being [better] educated" (Suh Hee-sook 1985, in Chun 1985, 48). Another worker wrote: "It was difficult to study after work, but I could not stand just working in the factory. I had a firm belief that by studying as hard as I could, I would be able to get out of this world" (Chang Nam-soo 1984, 27).

For most young workers, however, the primary motivation for attending night school or joining educationally oriented small-group activities under the auspices of church organizations seems to have been less instrumental than psychological and emotional. Most of them realized that obtaining a high school diploma by examination was almost impossible and that even if they did obtain their diplomas the chances of their moving up to white-collar positions were extremely slim. So, attending these schools was primarily to satisfy their psychological need to dissociate themselves from the label of *kongsuni*. It is important to note that it was primarily the young female workers who attended night school, most likely because women, unlike men, had no avenues for upward social mobility, both practically and psychologically, other than through education or marriage. In fact, attending night school or church-sponsored educational activities was very much motivated by a desire to acquire cultural skills, such as reading Chinese characters, arranging flowers, and cooking, that would enhance their marriage prospects, although they realized later that their efforts at cultural cultivation did not make any difference (Suk 1984, 20–27).

Interestingly enough, the strong exit orientation among motivated female workers gradually turned to the positive orientation of "voice" as they developed a sharper awareness of the structure of inequality under the guidance of night school teachers. Although most workers had been initially recruited to the night schools or church-sponsored small-group activities primarily through their aspirations for social mobility—most programs were originally geared to the completion of the regular high school curriculum—these educational activities gradually turned into a major arena for consciousness raising. The fact that female factory workers constituted the majority of the participants in these educational activities provides a clue as to explaining why women played a leading role in the 1970s grassroots union movement. It is an interesting irony in the history of the Korean working-class movement that women workers' strong exit orientation helped them become the vanguard in voicing workers' demands and lay the foundation for the democratic movement in the 1980s.

Han: Consciousness of Injustice

I have so far stressed the significance of the status and symbolic dimensions of class relations in Korean industry. This is certainly not to depreciate the fundamental structural reality of class grounded in the antagonistic relations of production. Nevertheless, recognizing the importance of symbolic and moral oppression in the lived experiences of Korean factory workers is crucial in understanding the distinct pattern of identity formation and the development of class consciousness among Korean workers. Simply speaking, Korean workers' deep resentment against symbolic oppression often acted as a catalyst in shaping their collective actions and class consciousness.

A Korean cultural concept that played an important role in the expression and shaping of Korean workers' daily experiences is *han*.[2] *Han* is an extremely complex concept, difficult to translate into English, but in broad terms it can be defined as long accumulated sorrow and regret over one's misfortune or as simmering resentment over injustice one has experienced (see Chun I-du 1993; Kim Yŏl-kyu 1980; Han and Kim 1988; Kim Kyong-Dong 1993, 239–70; Choi Sang-Chin and Uichol Kim 1992; Lee Jae Hoon 1994; Suh Nam-dong 1983; Freda 1998). *Han* is a concept of contradictions, involving both the passive acceptance of one's situation as fate and the intense desire to overcome it or to revenge oneself on those who are the cause. It is an intense feeling that accumulates over time, unresolved, coiled, and suppressed, yet yearns to be released. *Han*, therefore, has an explosive quality. *Hanpuli* literally means releasing *han*, either symbolically, through dance or music, or violently, through vengeful actions. Many students of Korean culture agree that the essence of indigenous forms of Korean dance and music is releasing *han* in an artistic form.

Korean factory workers used the word *han* very frequently to interpret their daily experiences and to express their frustration and resentment. They talked about the *han* of having been born into a poor family and *han*

2. George Ogle defines *han* aptly as follows: "There is a small word in the Korean language that carries a big meaning. The word is *han*. That one sound expresses the accumulated suffering and anguish of a people, or a person. It is the groan of the human spirit demanding release from oppression" (1990, 75). Nancy Abelmann defines *han* simply as "anger and resentment that build over time and under the weight of hardship" (1996, 36), while John Lie likens it to the French notion of *ressentiment* (1998, 114).

of not having received more education. They also shared a deeply felt *han* against the despotic inhumane treatment they experienced at work. The scornful labels *kongsuni* and *kongdoli* also caused them great *han*. For example, the resolution issued by Dongil Textile unionists in 1977 read, "Suffering from society's cold treatment and the employers' abuses, and tormented by *han* of poverty, *han* of being uneducated, and *han* of not living in a nice house like others, Dongil Textile workers are cheated even by their (official) union" (Dongil pangjik pokjik tujaeng wiwonhoe 1985, 71). And after a massive and successful demonstration in 1987, Hyundai workers proclaimed, "August 18 was the day when Hyundai workers and the entire workers of the nation were reborn, overcoming their *han*, into the masters of the nation, and a great solemn march toward the future of a truly humanlike life" (Lee Soo-won 1994, 103).

Han is certainly not a language of class. It does not involve an awareness of the structured nature of social inequality or a realization of common class interest among workers in opposition to capital. Yet it is a moral language that heightens the awareness of injustice and the spirit of resistance. In other words, *han* is a language of spiritual resistance, for *han* cannot occur when one accepts a given situation as natural or morally acceptable. Beneath the perception of *han* lies an egalitarian spirit and resistance to the hierarchical social order that has lost much of its historical legitimacy. The language of *han* tends to intensify feelings of oppression and promote strong feelings of affinity among the people who suffer the same experiences. Thus, although *han* is not a class language, it can promote class awareness and class feeling through its unique sensibility to social injustice.

A comment that one worker made about the prostitutes she saw on the street looking for customers nicely illustrates the consciousness of inequality imbued with the empathy of *han:* "You and I are from the same lot, all thrown out by this society. But is it right to live like this without making any protest against the world which treats us like worms?" (in Kim Kyŏng-sook et al. 1986, 106). She continued, "I want to kick this damn world, which extracts our sacrifices in order to maintain its shiny facade, although I know through my experience that it is only my poor feet that will get hurt. One cannot deny the very fact that we are also human." The boundaries of *han*-based solidarity do not necessarily coincide with class boundaries, instead embracing all those who suffer from the inequality and injustice of society. But, when class oppression was experienced by workers in the language of *han*, it could add a stronger emotional quality to their resistance and could deepen their feeling of solidarity.

Labor conflicts triggered by seemingly trivial matters could flare up into violent protests when they touched this deep-seated feeling of *han* in the minds of the workers, as was often the case in the 1970s and 1980s. Solidarity among workers became stronger when *han* was aroused and protesters often tried to stir up this emotional feeling deliberately in order to maintain a strong fighting spirit. For example, the letter of resolution read by the Y. H. protesters the night before the anticipated brutal police attack of August 10, 1979, contained more emotional content than resolutions:

> All children of poor farmers, we left our parents early and entered this cold society and have worked hard as builders of industry [*sanŭp ŭi yŏkkun*]. Although we have been treated badly and with contempt by society for not being educated, we simply blamed ourselves for being uneducated and just worked hard, trying to save money for our younger siblings so that they would not become like us, and we had pleasure and pride in sending money for our siblings' tuition and our parents' living costs and medicine expenses. . . . From now on, who is going to provide our mothers' medicine costs and our younger siblings' tuition fees? (Chŏn Y. H. nodong chohap and Han'guk nodongja pokjik hyŏpuihoe 1984, 233–34)

Workers broke out into "tears of *han*," and the newspaper reporters and other observers on the scene shed tears also.

Such emotional appeals were especially strong among the young female workers who led the 1970s union movement, but it was not restricted to women. Male workers were equally emotional when they took collective action, and the issues they raised were usually more comprehensive and diffuse than focused on economic issues. Much of the violent action that accompanied the Korean workers' wildcat strikes or sit-in demonstrations can be understood as a form of *hanpuli*. In fact, the massive waves of labor conflicts that erupted in the summer of 1987 in the wake of the sudden breakdown of political control were, by and large, a huge manifestation of *hanpuli*. At numerous plants, large and small, workers vented their long-suppressed resentment and anger on managers and employers and tried to get even with them by threatening and humiliating them. All these events demonstrate the significance of status oppression, and the compressed feeling of *han* it generated, in the development of working-class struggles in Korean society.

Many labor songs that were popular among factory workers carried deep pathos and a sense of *han* in their lyrics and rhythm. A good example is "Song of the Old Laborer," which was frequently sung by workers during their strikes in the 1980s:

> In this valley I was born and became a laborer
> Flowers bloomed and snow fell for almost thirty years
> What have I done? What did I wish for?
> When I die and am buried in this earth that will be the end

Ah, my youth gone never to return
My flower-like youth clothed in workers' rags.

My sons and daughters do not lament
You are the children of the proud laborers
So you wish to wear nice clothes and eat good things?
Stop and forget about it for you are laborers' children
Ah, my youth gone never to return
My flower-like youth clothed in workers' rags.

What was my life's wish?
To take our grandchildren's hands and see Mt. Kŭmgang
My youth has gone waiting
Waiting for the flowers to bloom and the sky to clear
Ah, my youth gone never to return
My flower-like youth clothed in workers' rags.

Under blue skies, past green mountains and blue rivers
Walked the black faces with blue hats on their white hair
What have I done? What did I wish for?
To take our grandchildren's hands and see Mt. Kŭmgang
Ah, my youth gone never to return
My flower-like youth clothed in workers' rags.[3]

Language of Class

The absence of an artisan cultural heritage for the working class in Korea is reflected in the paucity of class language. In Europe, as scholarship on the working-class formation stresses, craft organizations and cultural traditions played a key role in shaping working-class responses to industrial change and the development of class consciousness. These responses were primarily social and moral rather than economic—they were more concerned with preserving their independence, workmanship, and morally regulated work relationships than with narrow economic issues. This is because the work of European artisans was regulated by corporate rules and disciplines, conducted in an intimate network of social ties and communal sentiments. From these occupational communities, they drew material, social, and personal resources for a strong collective response to proletarianization.

Korean industrialization occurred in the absence of a similar artisan culture. Artisan production was not significant in Korea until the nineteenth century. Most artisans were employed by the government to produce paper, utensils, special garments, and other luxury goods for the court and aristocracy (Song 1973). In the traditional Korean Confucian status system, artisans and merchants ranked below farmers, near the bottom of the hierarchy. In fact, many had been slaves in Chosun society. When commercial

3. I would like to express my thanks to Jennifer Lee for translating this song for me.

and industrial activities began in the second half of the nineteenth century, artisans were far less active than merchants. Traveling merchants established fairly influential guilds based on their nation-wide networks. Also, some large merchants formed "capital associations" to protect and enhance their monopolistic positions in the market. No similar organizations were developed by artisans.

Thus, the first generation of South Korean factory workers experienced proletarianization without any proud working-class cultural heritage. Instead, they inherited a negative legacy, as reflected in the labels *kongsuni* and *kongdoli*. In the early period of South Korea's industrialization, factory workers were identified by various terms, such as *nodongja* (laborers), *kongjang nodongja* (factory laborers), *kongwon* (factory employees), and *kŭnroja* (workers or employees). Gradually, with the number of factory workers growing, government and management promoted the word, *kŭnroja* as a more or less official term for industrial workers, calling, for example, Labor Day *kŭnroja ŭi nal* rather than *nodongja ŭi nal*. But *kŭnroja* was too broad a term, referring to all categories of employed workers, including manual, nonmanual, and technical workers. In contrast, *nodongja* had a more specific reference to factory workers or physical laborers (*yukche nodongja*), but it carried a negative status connotation. Thus, until working-class identity began to develop in the late 1970s, Korean factory workers did not have an appropriate term to define their collective identity. Whereas *kŭnroja* was unsatisfacory because of its artificial ring and ambiguous reference, *nodongja* was disliked by most workers because of the inferior status image associated with physical and manual labor that it conveyed.

Interestingly, it was the state that created the new language that constructed a positive image of the industrial workers. From the late 1960s, new words appeared in the industrial lexicon, such as *sanŭp chŏnsa* (industrial warriors) or *sanŭp ŭi yŏkkun* (builders of industry), and *suchul ŭi yŏkkun* or *suchul ŭi kisu* (leading producers of exports). Clearly, these terms were coined to mobilize workers for an export drive using nationalistic ideology. In these new phrases, nationalism was combined with developmentalism and military rhetoric, equating industrial workers with soldiers fighting for national defense. Working with dedication for the promotion of exports was celebrated as a patriotic act that workers could be proud of. Not only were these terms used frequently by the government and mass media, but workers themselves used them, often with tongue-in-cheek. As the Y. H. workers' letter of resolution (quoted in the previous section) indicates, workers often called themselves *sanŏp ŭi yŏkkun* (industrial warriors): "All children of poor farmers, we . . . have worked hard as *sanŏp ŭi yŏkkun*" (Chŏn Y. H. nodong chohap 1984, 233).

Similarly, the ideology of nationalism penetrated the language of the Korean workers. Thus, the Wonpoong Union, one of the most independent and aggressive unions in the 1970s, issued the following union resolution in 1973:

> 1. We are the warriors of industrial peace and will make our utmost effort to increase productivity;
> 2. We will make every effort to improve our working conditions with strong solidarity among ourselves;
> 3. As champions of the working people, we will do our best to improve the quality of the union. (Wonpoong mobang haeko nodongja pokjik tujaeng wiwonhoe 1988, 84)

Even while protesting against unfair labor practices, workers felt obliged to use nationalistic rhetoric. For example, a letter that Kyungsung Textile workers sent to their employer complaining about unpaid overtime was prefaced with: "We would like to congratulate your successful effort for our nation's economic development. We wish you good luck this year and wish that our Kyungbang will become more prosperous" (Han'guk kidokkyo kyohoe hyŏpuihoe 1984, 379). And they continued, "We have worked hard day and night with you for the development of Kyungbang, and we are proud of being the family members of Kyungbang." (379) Here we see the powerful ideology of familism also creeping into the language of the workers.

However, all this nationalistic, developmental, and familistic rhetoric had presumably little effect on the consciousness of the workers. Although workers used these words themselves, mainly for lack of other positive terms to describe themselves, they had a great deal of doubt and suspicion. "They call us industrial warriors or producers of economic development," workers acknowledged, "but what about us? . . . Who dares, with a shred of sincerity, to use those words like industrial warriors or pillars of export to call us, when we are not even allowed to express our own feeling?" (Dongil pangjik pokjik tujaeng wiwonhoe 1985, 49). Their daily work life and the way they were treated by society belied such an exalted image of the industrial workers.

It was, however, not until the late 1970s and the early 1980s that workers began to debunk the state ideologies and search for language of their own. As industrial workers' self-identity began to grow in the 1970s, the old word, *nodongja* (laborer or worker) began to acquire more of a class meaning, in opposition to *kŭnroja*, which employers and the government preferred workers to use. By the early 1980s, Roh Hoe-Chan, a prominent labor activist in the 1980s, told me, using the word *nodongja*, instead of *kŭnroja*, for self-identification was tantamount to expressing a certain level of class consciousness. Gradually, the words *kongsuni* and *kongdoli* disappeared from the popular lexicon. But these pejorative terms did not completely disappear until after the Great Worker Struggle of 1987, and they disappeared only as an outcome of workers' self-conscious efforts to claim their own identity.

> I am a *nodongja*. I am not ashamed of the word "*kongsuni*." My line would be in great trouble if I were absent. If so, if everybody in our line is absent, the company won't be able to operate. However pompously the office workers behave in front of us, they will starve without us. So, I have pride. We have power. Although we are weak as individuals, we can overcome anything if we are united. Yes, I am a *kongsuni*. (in Kim Kyŏng-sook et al. 1986, 114)

Exactly how this change in the workers' self-conception occurred is difficult to document. The rapidly growing number of workers in similar positions, their concentration in a few industrial towns, rising wages, and, most important, experiences drawn from many collective struggles all must have contributed to an awakening of workers' consciousness. Also, as we have seen, many workers acquired a new perspective on themselves and their role in society through attending night school or participating in small-group activities, most of which were linked to progressive churches and activist students.

Workers' night schools provided a particularly important vehicle for promoting the new worker identity. Those who attended these schools frequently reported, "I hated the class whenever words like *minjung* and *nodongja* were mentioned. I couldn't help thinking that our teachers were ridiculing us because we were workers. Until then, I had been reluctant to reveal my job to anyone because I was ashamed of being a worker" (in Kim Kyŏng-sook et al. 1986, 77). Another worker confessed, "I did not believe it myself when I first heard at the night school that 'workers are the masters of society' or that '[workers] are the engine of history'" (117). But most of the workers who attended night schools echoed their colleague who said, "Previously I was afraid to be disclosed that I was a worker. But now I can say to others with confidence that 'I am a worker [*nodongja*].' And now I have pride and satisfaction in being a respectable member of society as a worker" (117).

Minjung Movement

Another important factor in the development of Korean working-class identity and consciousness is the populist *minjung* movement, which emerged from the second half of the 1970s (see Abelmann 1996; Koo 1993; Wells 1995). The term *minjung* means the "people" or the "masses." Both

internal political circumstances and external influences contributed to
the development of this movement. The most significant factor was the
hardening of the authoritarian regime of Park Chung Hee and, more specifically, the installation of a bureaucratic-authoritarian *yushin* (revitalization) regime in 1972. The *yushin* regime intensified students' anti-regime
struggles and triggered strong opposition from the intellectual community,
religious organizations, opposition parties, and a growing segment of the
new middle class. Along with this political change, the issues of distribution and widening class inequality came to the serious attention of the
public during this period.

The political and economic reality of the 1970s thus demanded an ideology that could articulate these problems and unite the diverse struggles
of students, workers, farmers, the urban poor, journalists, writers, and so
on. *Minjung*, a political term used by both nationalists and leftists during
the colonial period and in the post-war years, suited this purpose eminently. It contained strong nationalistic sentiment, it was not a Marxist
term (it was essential to avoid being labeled pro-communist), it was vague
and broad enough to include all popular sectors, and it was suitable for both
the political and cultural movements. *Minjung* included all those who
were politically oppressed, socially alienated, and economically excluded
from the benefits of economic growth (Han 1984; Yu Jae-Chun 1984).

External influences also played an important role—they included
liberation-oriented theologies (especially Latin American liberation theology), dependency theory, and other neo-Marxist theories that were very
popular among students in the late 1970s and early 1980s. Stimulated by
these intellectual ideas, Korean theologians developed *minjung* theology,
while academics proposed *minjung* sociology, *minjung* history, and
minjung literature. Although borrowing key concepts from foreign
sources, Korean intellectuals insisted on Korean history and culture as the
ultimate source of their inspiration and their search for emancipation
(Suh Nam-dong 1983a; Choi Chungmoo 1995; Abelmann 1996).

At the core of the *minjung* movement is an ideology that claims that
minjung is the master of history and that Korean history is a history of the
minjung's oppression by the dominant class and by external forces; hence,
the real national identity and authentic culture of Korea must be found in
the culture and daily struggles of the *minjung*. With this broad ideological
content, *minjung* became a dominant form of discourse, slogan, and strategic tool for uniting and mobilizing diverse political and social struggles in
the 1980s. To a great extent, South Korean politics in the 1980s was little
more than continual confrontations between the authoritarian regime and
a loose, but highly active and strong coalition of *minjung* circles.

The significance of the *minjung* movement, however, is not limited to
its effect on political mobilization. The *minjung* movement is at once a

political and cultural movement (Wells 1995; Abelmann 1996). As a cultural movement, it stimulated serious efforts among intellectuals and artists to search for the essence of *minjung* culture, which had long been overshadowed by Western culture and neglected or even suppressed by the authorities. These efforts led to the reaffirmation and reappropriation of Korean culture and history from a fresh perspective. Many of the best-selling novels in the 1980s belonged to the genre of *minjung* literature. Historical novels dramatized the agonies and struggles of the oppressed and drew new historical meanings therefrom, while those with more contemporary themes sought to disclose the injustices suffered by the lower classes (Kim Uchang 1993).

One of the most interesting developments brought about by the *minjung* movement was the rediscovery and re-creation of indigenous cultural forms practiced by the commoners, such as *talchum* (mask dance or play), *pungmul* (peasant band music and dance), *madang kŭk* (play performed in a village public space), and *madang kut* (shamanistic rites) (Minjung yesul wiwonhoe 1985; Kongdongche 1986) (fig. 7). Interest in these traditional cultural forms appeared first in the 1960s among a small circle of nationalistically minded, avant garde students who demonstrated against the

Figure 7. Image of the *minjung* culture. (From Oh Yoon 1996, 86)

normalization treaty with Japan signed by Park Chung Hee's military regime. At that time, students introduced old shamanistic rituals into their demonstrations to show their nationalistic sentiment. But with the greater articulation of *minjung* ideology in the 1970s, this cultural movement went beyond a mere reappreciation of traditional culture and made a serious effort to reinterpret and re-create *minjung* culture. The 1980s saw a blossoming of all genres of *minjung* culture, mask dance, *pungmul*, *madang kut*, and other peasant and shamanistic rituals. There was hardly a college without a mask dance group and hardly a student demonstration that was not accompanied by a playful performance of *pungmul* or *madang kut* or both. With dynamic dances and the loud sounds of music, these rituals played an effective role in student gatherings, stirring up the collective mood for a violent confrontation with the police.

In appropriating *minjung* culture, young intellectuals emphasized several features of commoner culture that demonstrated the authenticity of Korean culture and that were instrumental in raising the consciousness of the subordinate people (Minjung yesul wiwonhoe 1985). The first was the communal, corporate spirit that underlies all forms of *minjung* culture. In mask dance, *pungmul*, and *madang kut*, there is no fixed stage, no separation of the performers and audience, and no strict following of the written script; and actually there is no clear genre distinction among these cultural forms. Throughout the performance, participation by the audience is not only encouraged but is regarded as essential, and the end of the performance breaks down this separation completely, as the performers and the audience join together to dance with a heightened spirit of joy and release. Participation, spontaneity, naturalness, and a communal feeling of solidarity are all features that clearly distinguished *minjung* culture from that of the upper class, which stressed individual technique, refined performance, serenity, and the sharp separation of performer and audience.

The second important feature of *minjung* culture, most clearly shown in mask dance, was its use in exposing and criticizing social injustices rooted in the class system. Mask dances almost always involve two opposite classes of people—the dominant class (*yangban*, Confucian scholars, or monks) and the commoners—and the typical ploy involves ridiculing the misdeeds and hypocrisy of the dominant class. Using humor, satire, and witty metaphors, the mask dance performers feel free to criticize the corrupt and unfair system in which they all live and suffer. Mask dance, therefore, was an excellent tool for exposing the injustices of the system and raising people's critical consciousness.

The third feature, which in many ways represents the most distinctive feature of Korean culture, was *shinmyŏng* (a collective feeling of ecstasy). *Shinmyŏng* is an essential element of Korean shamanism and, as many scholars argue, shamanism is at the core of Korea's indigenous culture.

Korean shamanism is also intimately connected with the psychosocial state *han*—the long-accumulated feeling of sorrow, grief, resignation, and resentment. The life of the *minjung* during the Yi dynasty was regarded as *han*, and it was especially so for women. Shamanism brought comfort to them and released their long-accumulated grief and resentment. *Shinmyŏng* arises when this psychological release occurs. It is important to understand, however, that *shinmyŏng* is not just a shamanistic ritual but constitutes an overriding theme and ethos in all forms of Korean indigenous culture, in dance and music, and in games and other everyday play among the commoners. "Korean dance," as one observer notes, "can be nothing but the dynamic dance of *shinmyŏng* struggling to free itself from the sorrow of *han*" ("Shinmyong" 1988, 42–43). *Shinmyŏng* is also an integral aspect of mask dance and *pungmul* (peasant music and dance), as they cherish and encourage the participation of the audience in a festive mood of dancing and singing.

In short, the traditional culture of ordinary Koreans as it was appropriated and re-created by the *minjung* intellectuals and artists, contained the essential cultural elements eminently suited to struggles for democracy and social justice: corporate spirit, democratic participation, critical awareness of social injustices, and an exuberant spirit for a collective fight for change. One of the most interesting features of the working-class movement in South Korea in the 1980s and afterward was the ways in which this cultural movement and workers' economic struggles intermeshed to produce a dynamic working-class movement.

Growing Working-Class Culture and Institutions

The Korean working-class movement in the 1980s drew a great deal of ideological and cultural support from the *minjung* cultural movement. *Minjung*, of course, is not a class language in a strict sense. *Minjung* includes various categories of people, including industrial workers, poor farmers, service workers, small shopkeepers, and intellectuals. The *minjung* movement, however, contributed tremendously to the Korean working-class movement by providing an anti-hegemonic ideology and an alternative cultural framework and discourse. Given the absence of a working-class tradition and given the power of the anti-labor, pro-capitalist state, such a supportive political and cultural movement was critical in the development of the working-class struggle.

If the organized labor movement went through a cyclical development of expansion and contraction, working-class culture seems to have developed steadily on a linear path. The maturing of working-class culture can be seen in many areas. Probably the most salient is the rise of working-class literature. In the 1970s and early 1980s, workers' writings were mostly personal essays about their daily experiences or personal reports on some major labor strife. Gradually, the genres of workers' writings broadened to include poems, plays, and novels. As workers' writings grew in number and maturity, they sought to grow above their subordinate status within the larger *minjung* literature, still dominated by intellectuals and professional writers. Naturally, working-class writers were able to describe their daily experiences of despair, anger, and aspirations more accurately and with greater authentic feelings. Not surprisingly, they found the category of *minjung* too broad and vague to express and interpret their own work and social relations. In the 1980s, the growth of working-class literature as an autonomous genre stimulated intellectuals to look more critically at *minjung* literature. In this self-critique, early leaders of the *minjung* movement were now criticized for revealing a "petty citizen" (or petty bourgeois) mentality—vague humanitarianism, sentimentalism, and fatalism—and for lacking a firm, positive vision of the future.

The dominant trend in the progressive literature of the 1980s was, therefore, a shift from "*minjung*-oriented" literature to "*minjung*-led" literature (Kim Sa-in and Kang Hyŏng-chŏl 1989). What made this change possible was the appearance of several professional worker-writers and many others who demonstrated a highly sophisticated writing ability. Of them, the best known is the worker-poet Park No-hae.[4] His collection of poems, entitled *Nodong ŭi saepyŏk* [Dawn of labor], was published in 1984 and made a great impact in literary circles. His poems express workers' feelings of alienation, anger, and class awareness with great simplicity and cogency.

Maybe

Maybe I'm a machine
Absorbed in soldering subassemblies
Swarming down the conveyor,
Like a robot repeating,
The same motions forever,
Maybe I've become a machine.
Maybe we're chickens in a coop.
Neatly lined up on our roosts,
Hand speed synchronized in dim light,
The faster the music,
The more eggs we lay,
Maybe we've become chickens in a coop.
. . . . .

---

4. His real name is Park Ki-pyung. He was imprisoned in October 1990 on a charge of organizing a revolutionary communist labor organization. He was then released in 1998 on a special pardon from the Kim Dae-Jung government.

They . . .
They who extract and devour
Our pith and our marrow,
Maybe they are barefaced robbers,
Turning humans into machines,
Into consumables,
Into things buyable and sellable.
Maybe they are dignified
And law-abiding barefaced robbers.

Those gentle smiles,
That refined beauty and culture,
That rich and dazzling opulence,
Maybe all of that is ours.
(Park No-hae 1984, 89–91)[5]

Expressed in his poems is far more than mere working-class identity or class opposition; there is a firm structural understanding of class inequality and a hint of an alternative society. Park No-hae signified the emergence of what Gramsci calls "organic intellectuals" (Gramsci 1971, 5–14). By the second half of the 1980s, the Korean working class had produced a number of organic intellectuals, who produced a large volume of poems, songs, play scripts, and newsletters. But it is also true that a large proportion of these organic intellectuals were students-turned-workers and that workers' writing activities were fairly limited to the more easily accessible genres, such as short stories, nonfiction documentaries, and poems, and did not include serious novels. Intellectual dominance over *minjung* literature was still an undeniable fact.

Parallel to these changes in literature, the 1980s saw a remarkable development in working-class cultural activities (Kim Dae-ho 1986; Chung I-dam and Park Young-Jung 1991). By the mid-1980s, almost every labor union had developed a *pungmul* (peasant band music and dance) group, a *talchum* (mask dance) group, and other cultural activities. *Pungmul* and mask dance were taught at cultural centers run by progressive religious organizations such as the Urban Industrial Mission. These cultural activities played a very important role in recruiting passive ordinary workers into the labor movement, because the spirit and the content of these activities were all oriented to increasing solidarity among workers and sharpening oppositional attitudes toward management and the government. Many workers report that they participated in *pungmul* or theater groups just for the fun of these activities, but slowly came to develop a critical attitude toward industrial relations and a strong feeling of solidarity with fellow workers. "The feeling I often get while playing *pungmul* is the feeling

5. I would like to express my thanks to Chun Kyung-ja for translating this poem.

Figure 8. *Minjung* culture as part of the movement culture. (From Sahoe sajin yŏnguso [social photography institute] 1989, 209)

of 'togetherness'," a worker reports (Lee Sŏn-yong and Kim Eun-sook 1985, 53). These cultural activities also provided a vehicle through which labor activists maintained close ties across firms and geographical areas. Activist workers often participated in the picnics, festivals, and athletic games of workers at other factories, and in these activities simple drums, gongs, and peasant dance contributed to breaking down the psychological or social barriers among workers and implanting a feeling of togetherness (fig. 8).

Pungmul and mask dance thus became strategic tools for mobilization in the labor movement. There was hardly a sit-in or strike in the 1980s that was not accompanied by these activities. The mobilizing band music and dances were often performed by semi-professional *munhwapae* (culture cliques specializing in indigenous music and dance), which were a part of many of the independent unions in the 1980s. *Minjung* culture thus became a vital part of the South Korean democratic labor movement in the 1980s. As one labor leader observes, "The loud and resonating sound of *pungmul* equals the shouts of thousands of workers, and the giant hanging picture amounts to thousands of signatures, and the enthusiastic singing of the labor song with lost voices heightens collective spirit and emotional feeling more than any speaker's eloquent speech can do" (Yŏn 1989, 40).

Another important working-class institution that emerged in the 1980s was the workers' newspapers. The major workers' newspapers included *Minju nodong* (Democratic labor), *Nodongja shinmun* (Workers' newspaper), *Wonpoong hoebo* (Wonpoong union newsletter), *Chunggye nojo shinmun* (Chunggye union newspaper), *Sŏnoryŏn shinmun* (Newspaper of the Seoul Council of Labor Movements), *Ilkkun charyo* (Working people's data), and *Nodong chubo* (Labor weekly). These newspapers were biweekly or monthly and published by national-level or area-level union organizations as well as by labor-oriented Christian organizations. These newspapers included the news about current labor protests, which were normally not covered in the regular daily newspapers, informative educational columns on labor laws and workers' rights, critical analyses of the government's economic policies, and ample space for the readers' letters, essays, and poems. In addition to these regular newspapers, many newsletters and pamphlets were published by local unions and movement groups, all aimed at providing alternative channels of information to the established news media, which were directly or indirectly controlled by the government. For example, the inaugural issue of *Nodongja shinmun* (February 25, 1985) proclaims:

> Workers are forced to remain ignorant about every social issue by the government-controlled media which are contemptuous of the workers. We need newspapers to break the wall of this wrong reality. For the workers, as the subject of history, are deprived of their right to know the reality of this land correctly.

Of all the working-class institutions, these workers' newspapers were run by the most radical and politically oriented segment of the working class. Their explicit goal was to counter the official version of reality and to establish a counterhegemony of the working class in South Korean society (Kim Dae-ho 1986, 126–67).

Conclusion

The first half of the 1980s saw the emergence of opposition ideologies and anti-hegemonic discourse. The dominant ideologies of nationalism, familism, national security, and social harmony, of course, remained strong and continued to suppress workers' new consciousness based on their class experiences. Against these hegemonic ideologies, however, the new discourse of democracy, *minjung*, justice, and cultural authenticity emerged and spread through both the new middle class and the working class. This discourse, like all other discourses, was produced by the intellectuals with their own cultural and intellectual predilections. But its major structural sources were the growing working-class struggle at the grassroots level and the intensive opposition movement against the harsh authoritarian regime.

The growth of anti-hegemonic discourse in the 1980s in turn played a critical role in promoting workers' new collective identity and consciousness. In South Korea, as I have previously argued, the development of worker identity was critical in the formation of the working class. This is because Korean factory workers emerged without a traditional artisan culture or culture of mutuality, but instead with a menial and contemptuous cultural image. Both the cultural environment and the material conditions of factory work encouraged workers to adopt predominantly an exit orientation to their industrial employment, both physically and psychologically. It was difficult for them to develop a positive worker identity under such conditions; a strong worker identity could occur only when workers realized the futility of their aspirations for upward mobility from factory employment and when they obtained the appropriate language to forge a positive sense of their position in the industrial system and in society. In this regard, the new anti-hegemonic language provided by the *minjung* and other social and cultural movements played a critical role in advancing the workers' collective identity and class consciousness.

Given the dominant ideological and cultural environment, worker identity in South Korea necessarily represented a "resistance identity."[6] When a Korean factory worker said, "I am a worker [nodongja]" in the early 1980s, it was almost certain that he or she was expressing an assertive attitude about his or her position in the industrial system and society—an antagonistic and resistant attitude toward a society that treated factory workers as dirty and menial—and a sense of solidarity with other fellow workers. Worker identity is important because it is an essential element in transforming the workers' exit orientation to "voice." Worker identity is thus an essential element in producing class consciousness; if the class consciousness has more cognitive (or one might say scientific) elements, the worker identity contains more emotional and affective elements. But

---

6. Castells (1997, 6–12) makes a useful distinction among three types of identity: legitimizing identity, resistance identity, and project identity.

it seems essential that strong class feeling develops first before workers develop clear class consciousness.[7]

In any event, the structural, political, and cultural processes that occurred in the 1970s and 1980s produced a rapidly growing working class in South Korea with an emerging working-class identity and "culture of solidarity."[8] Yet all these processes were largely hidden under the surface of the industrial peace maintained by the repressive labor regime—until 1987, when a major crack in the authoritarian control system allowed all the tensions and simmering resentments to burst through in a gigantic wave of labor revolts.

7. Raymond Williams's (1977) concept "structure of feeling" seems appropriate in this regard.
8. Fantasia defines "culture of solidarity" as "more of less bounded groupings that may or may not develop a clear organizational identity and structure, but represent the active expression of worker solidarity within an industrial system and a society hostile to it" (1988, 19).

7   The Great Labor Offensive

> The twenty years at Hyundai Motors! In the sea of
> laborers that had ever been so calm, a huge mountain-like
> wave erupted suddenly. A solemn scene was staged in
> which the workers, who had been no more than mere
> parts in the continuously running conveyor belt, refused
> to be machines and proclaimed that they were human.
>
> (Lee Soo-won 1994, 74)

The massive wave of labor conflicts that erupted in summer 1987 marks a watershed in the history of the South Korean working-class struggle. It was an extraordinary period during which all the hidden contradictions of the Korean capitalist development and the long-accumulated grievances of the workers were brought to the surface by labor militancy. In three months, from July to September, more than three thousand labor disputes occurred, surpassing the total number of labor conflicts that had occurred during the previous two decades of rapid industrialization. Labor unrest swept across the country with alarming speed and ferocity, paralyzing industrial production in almost every large-scale industry. Hardly any region, any industrial sector, or any scale of enterprise was immune from labor unrest. The gigantic scale on which hundreds of thousands of workers were mobilized almost simultaneously across the country brought a new sense of collective identity and class consciousness to Korean industrial workers. In every sense of the phrase, the large scale of labor conflicts that erupted in the summer of 1987 represents the Great Worker Struggle (as South Korean workers and labor experts call it), and clearly it was the most critical juncture in the formation of the South Korean working class.

The Great Worker Struggle

As in previous periods of large-scale labor unrest, this unprecedented wave of industrial strife occurred in the context of abrupt political change brought about by the opposition movement to the authoritarian regime (Christian Institute for the Study of Justice and Development 1998). On June 29, 1987, Roh Tae Woo, then chairman of the ruling party, the Democratic Justice Party (DJP), made a surprise announcement that the DJP would accept the demands of the opposition party for a direct presidential election and constitutional reform. This was a major turning point in South Korean political history, paving the way for a transition to democracy after almost three decades of military rule. Chun Doo Hwan had attempted to transfer power to his hand-picked heir and old classmate at the Korean military academy, Roh Tae Woo, through an indirect election by the electoral college. In early June, Chun had arbitrarily cancelled negotiations with the opposition party over constitutional amendments and announced that he would hold an indirect election in order to avoid unnecessary political conflicts and instability. This authoritarian action intensified popular resentment, which had been building up after the revelations of the death of one student demonstrator due to police torture and of the sexual assault on a female student labor activist by a police interrogator. As student protests spread, a growing number of shopkeepers, white-collar workers, and other workers began to join the street protests organized by students, creating the specter of revolution (fig. 9). The June 29 declaration of democratization was a tactical surrender to the people's power by the Chun regime in an attempt to avoid the fatal consequences of this political crisis (Shin, Zho, and Chey 1994; Oh 1999; Diamond and Kim 2000; Sunhyuk Kim 2000).

Clearly, this democratic transition was not the product of the labor movement. The main actors, as in most other previous political upheavals in South Korea, were students, who had fought for democratization tenaciously throughout the 1970s and 1980s. But the success of the student-led democratization struggle in June 1987 owed much to the participation of a large number of citizens, including white-collar workers, small business owners, poor urban residents, and industrial workers. As street protests escalated across the country, several white-collar unions that had been recently formed began to participate in the democratization movement. In May and June, many white-collar workers employed in banks and other financial institutions in downtown Seoul could be seen joining the students' street demonstrations during their lunch breaks.

The role of the industrial workers in this struggle for democracy, however, is not so clear. Many analysts believe that the role of the industrial

Figure 9. A huge street demonstration combined with a funeral march for a student killed by police tear gas in June 1987. (Provided by *JoongAng Daily*)

workers and labor unions was minimal. One indication of labor's marginal role in the democratization movement is that labor leaders made up only a tiny fraction of the grand national coalition of democratization movements that led the civil protests against the Chun regime in spring 1987; of the total 2,200 founding members, there were only thirty-seven labor representatives (*Joong-ang Daily News*, July 7, 1987 in Lim Young-Il, 1998, 143). Unions played no particular role during the June civil uprising, and there is no evidence of any organized participation of manufacturing workers in street demonstrations, although many workers participated in protests as individuals.[1] The only action of the national center of unions, the FKTU, during this period was blatantly anti-democratic: it publicly endorsed Chun Doo Hwan's cancellation of the constitutional debate in April and supported his plan for an indirect presidential election. Many politically oriented labor groups that had been committed to the MPO (mass political organization) realized the importance of the political opportunity, but nevertheless failed to mobilize workers for the mass struggle in June 1987.[2]

Other analysts, however, stress a more important role played by the industrial workers in South Korea's democratic transition. They point out that a large number of wage workers, a number larger than the white-collar workers and shopkeepers, in fact participated in street demonstrations during June.[3] But more important than the actual participation by industrial workers was the potential threat of their mass participation. Choi Jang Jip (1993b) suggests that the Chun regime's calculated move toward political liberalization was influenced by the very real threat of thousands and thousands of factory workers pouring onto the streets (see also Chu 1998). Roh Joong-ki also argues that "The main reason why the ruling block hurried to announce the democratization plan at the end of June when the civil uprising began to spread to the working class was because they could not underestimate the potential threatening power of the labor movement" (1995, 81).

There is, thus, no disagreement among Korean labor experts that the principal agent that brought about the political opening for democratic transition in June 1987 was the student movement, and that the labor movement contributed to this political development mainly as a latent force or a potential threat rather than as an active participant in the strug-

1. Lim Young-Il argues that "Until the democratic coalition of students, urban middle classes, and the opposition party drew a major concession from the military ruling power through intensive acts of warfare-style resistance and enormous sacrifices, there was almost nothing that the Korean labor movement had done" (1998, 143).

2. During 1985 and 1986 these radical activist labor groups were divided among themselves and occupied in heated ideological and strategic issues (see Lim 1998, 144–46).

3. This is evidenced by the fact that the largest proportion of the people arrested during this period were laborers, although many of these might have been construction workers or casual laborers (see Kim Young-soo 1999, 207).

gle. Whether the breakdown of authoritarian rule could have taken place without this threat from the working class is clearly debatable. But it seems clear that organized labor in South Korea prior to 1987 was not able to act as an effective political force, whether due to internal organizational weakness or to the external constraints imposed by the state, which were considerably strengthened in spring 1987.

As soon as the Chun regime announced a plan for political liberalization, however, it was the industrial labor that was mobilized instantly on a large scale. A wave of violent labor conflicts erupted within two weeks of Roh's announcement of political liberalization. Labor unrest swept across the country like a prairie fire at an unprecedented level of intensity and fury. It started in the manufacturing industries and then spread to mining, transportation, the dockyards, and some service sectors. From July to September 1987, as many as 3,311 cases of labor conflicts occurred, virtually all of which involved work stoppages, wildcat strikes, or demonstrations. The number of labor disputes that occurred during that summer exceeded the total number of disputes that had occurred during the entire period of export-oriented industrialization since the early 1960s (chart 6). In the middle of August, when the labor unrest was at its peak, more than one hundred labor disputes occurred daily, the annual average during the Park

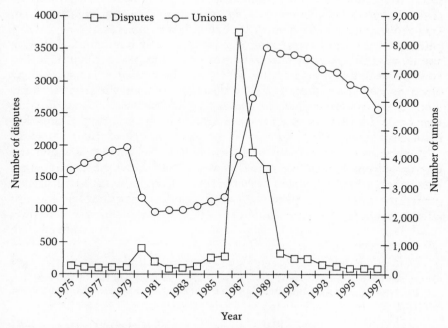

Chart 6. Number of Labor Disputes and Labor Unions, 1975–1998

and Chun periods. The total number of workers who participated in these labor actions is estimated to be 1.2 million, equivalent to approximately one-third of the regularly employed workers in enterprises with ten or more workers (Ministry of Labor 1988). (See table 7.1.)

Interestingly, the wave of labor unrest did not start in the Seoul or Kyungin regions, where labor had previously been most active, but in the southern industrial city of Ulsan. Ulsan was the center of the Hyundai conglomerate companies, and the majority of its inhabitants were the employees of Hyundai firms (including Hyundai shipbuilding, Hyundai automobile, Hyundai machinery, and their subsidiary companies) and their families. Like other *chaebol* groups, Hyundai had no union organized within its group structure and had seen only one serious labor dispute, a violent labor protest that occurred at Hyundai shipyard in 1974. But within two weeks of the June 29 declaration, virtually all the Hyundai firms were involved in labor disputes. Labor disputes at Hyundai spilled over into large street demonstrations and ignited labor conflicts at smaller firms affiliated with Hyundai firms. The wave of strikes quickly spread to other major industrial centers in the southern coastal region—to Pusan, Changwon, and Masan—where heavy industries were concentrated. By mid-August, the strike wave had reached the Seoul-Kyungin region, where the smaller light manufacturing industries were concentrated. Thence, labor unrest spread to smaller cities in the southwest region. By late August, the whole country had become engulfed in labor conflicts.

However, the 1987 Great Worker Struggle largely represented a spontaneous, unorganized, and uncoordinated explosion of labor conflicts. Despite some differences in time sequence, thousands of labor conflicts occurred almost simultaneously nationwide without systematic planning, strategy, or leadership. There was no national or regional organization that could have coordinated this great eruption of labor actions. With no organization and no leadership, workers nevertheless seized the opportunity created by the sudden relaxation of authoritarian control to vent their long-suppressed anger and grievances. This was, of course, not the first time that Korean workers had demonstrated this explosive quality; it had also happened in spring 1980 in the wake of the political vacuum left by Park Chung Hee's assassination. But this time, the labor conflicts were on a much larger scale, broader in scope, and far more militant and effective in achieving organizational goals.

The major demands of the workers in the great struggle concerned wages and the authoritarian industrial relations. In many of the bigger firms, workers were able to obtain 20–30 percent wage increases along with increased benefits. As in many previous labor protests, however, the demands for humane treatment and for more democratic industrial relations were as strong as the demand for fair pay. The list of workers' demands was

Table 7.1 Union Activity, 1963–1998

Year	Disputes	Unions	Union Members (thousands)	Organizational Rate* A	B
1963	—	1,820	224	20.3	9.4
1964	126	2,105	272	23.3	11.5
1965	113	2,255	302	22.4	11.6
1966	117	2,359	327	22.7	11.8
1967	130	2,619	378	22.2	12.4
1968	135	2,732	413	21.1	12.1
1969	94	2,939	445	21.3	12.5
1970	90	3,063	473	20.0	12.6
1971	109	3,061	497	19.7	2.7
1972	—	2,961	515	20.4	12.9
1973	—	2,865	548	20.4	13.2
1974	—	3,352	656	22.1	14.8
1975	133	3,585	750	23.0	15.8
1976	110	3,854	846	23.3	16.5
1977	96	4,042	955	24.3	16.7
1978	102	4,301	1,055	24.0	16.9
1979	105	4,394	1,088	23.6	16.8
1980	407	2,618	948	20.1	14.7
1981	186	2,141	967	19.6	14.6
1982	88	2,194	984	19.1	14.4
1983	98	2,238	1,010	18.1	14.1
1984	113	2,365	1,011	16.8	13.2
1985	265	2,534	1,004	15.7	12.4
1986	276	2,658	1,036	15.5	12.3
1987	3,749	4,086	1,267	17.3	13.8
1988	1,873	6,142	1,707	22.0	17.8
1989	1,616	7,883	1,932	23.3	18.6
1990	322	7,698	1,887	21.5	17.2
1991	234	7,656	1,803	19.7	15.9
1992	235	7,527	1,735	18.4	15.0
1993	144	7,147	1,667	17.2	14.2
1994	121	7,025	1,659	16.3	13.5
1995	88	6,606	1,615	15.3	12.7
1996	85	6,424	1,599	14.7	12.2
1997	78	5,733	1,484	13.5	11.2
1998	128	5,560	1,402	13.8	11.5

* Organizational rate: A indicates union members as a proportion of the total number of nonagricultural, regularly employed workers; B indicates union members as a proportion of the total number of employed workers.

typically long, including an increase in wages, more generous bonuses, reduction in working hours, termination of the arbitrary evaluation system by foremen, elimination of status distinctions between white-collar and blue-collar workers, improvement in the quality of meals, removal of restrictions on dress and hair styles, and discontinuation of compulsory morning exercises.

In many ways, the Great Worker Struggle of 1987 was an occasion in which workers' long-accumulated *han* exploded and was released. It was, in other words, a huge manifestation of *hanpuli* (releasing *han*) by workers,[4] when long-suppressed grievances and resentment are expressed, in an impulsive, emotional, and violent manner. Almost all the strikes in summer 1987 were illegal actions because workers purposely ignored the mandated cooling-off period and other legal requirements for a strike. Workers were not content with the regular channels of labor disputes and resorted to more militant actions such as occupying company buildings, holding street demonstrations, or taking managerial staff hostage. Violence occurred frequently as workers retaliated against the mean and arrogant managers and employers. Some employers were forced to make concessions to workers' extravagant demands due to fear of physical threats. As one Korean labor analyst describes it, the violent labor conflicts in 1987 resembled a "class war" waged by the deeply discontented and suddenly empowered workers against the oppressive labor regime they had endured so long (Song Ho Keun 1994b).

The Great Worker Struggle of 1987, however, was different from the previous outbursts of labor conflicts. In 1987 and in the following year, workers were not just interested in venting their grievances and gaining higher wages. They were equally interested in acquiring the organizational means to protect their long-term interests—union organization was at the top of their priorities. Where company unions existed, workers wanted to transform them into genuine representative unions. In almost all factories where intense labor conflict occurred, a focal point was the struggle to force management's acceptance of a newly formed union or a democratic union in place of a company-controlled (*ŏyong*) union. The strong union consciousness demonstrated during this period was no doubt the result of the past experience of struggles. Workers had learned through bitter experience that temporal concession by capital or the state did not assure long-term improvement in their conditions and that unions were the only effective means through which they could demand respect and human

4. This idea was first suggested to me by Park Dong, a student-turned-worker who later returned to graduate school at Korea University. In 1987 he was working in the Kuro industrial complex. I would like to thank him for offering me his insightful observation and also for arranging my visit to several factories in Seoul-Kyungin areas in summer 1995.

dignity in the factory. It was this new level of class consciousness that made the 1987 struggle much stronger, more militant, and tenacious.

Thus, the Great Worker Struggle resulted in a quantum jump in the number of unions and union members. Within a year of the labor uprising, as many as 4,000 new unions were formed, and some 700,000 workers joined unions (Kim Dong-Choon 1995; Lim Young-Il 1998). The total number of unions increased dramatically, from 2,675 at the end of 1986 to 6,164 by the end of 1988 (see table 7.1). More than half of the unions that existed in early 1989 were formed after the 1987 labor offensive. During this period, the number of unionized workers increased from 1 million to 1.7 million. Unionization occurred more successfully in large firms than in smaller firms. Practically all newly formed unions were democratic unions, and most company-controlled (or "ghost") unions were replaced by representative unions.

The labor uprising of 1987 brought about a drastic change in the main actors of the South Korean labor movement. As previously noted, the major sites of intense labor struggles in 1987 and 1988 were not the small enterprises in the labor-intensive, light manufacturing sector but the large firms in the heavy and chemical industries. This also meant there was a major change in the gender composition of the main actors of the labor movement, from predominantly female to predominantly male workers. Light manufacturing areas such as Kuro, Puchŏn, and Anyang, where many labor conflicts had occurred previously, were relatively quiet when this wildfire of labor unrest engulfed the large firms in southern cities of Ulsan, Changwon, and Masan. Almost overnight, the male semi-skilled workers of large factories in the heavy and chemical industries emerged on the front lines of the labor movement, pushing aside the female workers who had carried on the battles in the 1970s alone and had laid the ground for the democratic union movement.

The Great Worker Struggle was significant in another important respect. Unlike previous labor strikes, this labor struggle occurred without the initiation, leadership, or active guidance of the outside intellectual community. It was entirely the result of workers' voluntary and spontaneous participation in collective actions. The unionization struggles that started at Hyundai in July 1987, for example, were led by the workers, with little support from outside organizations. Not only in Ulsan but in all other industrial towns, the leaders of the labor protests and strikes emerged from within each factory. The students-turned-workers, who had played such a conspicuous role in the unionization struggles in the early 1980s, played no significant role in 1987 (Lim 1992, 138; my interviews with Hyundai workers in Ulsan in 1995 confirm this). Before 1987, most students-turned-workers had been working in the Seoul-Kyungin region, with some in Taegu; few of them had been able to enter the bigger firms in southern industrial cities.[5] The Great Worker Struggle of 1987 thus demonstrated that Korean workers had outgrown the need to be protected and represented by the intellectual community. The Korean working class had produced its own leaders and "organic intellectuals," as well as organizational resources, to become a class in its own right.

The Nature of Spontaneity

I have just described that the 1987 wave of labor conflicts was largely a spontaneous and unorganized explosion of labor conflicts; there is wide consensus among Korean labor experts on this point—that labor conflicts in summer 1987 occurred without premeditation or planning, and without preconceived objectives or strategic ideas. The explosion of labor militancy occurred so suddenly and on such a massive a scale, that even many intellectual labor activists who had been working for labor mobilization for a long time seemed to be at a loss and were unable to play a leading role. As a prominent labor scholar, Lim Young-Il, observes, "There was hardly any strike that had been planned, and even in a very few cases where some preparation had been going on by activists inside and outside the firms, the speed and size of the mass participation and its militancy made such a preparation rather meaningless" (1998, 89–90).

The explosion of labor conflicts in 1987 was largely the product of a sudden political opening created by the political dynamics of the civil society. The temporary suspension of authoritarian state intervention in the labor regime provided a golden opportunity for workers to vent their long-suppressed grievances. As Kim Dong-Choon, another astute labor analyst, points out, "the struggle occurred right after the relaxation of political control by the authoritarian regime following the 6–29 [democratization declaration] and dwindled in September with the return of repression. In short, like the past labor movement in Korea, it was the external factors, especially political factors, rather than factors internal to workplaces, that had a determining influence on the overall occurrence and disappearance of the labor disputes" (1995, 121). Thus, there is wide scholarly agreement that given the abrupt and unexpected arrival of this political opportunity, the workers' responses were largely spontaneous and unorganized.

It is important to realize, however, that this does not mean that workers simply responded to an opportunity provided by other groups without any prior effort or organization on their part. It is in fact difficult to imagine

5. Kim Ho-kyu, a student-turned-worker employed at a Hyundai factory in Ulsan, whom I interviewed in 1995, said that many of them had been planning to move to Ulsan before the outbreak of the Great Worker Struggle of 1987. Their activities had been concentrated in the industrial areas near Seoul and Inchon, and very few of the students-turned-workers went to Ulsan from Seoul. Kim himself moved to Ulsan after 1987.

that mobilization on such a massive scale could have occurred without prior experiences of labor resistance and in the absence of organizational activities among workers. And it is certainly incorrect to assume that the dominant pattern of these labor struggles—militant, aggressive, and aimed at organizing independent unions—had no relationship to the level of class consciousness that had developed among a significant minority of Korean industrial workers. The 1987 labor uprising was spontaneous only in the sense that a majority of the disputes occurred without premeditation, planning, or organizational leadership, not in the sense that workers simply reacted to the circumstances in a purely impulsive and irrational manner in the absence of prior efforts to organize collective resistance.

In this regard, it is useful to consider why the 1987 labor revolt occurred first in Ulsan at a relatively small firm, Hyundai Engine, within the Hyundai conglomerate group. On July 5, 1987, within a week of Roh Tae Woo's June 29 announcement of democratic reform, some one hundred workers of Hyundai Engine secretly met in downtown Ulsan and formed a union. Workers at other Hyundai plants quickly followed suit. Within a month of the announcement, nearly all twelve Hyundai firms had unions either already formed or in the process of being formed.

This was indeed a remarkable development, considering the level of passivity and quiescence that seemed characteristic of Hyundai workers in the previous twenty years.[6] Clearly such a dramatic change in workers' responses could not have been possible without a political crisis in the regime. But in actuality unionization struggles at Hyundai had not occurred completely spontaneously. There had been a number of workers at several Hyundai firms who had been secretly preparing themselves to organize a union to improve their working conditions through collective action. At Hyundai Engine, where the first union was formed, a small group of workers had been actively cultivating comradeship and class consciousness through a variety of small-group activities. Unlike the small-group activities in the light manufacturing sectors in the early 1980s, which had been initiated and led by students-turned-workers, the small groups at Hyundai grew out of the workers' own initiative and had only tenuous relationships with the outside intellectual community.[7]

6. Only once in 1980 had there been a preliminary attempt to organize a union at Hyundai Heavy Industry. Interestingly, the attempt was made not by workers but by a labor-oriented manager named Lee Min-woo. His courageous attempt was, however, crushed by the newly formed military regime before it had a serious effect on other workers (see Lee Soo-won 1994, 34–35).

7. This does not mean that these small groups received no help at all from outside organizations. In fact, they received organizational help from the Ulsan council of Social Missionary organizations (Ulsan sahoisŏnkyo hyŏpŭihoi), but they were not dependent on this outside group's support (see Lee Soo-won 1994, 23, 62).

Most significant among these groups was the study group organized at Hyundai Engine by Kwon Yong-mok, who emerged as a charismatic leader in the 1987 Hyundai workers' struggles. Kwon Yong-mok, like his fellow workers who participated actively in small-group activities, was a high school graduate, and had developed a keen sense of injustice toward despotic managerial practices at Hyundai and acquired a high level of class consciousness through contacts with dissident intellectuals and through extensive reading of the then-popular Marxist literature (Kwon 1988; Lee Soo-won 1994). He may be considered a prime example of what Gramsci (1971) calls "organic intellectuals." In the early 1980s, he organized a small leisure-activity group to visit sites of cultural heritage on the weekends. Gradually, the group's attention was turned to discussing the problems in their workplace and studying labor laws and Marxist literature. In 1986, Kwon and his colleagues succeeded in taking control of the labor-management council and transforming it from a pro-management agency to a more worker-representative organization. Their next step was to organize a union, and in spring 1987 they selected a few members for its preparation (Lee Soo-won 1994, 47–48).[8] It was this preparatory work that enabled the Hyundai Engine workers to move swiftly to organize a union as soon as the opportunity appeared in July 1987. Similar small group activities had been going on in other Hyundai firms in Ulsan, including Hyundai Motors, Hyundai Heavy Electrics, and Hyundai Heavy Industries (1994, 39–79).[9]

It is also important to understand that although the 1987 labor struggle occurred without systematic planning or guidance from outside activist organizations, once the spontaneous uprising had occurred the role of such outsiders became very important in supporting the democratic union movement. Striking workers during this period displayed enormous zeal for democratic unions, but had little practical knowledge of trade unions; they did not know how to organize a union, how to register it, or what the legal requirements were for union activities. With a hundred labor disputes occurring daily in July and August 1987, most of them involving unionization struggles, the Korean democratic union movement faced a crisis. In response there was a quick activation of many informal and formal labor-activist groups, church-based labor-consultation centers, or other regional labor organizations. In addition to the existing networks of activist organizations, many new groups were quickly created to meet the mounting demand for assistance from the workers engaged in the struggle for

8. According to Lee's report, Hyundai Engine labor activists had planned to attempt to organize a union in June or July 1987.
9. At Hyundai Motors in 1985, five politically conscious workers had formed a study group to awaken consciousness among their fellow workers. A similar group had been organized at Hyundai Heavy Electrics by Chun Chang-Soo, a college graduate.

unionization. A remark by one labor activist (a member of the Kyungnam Labor Association, created by workers who had been fired from their previous employment for their labor activism), in an interview with Lim Young-Il, is instructive:

> There was no time to think anything else. And there was no need to think anything. This [great struggle] was not what we created, nor what we dared to think we could create, but the goal was crystal clear. We must help them to organize a democratic union at every firm on strike. And the unions formed must be protected. And we must make them congregate. There were too many things to do and too few people and too little time to do it all. But it was not too difficult. Workers accepted it surprisingly all too easily. Immediately after they resolved the main hurdles in their firm, under the leadership of the newly emerged leadership during the strike, workers gathered at our office and took the leaflets and rushed to other firms in the neighborhood (Lim 1998, 93n).

As this activist's remarks clearly indicate, although the 1987 labor eruption occurred because of spontaneous participation by the masses of workers, the struggle did not progress haphazardly without organizational support or guidance. Where organizations did not exist, new organizations were readily formed, although mostly informally and on a small scale; and where leadership was absent, a new grassroots leadership quickly emerged out of the strikes. We can see that the organizational resources available to the South Korean working-class movement in 1987 were markedly different from those in 1980, as was the level of union consciousness and working-class solidarity. Undoubtedly, all these changes were the product of the pre-1987 struggles.

Worker Struggles at Hyundai

It is significant that the 1987 Great Worker Struggle was set off by a struggle at a Hyundai factory in Ulsan. Hyundai was the largest conglomerate group in South Korea and the biggest auto manufacturer and shipbuilder. Both in terms of its size and its role in the South Korean economy, Hyundai clearly represented the core of industrial power. As at other *chaebol* firms, unions had been considered taboo at Hyundai. The firm's founder, Chung Ju Young, was famous for his staunch anti-unionism; like the late Lee Byung Chul, the founder of Samsung group, he used to warn his workers, "I will never allow a union until earth covers my eyes" (Lee Soo-won 1994, 35). The formation of unions in Hyundai plants was thus a very significant event for labor activists in other firms. In many ways, the pattern of labor struggles that developed at Hyundai brings the most interesting features of the Korean working-class struggles during this period into sharp relief.

Labor unionization at Hyundai resembled an insurrection. On July 5, 1987, within a week of the declaration of political liberalization, some one hundred workers of Hyundai Engine secretly met at a discotheque in downtown Ulsan and formed a union. As already mentioned, this was the result of a small group of workers who had been preparing for union organization for some time.

Following this lead, unionization struggles occurred at all other twelve Hyundai firms within a month of the June 29 proclamation. Unionization at the other firms was, however, not as smooth or successful as it was at Hyundai Engine. After an initial shock, the Hyundai management recovered itself and tried to block the unionization drive. Hyundai management's first attempt was extremely crude and countereffective. On July 16, for example, when Hyundai Mipo Shipyard workers were just about to register their newly formed union at the city hall, several men suddenly appeared, snatched their registration papers, and drove away in a car waiting outside. This clumsy anti-union action was publicized in the media and invited a battery of criticism from all sectors of society. Thanks to this management blunder, the Mipo shipyard workers were able to register their newly formed union with official approval.

Such mistakes, however, did not discourage management at other Hyundai companies from trying other methods. The method used at Hyundai Heavy Industries and Hyundai Motors, the two largest firms within the Hyundai Group, was more sophisticated and effective. The tactic was to maneuver the formation of a union by pro-management workers in advance of the formation of a strong independent union. Since multiple unions at a single firm were prohibited by Korean labor laws, this tactic was effective in denying legal status to the representative union that was formed later. This method failed to prevent the formation of a strong independent union at Hyundai Motors, but succeeded in debilitating the independent union at Hyundai Heavy Industries and dividing its workforce for a long time. The fiercest worker struggle thus occurred at Hyundai Heavy Industries over the recognition of a genuinely representative union.

Nonetheless, once unions had been successfully formed, Hyundai workers voiced their long-suppressed grievances in a lengthy list of union demands; in addition to 25–30 percent wage increases, workers' demands included the elimination of the invidious system of wage competition among workers, the abolition of the restriction on hair length, termination of compulsory morning exercise, and improvement in the quality of the daily lunch. Interestingly, the demand for personal freedom as to hairstyle and pre-work exercise appeared at every strike at Hyundai firms, demonstrating the workers' strong resentment against the military-style work environment. Hyundai's military-style disciplinary practices were quite well known, although certainly not unique in the bigger Korean manufacturing firms. Workers were often stopped by security guards at the entrance to have their hair length measured, and if their hair was found to be longer than allowed by the company hair code, the guards used big scissors to cut their hair on the spot (Lee Soo-won 1994, 30). Production workers were also subjected to body searches when they left the plant. It is no wonder that Hyundai workers smashed the guards' office first when they went on a strike.

The unionization movement at individual Hyundai firms quickly converged into a solidarity struggle at the group level. On August 8, 1987, union representatives from twelve Hyundai firms gathered and formed the Council of Unions of the Hyundai Group. Kwon Yong-mok of Hyundai Engine was elected to the chair of the council. Unionists wanted to take a coordinated approach in dealing with the highly centralized authority structure at the Hyundai Group, where, they knew, all important decisions were made at the group level and ultimately by its monarchical chairman. The Council of Unions at Hyundai immediately clashed with management over two issues: a demand for group-level wage negotiations between management and the council, and the recognition of the bona fide union that had been formed at Hyundai Heavy Industries.[10] But management refused to negotiate with what they considered to be an unlawful organization. Workers were ready to show their muscle. On the morning of August 17, thousands of Hyundai workers gathered at the Hyundai Heavy Industries plant and marched toward the city (fig. 10). At the front of the march were dump trucks, forklifts, fire engines, and sand-blasting machines. Accompanied by drums and gongs, the crowd sang newly learned songs and shouted, "Down with Chung Ju Young!" On the streets they were met by the riot police. The police fired tear gas at the protesters, but soon they found themselves fleeing in panic from the angry crowd. The police chief offered to negotiate. He sat down with Kwon Yong-mok in the middle of the four-lane road to do so. With Kwon's promise to maintain a peaceful demonstration, he allowed the demonstrators to walk to Namok Hill (midway to downtown) and walk back to Hyundai Heavy Industries. Workers walked the 3 kilometre to Namok Hill, shouting and chanting, and walked back to their workplace peacefully.

10. Just before this bona fide union was formed, with support from the absolute majority of workers, Hyundai Heavy Industries management helped a small group of pro-management workers to organize a union and register it as the sole legal union. Although workers then replaced the pro-management officers with new independent leaders by an almost unanimous vote, Hyundai management refused to acknowledge the new leadership as legitimate.

Figure 10. Hyundai workers marching to Ulsan public stadium, August 1987. (Provided by *JoongAng Daily*)

The demonstration became bigger and better organized on the following day. Workers from various Hyundai companies in Ulsan gathered in the grounds of Hyundai Heavy Industries in the early morning of August 18. Some forty thousand workers were estimated to have gathered. By mid-morning they were joined by some thirty thousand wives and children. They set out toward the city, again led by dump trucks, forklifts, and other heavy vehicles. The lead group was armed with gas masks and fiber hats; their destination was Ulsan Sports Stadium. The demonstrators were met by 4,500 police, but the police realized that they were not a match for forty thousand demonstrators led by heavy vehicles. The police had no alternative but to allow the marchers to proceed. The workers had suddenly become invincible. The demonstrators had increased to sixty thousand when they arrived at the city stadium peacefully. Mothers, wives, and children marched alongside the workers. The parade stretched for two miles and it took five hours to complete the 10-mile journey to the stadium.

At the stadium, workers were later greeted by a government representative, but not by Hyundai managers. The Deputy Minister of Labor had flown down to Ulsan from Seoul to negotiate with the workers. He directed the negotiations between Kwon Yong-mok and the chief officer of the Office of Labor Affairs. The agreement, announced by the deputy minister himself, was the acceptance of practically all of the workers' demands including a significant wage increase and the recognition of the independent union at Hyundai Heavy Industries. The sixty thousand workers and their family members in the stadium cheered wildly and headed back home. It was the first victory Hyundai workers had achieved through collective action. As one of the leading labor activists at Hyundai later wrote, "August 18 was the day when Hyundai workers, or all the workers of the nation, were reborn, overcoming their *han*, into the masters of the nation, and a great solemn march toward the future of a truly humanlike life" (Lee Soo-won 1994, 103).

However, it was only a symbolic victory and a short-lived one. Hyundai management simply decided to ignore what had been promised by the Deputy Minister of Labor and denied the legitimacy of both the new union leadership at Hyundai Heavy Industries and the Council of Unions of Hyundai Group. Consequently, wage negotiations were stalled and labor unrest continued.

THE second episode of the Hyundai workers' struggle occurred at Hyundai Heavy Industries toward the end of 1988. Labor disputes occurred over a contract negotiation and the reinstatement of four dismissed union leaders. Neither side was willing to compromise, and the union called a strike on December 12, which turned out to be the longest strike in South Korean labor history, lasting 128 days. Part of the reason for the long duration of this strike was the lack of cohesion in the union leadership and management's strategy to cripple hard-line union leaders. Just before the strike, Hyundai Heavy Industries workers had elected a new union president, Suh Tae-soo. Suh, however, betrayed the union members by signing a new contract with management on his own, without seeking the members' approval. Angry workers voted to nullify the contract. They also voted Suh out and elected a new president, Lee Won-keun. But the company refused to accept this election and Suh did not step down, causing continual organizational problems for the union.

While the strike went on at Hyundai Heavy Industries in Ulsan, 171 workers went to Seoul to see Chung Ju Young on December 15, 1988. This was the third time Hyundai workers had gone to the Hyundai conglomerate's main office in Seoul to see Chung. The first occasion had been in August 1987 when the officers of the newly formed union at Hyundai Heavy Industries came to him to plea for the recognition of the democratic union. The second time had been in November 1987 when Hyundai Engine workers came to see Chung to ask for the release of their jailed leader, Kwon

Yong-mok. The Hyundai workers knew that Chung was the ultimate authority for important decisions at Hyundai and they believed that even the arrests and releases of workers by police were more or less in his hands. Chung, however, refused to see the strikers. The protesters carried out a sit-in demonstration in front of the Hyundai main building in Seoul, but had to end their protest because of an attack by police on December 29.

On December 28, 1988, President Roh Tae Woo made a "Special Announcement on Maintaining Civic Security and Law Order," signalling the government's resumption of repressive measures and the end of the relatively liberal political atmosphere that had prevailed since June 1987. Both the changing political atmosphere and the New Year's holiday necessarily dampened the spirits of Hyundai strikers in Ulsan.

But a new incident occurred in January 1989 that poured gas on the flickering flame. At dawn on January 8, a number of armed men broke into the office of the Association of Dismissed Hyundai Employees, beat the people sleeping there with baseball bats and wooden clubs, and smashed the furniture to pieces. The association had been formed in February 1988 by union leaders who had been jailed and were subsequently laid off by the Hyundai companies, including Kwon Yong-mok and other hard-core leaders. In 1988, the Association of Dismissed Hyundai Employees had taken over the role of the Council of Unions at Hyundai and played a central role in guiding union actions at the individual firms.[11] Apparently, the Hyundai management wanted to break up this outside militant labor organization and sever its ties with shop-floor union leaders. Interestingly enough, this raid was organized by a Korean-American professional union buster hired by Hyundai Heavy Industries, James Lee. The revelation of this incident made workers in Ulsan furious and also brought thirty thousand workers from other regions for a huge rally in Ulsan to denounce the terrorist actions by Hyundai management and to pledge a solidarity struggle with the Hyundai Heavy Industries strikers.

Bitter confrontations between workers and management continued through spring 1989. The protracted period of the strike was rife with violence, between workers and management and between anti-management and pro-management workers. As in many other Korean firms, Hyundai Heavy Industries management organized the *kusadae* (save-the-company corps)—made up of managerial workers, factory guards, and hired thugs—and used this organization to try to discourage participation in strikes by passive workers. But unlike the female unionists in the 1970s who often fell victim to male violence, male workers at Hyundai and at other heavy

11. The Association of Dismissed Hyundai Employees maintained a close relationship with the Ulsan Association of Social Missionary, and the two organizations included several students-turned-workers who actively supported Kwon Yong-Mok and other labor leaders (see Lee Soo-won 1994; Ulsan nodong chŏngchaek kyoyuk hyŏphoe 1995).

industry firms were not such easy prey. The ways in which the Hyundai workers responded to police intervention vividly demonstrated the changed terrain of labor conflicts. Not only their massive numbers, easily reaching tens of thousands, but also their use of a variety of defensive weapons made them an intimidating crowd to control. Police violence was bound to lose much of its effect in controlling these kinds of strikers. It is in this physical sense, if not in a more profound sociological sense, that the post-1987 Korean labor movement differs sharply from the previous female-dominated struggles for democratic unions.

At the request of the company, the police announced its plan to invade the Hyundai Heavy Industries compound on March 30, 1989, to end the strike. The strikers, however, voted to fight until the end. The day before this D-day, strikers held a press conference, where they impressed reporters with a display of homemade weapons, including fire bombs, trench mortars, and many other ingenious weapons they had produced. At dawn on March 30, on the 109th day of the strike, a massive military-style operation started with a signal of multiple gunshots fired into the early morning sky. It was an operation by land, sea, and sky. On land, the riot police who had gathered earlier in front of the Hyundai Heavy Industries plant began to move in while firing tear gas. From the sea, marine boats arrived carrying eight quadrons of riot police. And from the sky, helicopters swirled around over the factory compound and announced to the workers, "You are all surrounded. Law-violating workers, please surrender voluntarily." It was a huge military operation, called the Ulsan 30 Operation, with the code name "morning dew." Some fifteen thousand policemen were mobilized for the operation.

When the police force entered the factory compound, however, there were hardly any strikers because they had sneaked out of the compound at midnight and reassembled in front of the Hyundai dormitory building, the *ojwabŏl* residence hall. At noon, the riot police, accompanied by a band of notorious *paikgoldan* (a police unit specially trained in the martial arts) invaded *ojwabŏl*. The *paikgoldan* beat resisting workers mercilessly and arrested hundreds of them. But that was not the end of the strike. By the late afternoon, workers' resistance had developed into a large-scale street battle. Some 1,500 fellow workers at nearby Hyundai Engine declared a one-day strike in sympathy and poured on to the streets. Hundreds of workers from Hyundai Motors, Hyundai Mipo Shipyards, and Hyundai subsidiary firms also poured on to the streets. The eastern section of Ulsan turned into a war zone.

The street battles grew larger and more violent on the following day. Several dozen students from nearby areas arrived to join the Hyundai workers' struggles. A large number of residents also joined the street protests. Having seen how cruelly the *paikgoldan* attacked their husbands and fathers, many wives and children of Hyundai workers were enraged and became

direct participants in the street battles. They blocked the police from entering their street alleys in pursuit of fleeing workers, they collected
money and hid in their homes students who had come to assist the workers, and they collected empty bottles for manufacturing Molotov cocktails.
The street battle lasted for more than ten days, and ended on April 18,
1989, with the arrests of fifty-two union leaders and dismissals of forty-
nine workers. Workers later wrote about this painful ending, "The 128-
day-long strike, which was the point of Hyundai Heavy workers' pride,
who had carried the flag of democratic unionism since 1987 despite so
much sacrifice, was trampled by Hyundai's cruel terrorism and the formidable power of the police and came to an end, once again leaving great *han*
deep in the minds of the Hyundai workers" (Lee Soo-won 1994, 255).

The 128-day strike at Hyundai Heavy Industries was, however, far from
being a failure. Workers failed to achieve their demands for the release of
their union leaders, but they succeeded in achieving something very precious through this struggle. Solidarity was born, and a high level of class
awareness and political consciousness was in evidence among the growing
number of workers who participated in the struggle. The union became
stronger and more democratic in operation, and union membership increased significantly. On the shop floor, too, workers were organized
into small groups or committees and began to have a voice in many job-
related issues. All these changes meant that managers had lost substantial
power over workers on the shop floor; they even became afraid of militant
workers.

THE third major episode of the Hyundai worker struggle, known as the
Goliat struggle, occurred again at Hyundai Heavy Industries over what
appeared to be relatively minor issues. In January 1990, Hyundai Heavy
Industries workers elected the fifth slate of union executives. This frequent changeover of union leadership, five times in two and a half years although the term for union officers was two years, was due to the frequent
arrests of union leaders during strikes and to internal division in the union
leadership. As the union movement evolved at Hyundai Group, most
unions were divided between militant *minjupa*, who stressed class solidarity beyond the firm level and the importance of political struggle to
reform the repressive labor policies, and moderate pragmatists (*silipa*) who
wanted to confine their collective actions to more immediate firm-level
objectives. Whereas the Hyundai Heavy Industries union was dominated
by radical members, the Hyundai Motors union was led by a more moderate, pragmatically oriented leadership.

Labor friction occurred when the Hyundai Heavy Industries workers
wanted to hold an inauguration meeting for the newly elected union officers during working hours and the company denied the request. The com-

pany also denied the union's request to allow workers to leave early to attend the court hearing of five of their union leaders who had been arrested during the 128-day strike. The new union leaders decided to ignore the management decision and they went ahead with their plan. The company immediately reported them to the police, who arrested the union leaders. The radical union members saw this unfriendly action as management's deliberate attempt to pick a fight and debilitate the union. They decided they had no choice but to fight.

Workers were further angered by the heavy sentences given to their previous union leaders who had been jailed, especially compared to the light sentences given to the participants in a strike that had occurred at the KBS broadcasting station a little earlier; the some one hundred broadcast workers who participated in the strike had all been released. Hyundai workers were angered because they believed that the government (and society) was discriminating against factory workers. As a union leaflet charged, "this time we must correct, once and for all, their attitude that pen and broadcasting are to be feared but workers with hammer and welding machine are to be ignored" (Lee Soo-won 1994, 292). Clearly, what was at stake was more than the immediate economic interests of the workers. As Lee Soo-won notes, "It was the shared feeling of societal discrimination against the uneducated workers that prompted the strike at Hyundai Heavy Industry" (291). A later strike leaflet defined the strike as "not simply a struggle of the Hyundai Heavy Industries union but a major fight with the dictatorial regime with the trust and pride of the twenty-five million workers at stake" (Ulsan nodong chŏngchaek kyoyuk hyŏphoe 1995, 71). Pride and fidelity (ŭili) of the working class were the overriding values that strikers at Hyundai attached to the meaning of their collective action, and this was a general characteristic of the working-class struggle in South Korea during the post-1987 period (Kim Dong-Choon 1995, 445–48).

Having decided to go on strike, however, the union faced a serious problem with its leadership; many of its leaders were either in jail or reluctant to lead the strike. Two men who had been selected to head an emergency planning committee declined to accept the position for family reasons. (Both men had been recently released from prison and were understandably reluctant to assume a role that would almost certainly send them back to prison.) Two more people recommended for the chair of the emergency committee then declined, and finally Lee Kap-yong agreed to accept the responsibility. Thus the Goliat struggle began; it was another spectacular worker struggle at Hyundai Heavy Industries, which set off a general strike joined by many democratic unions across the country. As in previous years, this labor protest was possible not necessarily because of a strong union leadership but because of the strong bottom-up push from radical groups of rank-and-file workers. The substantial growth in the number of class-conscious workers (*sŏnjin nodongja*) and the existence of radical labor leaders outside the factories were critical factors in determining the labor struggles in the 1987–1990 period.[12] Although union leaders at the Hyundai firms were more inclined toward a moderate and pragmatic approach, they were often forced to take a militant confrontational approach by the radical rank-and-file union members (Ulsan nodong chŏngchaek kyoyuk hyŏphoe 1995; Lim Ho 1992, 185–86; Kim Dong-Choon 1995, 342–60).

From the beginning, the 1990 spring strike at Hyundai Heavy Industries had the character of a political struggle, fighting directly against labor-repressive state agencies. Militant members of the union did not have a well-devised strategy, but they did have an exceptional determination to resist. They swore, "We could die but would never surrender." When a police attack was imminent, a core group of seventy-eight protesters climbed up a huge crane, 82 meters above the ground, where they hoped to continue their struggle indefinitely. On the ground, thousands of workers confronted the massive police forces. On the morning of April 28, another huge military-like operation started. Some twelve thousand police and *paikoldan* poured into Hyundai Heavy Industries. Again, the eastern sections of Ulsan city turned into a violent battleground.

The Hyundai Heavy Industries workers' Goliat struggle was not a simple strike at a single workshop. Militant labor groups in the country all saw it as a political struggle of the entire working class against the repressive state and the capitalist class. So, immediately after the strike began at Hyundai Heavy Industries, radical leaders elsewhere organized sympathy struggles. Starting with the Hyundai Motors workers' attempt to block the riot police on their march to Hyundai Heavy Industries on the morning of April 28, four Hyundai unions decided to go on solidarity strikes. On April 30, the newly formed National Congress of Trade Unions (NCTU or *Chŏnohyŏp*) decided to call a general strike. On May 4, some 120,000 workers at 146 enterprises participated in the general strike across the country in support of the Hyundai Heavy Industries workers' struggle.

These sympathy strikes, however, lasted only a few days. Even the Hyundai Motors union, the largest and the most influential union in the Hyundai Group, decided to end its strike and return to work on May 4. The NCTU, despite its stature within the democratic union camps, was a relatively feeble organization and was unable to mobilize a large-scale general strike in support of the Hyundai Heavy Industries struggle. As outside support dwindled, street battles also diminished, leaving the core group

12. The Association of Dismissed Hyundai Employees played the most important role in coordinating and guiding union activities at Hyundai, especially during periods of violent labor strife.

of protesters on the Goliat crane, isolated and dispirited. They continued to resist with a hunger strike, but had to surrender eventually on May 10. "At 2 o'clock on May 10," Lee Soo-won writes, "51 'lonely wolves' were climbing down the stairway of the 82 meter Goliat one by one. Uncontrollable tears flowed continuously from their eyes . . . For the historical struggle that carried a torch for the nationwide labor struggle was nevertheless a complete defeat for them" (1994, 299).

Solidarity Is Born

One of the most significant outcomes of the Great Worker Struggle was the rapid growth of worker identity and worker solidarity. No longer were the factory workers the objects of social ridicule as *kongsuni* or *kongdoli* (although the words had not completely disappeared from the popular lexicon), no longer were average workers shy about identifying themselves as factory workers, and no longer was it likely to be merely a self-affirmatory remark when a worker asserted, "I am proud of being a worker." The changing demography of industrial workers (with a growing proportion of workers from urban backgrounds with high school educations) and their improved economic status over time contributed to establishing a more positive worker identity in the second part of the 1980s. The influence of *minjung* discourse and the slowly growing working-class communities also played instrumental roles in promoting class solidarity. But it was the massive and powerful way workers rose up to demand respect from society that provided the most critical ingredient for the growth of a strong working-class identity among Korean industrial workers.

If a strong working-class identity had been limited to a relatively small number of advanced, class-conscious workers (*sŏnjin nodongja*) prior to 1987, the experience of the Great Worker Struggle brought it to the masses of industrial workers. By actively participating in the struggle and by achieving substantial victories in their struggle, workers were able to obtain a sense of power vis-à-vis their employers and managers. They realized that workers could shut down the factories and paralyze the whole economy; and they saw that they could indeed make the capitalists kneel down in front of them. The Great Worker Struggle provided an opportunity for society, and for the workers themselves, to understand how much raw power workers could wield when they were mobilized en masse. This new sense of power must have facilitated their class identity, for class identity does not simply grow out of sharing a common position, but requires a certain degree of positive evaluation of the group with which one identifies. The experience of the Great Worker Struggle thus played a vital role in helping workers overcome the sense of defeatism and escapism that had dominated workers for a long time.

The working-class solidarity thus born was not limited to workers at the same workplace, but was also extended to fellow workers in the same business group or in the same geographical area. As we have seen in the case of Hyundai, workers employed at different firms of the same *chaebol* group organized group-level joint union councils as soon as they had succeeded in establishing the firm-level unions. A few months after the Council of Unions of Hyundai Group was formed, group-level, interfirm union organizations were also formed at the Daewoo, Sunkyung, Kia, and Ssangyong *chaebol* groups. These enterprise councils were not legally recognized organizations, but nevertheless played an active role in reinforcing solidarity among affiliated unions and supporting collective bargaining at the group level.

A more significant development, however, was the growing worker solidarity across firms located in the same geographical area. Area-based solidarity struggles had begun to appear in the early 1980s, as most prominently displayed in the Kuro solidarity struggle. If such solidarity struggles occurred in trickles in the early 1980s, by the late 1980s it had become a major stream of the democratic labor movement. Also, if earlier interfirm solidarity had been based mainly on a small network of labor activists working in the same region, the new form of solidarity struggles was based on the growing feelings of solidarity among ordinary workers across firms in the same area. Not only in Ulsan but also in other industrial towns around the Masan-Changwon and Seoul-Kyungin areas, it was relatively common for workers to visit other neighborhood plants in order to assist fellow workers' strikes or demonstrations (Ulsan sahoe sŏnkyo silchŏn hyŏpŭihoi 1987; Han'guk kidokkyo sahoe munje yŏnguwon 1987). Worker solidarity was expressed in several forms: protest visits, joining street demonstrations, collecting strike funds, and engaging in sympathy strikes. Interfirm solidarity struggles occurred more frequently at the smaller firms. When union members at small firms found it difficult to defend their newly formed unions against hostile management actions, they often sought help first from fellow workers at neighborhood factories before soliciting help from the FKTU or other organizations. The "culture of solidarity," to borrow Fantasia's (1988) term, was born and visible in many industrial towns in South Korea in the late 1980s.

In contrast to earlier periods, the worker solidarity that appeared in this wave of labor conflicts did not evaporate. Workers had learned the great importance of building class organizations. After the 1987 struggle, labor leaders quickly set out to build interfirm regional consultative organizations. The first regional council was formed in the twin industrial cities of Masan-Changwon, where heavy and chemical industries were concentrated and where many militant unions had been formed at medium- and small-scale manufacturers. The Council of Masan and Changwon Unions was established in December 1987 and forty local unions in the region joined the council. Other regional unions followed suit, starting in the Seoul, Inchon, and Sungnam areas in spring 1988. By the end of 1988, eleven regional councils had been formed, incorporating 403 local unions and 113,500 union members (Huh 1989, 162).

The establishment of these regional associations greatly facilitated interfirm cooperation in labor education and public relations activities, as well as the coordination of strike activities among local unions. But they represented only loosely organized, consultative organizations and had little internal unity or organizational strength. As Lim Ho observes, "The majority of regional councils of unions had a relatively low level of solidarity, because they were formed on the basis of interactions among union leaders rather than broader interactions and close ties among rank-and-file workers" (1992, 147).

Alongside this organizational development among blue-collar unions, a significant development also occurred in the white-collar union movement. In addition to financial workers who had been organized earlier, white-collar and professional workers employed in the media, hospitals, printing industry, and government-sponsored research institutes also succeeded in organizing unions. The active white-collar movement during this period was derived primarily from two sources. The first was the deteriorating job market for white-collar workers. With the rapid increase in the number of lower-level white-collar workers in the process of industrial deepening and with the continuing introduction of automation and the rationalization process into clerical work, white-collar workers in Korea had become increasingly proletarianized, in terms of both the nature of their work and their economic status. Particularly hurt by this proletarianization of white-collar workers were those employed in the financial sector, especially those without college degrees who could not rise any higher on the promotion ladder. As their work became increasingly routinized and their economic status became marginalized, Korean clerical workers began to develop the same collective responses as their counterparts in other industrial societies. They realized that unions were the best means for fighting against their deteriorating job market.

In South Korea, however, the white-collar union movement was more than an expression of "instrumental collectivism" (Goldthorpe et al. 1969). A second equally important, or possibly more important, source of the movement was political. The aggressive unionization struggles among media workers, teachers, researchers at government-sponsored institutes, and printing-industry employees were their reactions to the lack of democracy in Korean workplaces and to the state's political and ideological control over intellectual production. It was not only the blue-collar workers but also white-collar workers who suffered from the highly authoritarian culture in South Korean organizations. Long hours of work, arbitrary work assignments, irrational work procedures, the lack of a voice, and generally poor industrial relations characterized the work situations equally for blue-collar and white-collar workers (Janelli 1993; Choong Soon Kim 1992). Moreover, journalists, teachers, and researchers were also subjected to the state's ideological control over their work and were often forced to produce state-dictated materials.[13] Although ideological control over intellectual work had been present in Korea since the colonial period, the new generation of intellectuals who had gone to college during the highly politicized decade of the 1980s reacted against it (fig. 11). They brought the culture of student activism to their occupational world and were keen to make their workplaces more democratic and humanitarian. The active white-collar union movement thus became another pillar of the South Korean democratic union movement beginning in the late 1980s (see Suh Kwan-mo and Shim Sŏng-bo 1989; Minjuhwa undong chikjang chŏngnyŏnhoe 1989; Cho U-hyun and Yun Jin-ho 1994; Kim Jin-young 1994; Suh Doowon 1998).

At a very early stage, white-collar unions were organized into occupational or industrial federations. This was mainly because white-collar workers in the same occupational or industrial category were subject to the same market pressure and had often to deal with the government in order to protect themselves. Thus, by the end of 1988, eight occupational/industrial federations had been formed, including the Federation of Clerical and Financial Unions, the Federation of Journalists' Unions, the Federation of Hospital Unions, the Federation of Democratic Publication and Press Unions, the Federation of University Employees' Unions, and the Federation of Construction Workers.

The ultimate task of the democratic union movement in this florescence of unionization activities was to establish a national center of "democratic unions," separate from the conservative FKTU. Following many internal debates and controversies,[14] the democratic labor movement groups formed a new national center, the National Congress of Trade Unions

13. Noteworthy in this regard were the struggles of public media employees at two major broadcasting companies, KBS and MBC, against government interference in the content of the media. The most serious ideological challenge, however, came from school teachers who had long sought to organize a union as a vehicle for freeing education from government ideological control. The teachers' union movement had a strong leftist pedigree from the post-war period, and the state had been especially harsh in suppressing it. The government forced the expulsion of hundreds of school teachers from their jobs for joining the illegally formed Teachers' Union, but the movement continued until the union was finally approved in 1998 during the Kim Dae Jung government.

14. Unionists in the post-1987 period were divided into several camps (see Kim Dong-Choon 1995, 365; Kim Yong-ki and Park Sŭng-ok 1989; Kim Keum-su 1995, 46–53).

Figure 11. A white-collar workers' hunger strike. (From Sahoe sajin yŏnguso [social photography institute] 1989, 302)

(NCTU; *Chŏnkuk nodong chohap hyŏpŭihoe* or *Chŏnohyŏp*), on January 22, 1990. At the time of its establishment, the NCTU included 456 unions (5.8 percent of the nation's total unions) and some 160,000 union members (8.6 percent of total union members) (Kim Dong-choon 1995, 400). Fourteen regional councils of blue-collar unions and two occupational/industrial federations joined the NCTU.

The NCTU, however, was a relatively feeble organization. Despite its claim to being a national center, it comprised a relatively small number of unions representing primarily medium- to small-scale manufacturing firms plus their regional consultative councils. It failed to include unions at large conglomerate firms, such as Hyundai and Daewoo, and most white-collar unions. That these two large and powerful groups of trade unions expressed symbolic support but decided not to join the NCTU revealed the internal divisions within the democratic union movement and portended the serious organizational difficulties that would be faced by this new radical union center. Organizationally weak, and severely repressed by the government, the NCTU nevertheless represented the most authentic voice of labor, supported by dedicated local union members (Kim Keum-su 1995, 49–51).

180   *Chapter 7*

Marginalization of Women in the Labor Movement

The 1987 Great Worker Struggle brought a significant change in the main actors of the Korean labor movement. The workers who first set the fires of the labor struggle in summer 1987 and set the tone of nationwide labor unrest were primarily workers who had been relatively quiet before this—the semi-skilled male workers employed in the heavy and chemical industries. They suddenly came on the scene and took over the leading role from the female workers who had been the mainstay of the grassroots union movement in the 1970s and up to the mid-1980s.

To a certain extent, this shift in the gender composition of the Korean labor movement was to be anticipated given that the dominant trend of the Korean economy at the time was away from female-dominated light manufacturing to male-dominated heavy and chemical industry. Although the number of female factory workers had increased faster than the number of male workers in the 1960s and 1970s, the trend reversed beginning in the mid-1980s. By the early 1980s, the core of the Korean industrial structure was represented by the heavy and chemical industries, and by predominantly semi-skilled and skilled male workers employed in this sector.

But this macro-structural change is insufficient by itself to explain why workers in the Seoul and Kyungin region, a center of earlier labor activism, were quieter and slower in responding to the political opportunity of the summer of 1987 than the male workers in the southern industrial cities. Other political and economic factors must be included to explain this relative passivity. The first factor was the negative consequences of past activism. In the industrial complexes in Kyungin area where a high level of labor activism had occurred in the past, such as the Kuro industrial district, most of the unions had been crippled by severe repression and workers had become more passive and skeptical about the efficacy of collective action (Kim Dong-Choon 1995, 114).

A second factor was the trend in student activism. In the mid-1980s, especially after the Kuro solidarity struggle, student activism shifted from shop-floor-based unionization to the broader political organization of class struggle. Many students-turned-workers left the factories, and the student movement in the mid-1980s spent a lot of time and energy in heated ideological debates and became somewhat disengaged from shop-floor activities. Thus, when the civil uprising brought about a sudden political opening, the vanguard labor activists who could have mobilized workers in the Seoul-Inchon region were not prepared for the opportunity.

A third important factor was the generally grim economic conditions of most small enterprises in the region in the 1980s. The labor-intensive sector of the Korean export industry had been continuously declining during the 1980s and created a vulnerable market position for workers employed in textile, garment, and other light manufacturing firms—a far inferior market position than workers in the large heavy and chemical industries.

It must be realized, however, that although a little slower and weaker to respond, workers in the Seoul-Kyungin area also arose and participated in the Great Worker Struggle of 1987. In fact, during this period, a greater number of labor disputes occurred in small- and medium-size firms. Official labor statistics indicate that of 3,494 labor disputes that occurred in 1987, 37 percent occurred in firms with fewer than one hundred workers, and another 40 percent in medium-size firms with 100–299 workers. Only 229 cases occurred in large firms with one thousand workers or more (Han'guk kidokkyo sahoe munje yŏnguwon 1987b, 44). Given the large proportion of female workers in small- and medium-size firms, it can be estimated that the participation of female workers in the 1987 labor conflicts was not significantly different from that of male workers. Indeed, most textile and electronics firms in Inchon, Taegu, and Masan industrial parks were involved in labor conflicts in August 1987. In particular, the Masan free export zone (MAFEZ) became a new site for intense labor struggles, some of which were led by students-turned-workers (Seung-kyung Kim 1997, 113–28; Jeong-Lim Nam 2000). In the Seoul-Inchon region, many married women workers, who tended to be more conservative and passive than single women, became involved in protest actions. Furthermore, the wives (who were not themselves factory workers) of striking male workers also frequently participated in strikes during this period (Han'guk kidokkyo sahoe munje yŏnguwon 1987b, 70–105; Nam 2000).

Thus, if there occurred a gender shift in the main actors of the Korean labor movement, it does not necessarily mean that women suddenly became passive and inactive while men became active. Rather, it means a shift in the cast of the leading roles and with this an important shift in the dynamics of labor struggles. The emergence of the new male actors was welcomed by activists and scholars alike because they appeared to be more militant, more class conscious, better educated, and more powerful in resisting violent repression than female workers had been. Given that violence had been a major means of suppressing labor in South Korea, the male workers' superior ability to fight back was often noted in descriptions of the post-1987 labor struggles. A report prepared by a Christian-based labor organization notes that in large firms where strikes were led by male workers, the companies were generally afraid to organize kusadae to break the strikes (Han'guk kidokkyo sahoe munje yŏnguwon 1987b). Highlighting the Hyundai workers' ability to fight back against the police on their own terms, the report continues, "This makes an interesting contrast with the cases of Kukje Sangsa and other female-dominated firms in Pusan where the strikes were smashed at the very early stage by the kusadae and the police and portends that the future Korean labor movement must inevitably be led by male workers in the heavy chemical industry" (1987, 85–86).[15]

Other scholars have pointed out other important differences in the patterns of labor disputes that occurred in the light manufacturing and heavy industrial sectors. It has been observed, for example, that "in Taegu area where a majority of the enterprises were in textile industry, labor disputes during the Great Struggle occurred in large numbers only after August 10, but ended quickly on the same day or within a few days, and furthermore most of them did not develop into the formation of democratic unions. In contrast, labor conflicts in Ulsan area were distinguished by the fact that they occurred first in the nation and that a majority of them developed into the organization of new unions" (Kim Dong-Choon 1995, 119). Of course, this divergence derived from differences in the type of industry and firm size rather than from the difference in gender, but given the sex-segregated distribution of the industrial labor force, the characteristics of light manufacturing workers can easily be conflated with the presumed gender characteristics of female workers. In any event, the militant and aggressive labor actions in Ulsan, Masan, Changwon, and Kŏje came to overshadow the numerous labor conflicts and unionization struggles that occurred throughout the country and in which a large number of women participated as actively as male workers.

Once the male workers captured the center stage of the working-class struggle in 1987, women workers were quickly pushed aside. Many unions that were formed during 1987–1988 represented predominantly male workers in the heavy and chemical industries, and they enjoyed greater influence in the labor movement as a whole. The new union leadership at both the local and national levels was captured by militant male workers who had led the violent strikes during the Great Worker Struggle. In 1989, according to a survey by the Ministry of Labor, women workers constituted 27.4 percent of total union membership, but women represented only 3.6 percent of the local union presidents nationally (Park Ki-Sung 1991, 78). The National Congress of Trade Unions (Chŏnohyŏp), the most militant and politically oriented organization, had a large proportion (43 percent) of women in its membership because it represented unions in small- to medium-size enterprises. Yet it was primarily run by male leaders, although several women occupied high-ranking positions in the organization hierarchy (Rho Hoe-Chan and Kim Ji-Sun, personal communication). Thus, the post-1987 South Korean labor movement reveals

15. In this regard, Kim Hyun Mee argues: "The image of labor which emphasizes masculine qualities idealizes violence as a natural part of masculinity. . . . The labor movement develops and secures laborers' militancy by advocating this image of the ideal masculine laborer. A natural consequence of this is that workers interpret the intensity of their physical resistance as indicative of their class consciousness" (1997, 64).

the same trend as in other industrial societies—the domination of the labor movement by male workers in the metal and chemical industries and the marginalization of women workers and women's interests within this male-dominated labor movement.

This marginalization of women occurred, however, not just in the dynamics of the labor movement, but, more important, in the popular representation of and scholarly discourse on the women's labor struggle. As feminist critics point out, both labor activists and scholars tend to depreciate the historical and current role of women workers in the Korean working-class struggle. Kim Seung-kyung, for example, argues that since the 1987 struggle, "women's activities were quickly relegated to secondary status, even by activists and sympathetic observers" (1997, 130). Kim Hyun Mee makes a more potent criticism of the gendered representation of the women's labor activism: "It is often described as if female workers had been once engaged in the unsuccessful democratic union movement (the 1970s) in the Korean labor history, both qualitatively and quantitatively, but then failed to participate actively in the intense labor movement that occurred nationwide in the 1980s. In fact, the women-led democratic union movement has hardly ever been included in the mainstream discourse since the 1987 great struggle" (1999, 139–40).

Gender-biased representations of women's labor struggles are not confined to women's roles after 1987. In many writings on the pre-1987 labor movement, there is a distinct tendency to downgrade the significance of the 1970s union movement led by women workers. In general, the 1970s labor struggles are presented as spontaneous, economistic, passive, and lacking class solidarity and political consciousness. This characterization had already appeared in the mid-1980s when student activists criticized narrow economistic trade unionism in comparison to political unionism. Enterprise-based economic unionism was described as a flawed strategy to be overcome. Explicitly or implicitly, this flawed strategy was attributed to its being based predominantly on female workers in the light manufacturing industries. In retrospect, some writers even argue, "In any event, the fact that the 1970s labor movement was based on female workers in the light manufacturing industries became a major obstacle to the qualitative development of the labor movement" (Yang Seung-jo 1990, 137). Other writers appreciate the role played by female workers in earlier labor struggles, but tend to depreciate the class character of these struggles.[16] In general, the current writings on the contemporary history of the South Korean labor movement, as Kim Hyun Mee argues, "tend to disclose the

16. For example, Lim Young-Il argues, "The labor movement led by the unskilled single women in the labor-intensive manufacturing sector during this period [the late 1970s] had no more than a symbolic meaning as a 'working-class movement.' In many ways, it shared the same meaning as being part of the democracy movement led by the progressive intellectuals and church organizations during this period" (1998, 80).

limits of women-centered labor movement and renders female workers' participation in the late-1980s invisible in order to stress and glamorize the political orientation and class character of the 1980s labor struggles" (1999, 140).

Although most of the feminist critiques of the current discourse on the Korean labor movement are correct, I tend to believe that such a representation is not entirely due to gender bias, or to a "patriarchal conspiracy," as Kim Hyun Mee suggests (1999, 140). There is also, I believe, a myopic historical vision that produces this lack of appreciation of the pre-1987 struggle and of the role of women in it. It is easy to depreciate the significance of the 1970s labor movement if it is compared with the 1987 struggle only in terms of scale, intensity, militancy, and political character. In these aspects, clearly there was a quantum jump and a qualitative change. Also, because the 1987 labor conflicts exploded so suddenly with spontaneous actions by workers who had not participated in previous struggles, it is easy to assume that it had little continuity with the pre-1987 Korean labor movement. Indeed many young scholars seem to believe that the post-1987 labor movement owes little to the earlier struggle and that Korean workers arrived at this stage largely because of structural changes in the working class and the democratization process. This is probably why almost all books and Ph.D. dissertations on the South Korean labor movement written after 1987 take the Great Worker Struggle as their point of departure. I have been told that the labor-history education conducted at the Korean Confederation of Trade Unions (KCTU) also focuses mainly on the post-1987 period. Even some of the most thoughtful labor experts seem to slight the significance of the pre-1987 struggle in the historical process of class formation in South Korea. For example, Lim Young-Il argues, "Prior to the 1987 Great Worker Struggle, the Korean working class had never become a major actor or a variable in class politics" (1998, 76). And he further argues that "During the entire period from 1961 to the 1987 Great Worker Struggle, the Korean labor movement had not shown a process of advancement to even the lowest level of 'political labor movement'" (78).

Many old-time labor activists, both female and male, whom I have interviewed over the years were very displeased at the way the 1970s union movement has been characterized in more recent writings—as having been too economistic, being too narrowly enterprise unionist, and lacking political consciousness. They regreted that people do not seem to understand just how difficult the circumstances were when they had tried to organize independent unions. "It was a death-defying struggle we had to fight in the 1970s," Suk Jung-nam of Dongil Textile union said (interview, June 2000). Forming an independent union and protecting it from vicious management attacks to destroy it, in itself, required an incredible amount of courage and sacrifice. "What more could be expected in such a situation?" Bang Yong-Suk, a male president of Wonpoong Textile union, asks of those who criticize the narrow trade unionism of the 1970s (interview, June 1994; see also Bang 1994). He claimed that it is totally unrealistic to have expected a class-conscious political struggle from workers in the 1970s, and he argued that it was in fact the students' political adventurism that helped destroy the democratic unions that the workers had established with so many sacrifices. Min Jong-duk, a male union leader at Chunggye Textile Union in the early 1980s, also expressed regret that a "shortsighted understanding" tends to slight what they had actually contributed to the Korean labor movement. He wondered whether the current working-class status could have been achieved without their earlier struggles (interview, June 2000).

Thus, both a gendered representation and a myopic historical vision have rendered the role of women in the South Korean labor movement marginal and invisible.[17] In reality, most women who had been active in grassroots union movement up to the mid-1980s left the industrial arena. Many of them became housewives, but most of them refused to become just housewives and continued to be engaged in some forms of social activism (such as feminist organizations, the environment movement, or other social movements). And none of them lost their keen awareness of class inequality and a sense of strong identity with the working class.[18]

Conclusion

The explosion of labor militancy in 1987 clearly marked a watershed in the South Korean working-class struggle. The post-1987 labor movement became qualitatively different from the previous struggles, not only in terms of the patterns of conflicts and organizational strength, but also in terms of the main actors, regions, industries, and gender composition. Since the eruption of this massive labor offensive, the Korean labor movement became better organized, stronger, more aggressive, male-led, and relatively independent of the outside intellectual community. The 1987 labor militancy thus brought a significant change in the balance of power between capital and labor and in working-class identity and consciousness among ordinary industrial workers.

17. My good colleague, Cho Uhn, pointed out to me that what I call "myopic historical vision" itself might be due to "gender blindness." She has a point, but I still believe that gender bias is only part of the story.

18. This is the most vivid impression I received when I interviewed a dozen women who had formerly been workers actively involved in the grassroots union movement in the 1970s.

It would be wrong, however, to look at Korean labor history after 1987 as representing a discontinuity, that is, to assume that the full-fledged labor movement in South Korea began only after the spontaneous eruption of labor militancy in 1987, with little or no connection to what had occurred before. That would be an ahistorical understanding of the evolution of the working-class movement in South Korea, grossly underestimating the contribution of the labor struggles that occurred in the 1970s and early 1980s in which young women workers played a dominant role. It is through the many lone and bitter struggles waged by courageous workers in the earlier period that Korean workers acquired a growing sense of their rights and collective identity, and became aware of the importance of solidarity and of organizing representative unions. The militancy and class solidarity demonstrated in the 1987 Great Struggle did not occur accidentally, but was the outcome of accumulated past struggles, a few victories and many defeats, in which workers' class awareness and political consciousness grew continuously. This gradual change in workers' consciousness, largely hidden beneath the surface, prepared the fertile ground for the volcanic eruption in 1987.

Another important way in which earlier "economistic" struggles contributed to the post-1987 "new unionism" is through the formation of clandestine networks of activists. Although workers in the southern industrial belt seemed relatively isolated from the activist culture and social networks, they were not completely disconnected. In fact, as shown in the case of the Hyundai workers, a significant minority of intelligent and politically conscious workers had emerged and were linked to or influenced by political activists who were mainly concentrated in the Seoul-Inchon areas. Through direct and indirect contacts, a radical political culture spread far beyond the center of early labor activism. Of course, this new "culture of solidarity" had not penetrated the masses of workers, but it did penetrate a significant minority of *sŏnjin nodongja* (workers with advanced class consciousness). The emergence of these indigenous leaders of the working-class movement would not have been possible without the earlier struggles of workers in the female-dominated light manufacturing industries.

The pattern of labor struggles in 1987 and in the following years clearly demonstrates the legacy of despotic labor relations and authoritarian labor control. When the tight grip was loosened momentarily, workers' long-suppressed anger and grievances exploded into spontaneous and violent actions. Long years of accumulated *han* was released, and this *han* was not just against low wages or poor working conditions but against the inhumane treatment by managers and against the contemptuous attitude shown by society toward laborers. As in previous periods, labor actions during this period were also highly emotional and moralistic. Workers were more interested in restoring their human dignity and social respect than in achieving specific material objectives, and they fought for unions because they understood that unions could assure workers' pride and human dignity. Labor actions were most often accompanied and propelled by strong anti-capitalist sentiment among workers and by their deep mistrust of management and the government. Thus, collective bargaining often took the form of a class war in which any concession was interpreted as total surrender (Kim Dong-choon 1995, 444–45). All these aspects were obviously the product of the extremely repressive and exclusionary labor regime of earlier years. The significance of the 1987 struggle is that workers arose en masse to make a frontal attack *on* this harsh authoritarian labor regime that had led the spectacular economic growth in the previous two decades.

8 The Working Class at the Crossroads

Classes are never made in the sense of being finished or
having acquired their definitive shape. They keep on
changing.

(Hobsbawm 1984, 194)

. . . classes are always in the process of becoming or
disappearing, of evolution or devolution.

(Kocka 1986, 283)

The two years of unprecedented labor struggles following summer 1987
brought significant changes to the Korean working class. Many labor conflicts that occurred during this period exhibited a solidarity reaching beyond individual firms and workers' demands represented their heightened
awareness of their collective interests and their rights in the workplace.
The balance of power on the shop floor shifted toward labor, and in many
factories management had to relinquish its power to the unions.

Efforts to build unions at the regional and national levels continued. It
seemed that workers had finally begun to see themselves with new eyes,
not as members of a stigmatized low class but as respectable members of
society and as an important agent of social change in Korean society. Thus,
the huge labor uprising in 1987 did more than any other event to facilitate
the formation of the Korean working class. We might say that the making
of the Korean working class as a class of its own was in sight at the end of
the 1980s.

Significant changes occurred in the 1990s, however, that either halted or retarded this development. The 1990s saw renewed efforts by the state to stabilize labor relations and new offensives by capital to regain control over labor. Their strategies to debilitate the newly empowered unions and dissolve worker militancy became more systematic and sophisticated as the years went on. Important changes also occurred in the Korean industrial structure and in the global economy that had detrimental effects on the Korean labor movement. Partly as a consequence of structural changes in the economy and partly due to the new capitalist strategy of labor-market flexibility, the Korean working class became increasingly differentiated within itself in terms of material conditions and consciousness. Improvement in material conditions for workers and improved industrial relations in the factories also had an appreciable effect on collective identity and consciousness among industrial workers.

State and Capital Offensives

The state has always been a critical variable in the development of the South Korean labor movement. Undoubtedly, the most critical factor that made the Great Worker Struggle possible was the temporary breakdown of authoritarian control in 1987. During the explosive years of labor militancy in 1987 and 1988, the state withdrew from the industrial arena for the first time and proclaimed a hands-off policy toward labor relations, leaving the capitalists suddenly naked and unprotected in the face of furious labor offensives. Totally unprepared for this situation, capitalists had to make substantial concessions to the demands of a labor force that had suddenly gained control of the situation. Workers obtained wage increases of over 20 percent in many large factories in 1987. Fortunately, the South Korean economy during 1986 to 1988 benefited tremendously from the favorable economic conditions of the so-called "Three Lows"—low interest rates, low oil prices, and low dollar-yen and won-yen exchange rates—so Korean firms were able to buy industrial peace by conceding to demands for big wage hikes. But these favorable external conditions ended by the conclusion of the 1980s and the South Korean economy began a downward slide from then on.

The state's resumption of its interventionist policy toward labor relations began at the end of 1988, with Roh Tae Woo's Special Announcement Concerning Civil Security. In spring 1989, the government sent police to crack down on strikes at Poongsan Metal Company, Seoul Subway Station, and Hyundai Heavy Industries. A series of political events during that year provided a good excuse for the government to revive the security regime, including the illegal visit to North Korea by Reverend Moon

Ik-Hwan, a prominent opposition leader, and the collapse of the communist regimes in eastern Europe. The government's renewed repression
was particularly focused on the militant labor groups' attempt to organize
a new national center separate from the official national union, FKTU.
The security agency and police were intent on demobilizing democratic
union leaders by interrogating, arresting, and jailing the most active of
the radical leaders. Thus, when the National Congress of Trade Unions
(NCTU, Chŏnohyŏp) was formed in January 1990, the majority of its leaders were either in jail or in hiding. Even after its de facto formation, the
government denied its legal status and harassed its member unions with
tax audits and other similar threatening measures. Partly because of this
government pressure and partly because of the economic downturn that
hurt small enterprises severely, the NCTU lost almost half of its members
within a year of its establishment; between January 1990 and January 1991,
it lost 48 percent of its member unions and 45 percent of its union
members.

The state's labor policy did not, however, remain completely unchanged.
Rather than maintaining the past blatant pro-capital stance in labor disputes, the state tried to maintain a neutral stance in labor-capital relations
and to steer trade unionism in a peaceful and "responsible" fashion. Its approach now was to restore industrial peace and develop a stable coopera-
tive industrial-relations system in Korean industries within the framework
of an atomized enterprise union system. To achieve this, the state changed
the labor laws in December 1987, making it easier to form unions and to
engage in collective bargaining. Allowing greater space for trade unionism,
the state, however, refused to abolish the clauses that disallow multiple
unions and third-party involvement in union matters. The goal was always
to keep trade unionism within the bounds of enterprise unionism and
to obstruct the formation of inter-firm solidarity among unions or of a
possible national center in competition with the government-controlled
FKTU. In short, a major shift in the state policy was a gradual change from
the crude repressive approach to a more sophisticated legal and administrative approach, while intensifying educational campaigns for harmo-
nious industrial order.

Supported by the state's resumption of labor control, capital launched its
own offensives against organized labor. After many blunders and crude responses to labor offensives in the first two years of labor unrest, as we have
seen in the Hyundai management example, Korean capitalists gradually
devised new strategies for regaining control over labor. One of the first responses from the capitalists was to establish more effective organizations
to coordinate their responses to labor challenge. In December 1989, one
month before the formation of the NCTU (Chŏnohyŏp), they organized the
Korean Association of Industrial Organizations (KAIO; Chŏnkuk kyŏngje

tanche chonghyŏpŭihoi or *Kyŏntanhyŏp*).[1] The first major policy recom-
mendation it made was the "no work, no pay" rule. Given the general
poverty of unions (union dues were not allowed to exceed 2 percent of the
members' monthly wages), this policy acted as an effective constraint on
strike actions as well as saving labor costs for employers. Despite strong
union resistance, the policy was gradually instituted beginning in the early
1990s. The state's role in implementing this policy was to apply negative
sanctions to those firms that failed to abide by this rule under pressure
from militant unions.

More important changes occurred in the ways Korean capitalists reorga-
nized the production process. In order to curb growing union power and
escalating wages, management at large firms actively sought to borrow
from advanced managerial techniques used in Japan and the United States.
These "new managerial strategies," which became popular in large Korean
firms in the 1990s, had four components: new personnel policies, flexible
labor use, labor-union strategy, and company culture.

First, employers tried to implement a set of new personnel policies,
including the introduction of a merit-based or performance-based wage
system in place of the traditional seniority-based wage system and the
restoration of a job-evaluation scheme (which had been discontinued
under pressure from labor). Many large firms established a personnel or
human resources management department to implement these new policies (prior to 1987, there had often been no independent personnel department, even at many large manufacturing firms) (Lee Kyun-Jae 1997).
A major emphasis of the new personnel policies was the reduction in
the harsh authoritarian aspects of industrial relations, which all managers
recognized as the basis of workers' strong resentment against management. As the director of human resources development at Hyundai Heavy
Industries told me, "We know that everything depends on human relations. But we realized that we did something wrong in the manner
we treated our (production) workers. So, we tried to do our best to make
workers more satisfied by showing the company's concern and respect
for them" (Suh Mun-Hwa, interview, June 2000). Managers and foremen
tried not to unnecessarily antagonize workers and many regulations
restricting workers' personal freedom (such as the hair code and compulsory exercise) were abolished. Company practices based on manual-
nonmanual status distinctions were minimized, such as different name
tags, different sections and utensils in the cafeteria, and different access
to commuter buses. Many companies adopted one label, *sawon*, for both
white-collar and blue-collar workers distinguished only by a qualifier

---

1. After two years, the KAIO's functions were taken over by the significantly expanded
Korea Employers Federation (which had been in existence since 1970).

indicating technical or clerical positions (for example, *kinŭgjik sawon* or *samujik sawon*).

Second, management adopted several new strategies to increase flexibility in their use of workers. One of these strategies was the introduction of automation in order to promote flexibility in the labor process and increase productivity. Automation of production processes occurred rapidly in the heavy industries, such as steel and automobile, replacing human labor with robots. At the same time, management at large firms sought to increase flexibility by hiring more temporary and part-time workers and by developing an expanded system of subcontractor production. Small manufacturers increased the number of poorly paid foreign workers on their payrolls.[2] Along with these efforts to increase "numeric flexibility," managers also sought "functional flexibility" by adopting Japanese-style human resource management techniques, such as the QC circle, zero defect, and just-in-time system (see Song Ho Keun 1994a; Park Joon-Shik 1996; Lee Chang-Hee 1998). A flexible teamwork system of production was also implemented in many large firms, moving away from the rigid hierarchical structure (see Park Joon-Shik 1996, 141–69).

Third, many employers, despite their antipathy toward unions, began to accept unions as an unavoidable reality and attempted to live with them. Thus, rather than trying to destroy the independent unions, they now tried to tame or coopt union leaders and to restrict their actions by invoking legal sanctions. The "no work, no pay" rule was effective in this regard. Many restrictive clauses in the labor laws also provided management with convenient tools to curb union actions. Employers frequently brought law suits against union leaders who organized illegal strikes and caused material damage or a loss in production to the employers. Increasingly, militant unions found themselves cornered not only by the hard-line approach of the state but also by highly restrictive legal and institutional mechanisms.

Fourth, the capitalist ideological offensive became stronger and more sophisticated. At the national level, capitalists made a concerted effort to influence the media to create an unfriendly atmosphere for the militant union movement. Given the conservative nature of South Korean newspapers and the deteriorating South Korean economy, the media took an active role in representing the views of capital. The dominant tone of the media echoed the theory of "worker responsibility" for the ailing economy, blaming industrial disturbances and escalating wages as the main factors behind the declining competitiveness of Korean industries and thus tacitly supporting the government's crackdown on militant labor (Koo 1991; Lim and Kim 1991; Choi Jang Jip 1993a; Shin Kwang-Yeong 1999).

2. The number of foreign workers increased from 81,824 in 1994 to 267,546 in 1997 (see Uh Soo-Bong 1999).

A more systematic ideological approach was found in large manufacturing firms, led by the *chaebol* groups. Beginning in the early 1990s, the management of these large firms sought to cast off the image of harsh authoritarianism and regain control over the minds of their employees through a "company culture movement." With some variation, all these company cultures used paternalistic language and symbols to recreate the sense of pseudo-family sharing a common economic fate among the members of the company. Large companies invested a fairly large sum of money to implement educational programs, recreational clubs and other small-group activities, festivals, song contests, retreats, and overseas trips for union leaders (mainly to ex-communist countries). For example, Hyundai Heavy Industries took managers and workers on a two-day retreat at a nice resort area; there they were divided into small groups and involved in challenging group activities to cultivate team spirit and a sense of family membership across the status hierarchy (Lee Kyun-Jae 1997). The company culture movement was also targeted at the family members of the employees. By organizing wives' visits to the factory and by encouraging them to participate in cultural activities organized by the company, management skillfully tried to promote company loyalty among both workers and their families.

The state also played an important role in the new campaign through *Tamul* ideology, which appeared in the 1990s and was used frequently in the ideological education of workers. This relatively new ideology, supposedly derived from the ideas of Tangun (the mystical founder of the Korean people) (see Lee Myung-sook 1993), was strongly nationalistic and chauvinistic. *Tamul* ideology reminded Koreans of the much larger territory that the ancient Koreans had occupied, including much of the Manchu area, and of the splendid culture their forefathers had developed. *Tamul* ideologues insisted that the Korean people try to restore the grandeur of their history and culture; in order to do this, workers needed to understand the precarious position that their nation and economy occupied in the ever-competitive and hostile international system and "get out of small discontents, small anger, and small sorrows and have pride in being the principal agent of rebuilding Korea's history" (Lee Myung-sook 1993, 163). *Tamul* educational programs skillfully combined lectures with traditional music, art, and martial arts classes. Many companies enrolled their workers in these programs with apparently very satisfactory results.

Setback and Advance in the Union Movement

As a consequence of these state and capital offensives, and the adverse structural changes in the economy, the Korean labor movement faced great difficulties in the early 1990s. The weakening of the labor movement appeared on several fronts. First of all, the number of unions began to decline noticeably. The number of unions reached a peak in 1989 (7,883 unions), but began to decrease after that. The number of union members decreased from 1,932,000 in 1989 to 1,667,000 in 1993 to 1,484,000 in 1997. Consequently, the unionization rate dropped from 18.6 percent in 1989 to 14.2 percent in 1993 to 11.2 percent in 1997 (see table 7.1).

Second, a more dramatic decline occurred in the number of collective actions. The number of labor disputes was still high in 1989, with as many as 1,616 strikes. But the number dropped sharply to 322 in 1990 and continued to decline, to 144 in 1993 and to 78 in 1997. Militant unionism was definitely in retreat in the early 1990s, and many local unions selected moderate leaders who favored a more pragmatic and conciliatory approach, rather than a militant and solidarity-oriented one. Growing concern about the vulnerability of the Korean economy in the 1990s created a conservative atmosphere in industry and made the wisdom of labor-management cooperation more persuasive to union leaders. In 1993 and 1994, the FKTU and the Korea Employers Federation (KEF) reached an agreement on wage increases at the national level and some trade unions issued the "no labor dispute declaration" (Lee Won-Duck and Choi Kang-Shik 1998, 57–86).

Democratic unions faced formidable obstacles to creating industrial unions or a new national center. The NCTU (*Chŏnohyŏp*) was subject to severe government repression and surveillance and was unable to expand its organizational base beyond small-scale, labor-intensive industries; *chaebol* unions and white-collar unions remained outside the NCTU.[3] In addition to losing approximately half of its membership in one year, the NCTU had great difficulty finding leadership due to the continual arrests of its leaders. Pushed into a corner, the NCTU took a militant confrontational approach with the state, at the risk of further narrowing its organizational base to militant unions and alienating the conservative sectors of society.

The failure of organized labor to make significant progress after the late 1980s was most evident in the realm of institutional reform. Despite many rallies and petitions, labor groups failed to get the labor laws revised as they demanded (fig. 12). Except for allowing a few changes that made unionization and union actions easier, the government held firm on maintaining the basic restraining clauses in the labor laws, forbidding the formation of alternative unions where there were official unions, the involvement of third parties in labor disputes, and political activities by unions. Also, teachers and civil servants were still barred from forming unions.

3. White-collar unions not affiliated with the FKTU joined together to establish an independent national federation, the Council of Occupational Trade Unions (COTU) in the late 1980s.

Figure 12. Scene of labor protest demanding labor law reform (in the late 1980s). (From Sahoe sajin yŏnguso [Social Photography Institute] 1989, 32)

Thus, by the mid-1990s early optimism about the Korean labor movement was replaced by pessimism and a sense of disappointment. Scholars and labor experts describe the labor trend in the 1990s as a "reversal" or "retreat" from the great labor advance in the late 1980s and characterize the outcome of the struggle as "a double failure to expand organizational space and political space in the transition to democracy" (Song Ho Keun 1994b, 3). Several factors are mentioned by analysts to account for this failure, including the resumption of state repression, capitalist offenses, leadership problems within the radical union movement, and the "betrayal by the middle class" (Lim and Kim 1991; Choi Jang Jip 1992).

A closer look, however, indicates that the state of the Korean labor movement in the 1990s was more complex than these pessimistic appraisals suggest. Although it is true that the overall rate of union organization had declined continuously from 1989, this statistic hides an important countertrend. A careful analysis shows that the decline in union membership was restricted to the labor-intensive, small-scale light manufacturing industries, which faced great problems in the globalized economy (Park Joon-Shik 1996; Lee Won-Duck and Choi Kang Shik 1998). Many small factories in the labor-intensive sector closed down or moved their plants to China or to Southeast Asian countries. In contrast, union membership in large firms changed very little and remained relatively high. The unionization rate in companies with three hundred or more workers at the end of 1989 was 60 percent, whereas the rate for small companies with 50–99 employees was 9.5 percent. (The unionization rate for the medium-size firms, with 100–299 workers, was 26 percent; Lee Won-Duck and Choi Kang Shik 1998, 64.) These data indicate that the unionization rate at large manufacturing firms had reached a saturation point by the early 1990s. The unionization drive and the organizational strength of unions at small- and medium-size companies suffered more from the economic difficulties facing these small firms than from the state's anti-labor policies.

Furthermore, it is important to note the counter-trend of the rapid growth of white-collar unions in the 1990s. The white-collar union movement appeared among financial workers and some sectors of professional workers immediately after the 1987 political liberalization, but it increased in the 1990s and spread to diverse occupational groups in the service industry. Successful unionization occurred among hospital workers, transportation workers, communication industry workers, newspaper and television employees, researchers at government-funded research institutes, university staff, employees of foreign-invested firms, and financial workers. Efforts to organize civil servants were continually blocked by law, but nevertheless progressive teachers formed the National Teachers' Union (NTU) and fought tenaciously to obtain a legal status for their illegally formed union. Some 1,500 teachers were dismissed from their schools for participating in this unionization struggle.[4]

The goals of the white-collar unions were not confined to the material conditions of the workers, but included institutional changes to enhance the democratic process in the company and to ensure autonomy from state control. Social democracy was thus a major agenda in the white-collar union movement beginning in 1987. Autonomy from the state's ideological control was a particularly important goal for the movement among intellectual workers. The rapid rise of white-collar unions can be seen in the changing rank order of the largest five industrial federations. Prior to 1980, the largest industrial federation was that of the textile unions. From 1988, the top position was held by the metal union federation, followed by the chemistry industry federation. The financial federation, which had not been included in the largest five federations before 1980, occupied the fourth position by 1990 and moved to the third position in 1996.

A steady progress in the democratic union movement could also be observed in efforts to organize a new national center to counter the conservative FKTU. In the early 1990s, the democratic union camp was divided into three groups: the NCTU (*Chŏnohyŏp*), the Council of Occupational Trade Unions, and the Alliance of Large-Firm Trade Unions (composed of unions representing workers at Hyundai and Daewoo). In October 1991, on the occasion of South Korea's admission to the International Labour Organization (ILO), democratic labor groups formed a national alliance to exert concerted pressure on the government for labor law reform. This loose alliance developed into the Congress of National Trade Union Representatives in June 1993. In November 1995, based on this national alliance, a new national center of democratic unions, the Korean Confederation of Trade Unions (KCTU) was finally formed. The KCTU included 862 labor unions and 420,000 union members at the time of its establishment. Although not legally recognized, the KCTU nonetheless quickly emerged as a powerful union center with many strong unions among its members, notably the metal unions, Hyundai unions, Korea telecommunication unions, and other public-sector white-collar unions. Despite strong state repression, its membership grew to 500,000 within a year of its formation.

Along with this steady development in establishing a national center of democratic unions, several attempts were made to represent and organize labor in the political arena. It must first be mentioned that party politics after 1987 showed little change from the previous period. Political parties were very reluctant to ally with labor for fear of losing the support of the

4. The NTU became a legal union in 1998 and the majority of the dismissed teachers were reinstated after suffering several years of hardship.

middle classes. Opposition parties were no different in this regard from the ruling party. Unrepresented by any party, and legally prohibited from acting as a collectivity, workers were absorbed into the electoral process as atomized individuals or, more likely, as members of pre-established social ties based on regions, towns, schools, clans, and the like (Choi Jang Jip 1993a). But there were a few political experiments during the period of democratic transition. A few months after the political liberalization of 1987, many intellectual labor activists joined other political activists to form progressive political parties, the Party of *Minjung (Minjungŭi dang)* and the Democratic Party of Hankyŏre *(Hankyŏre minjudang)*. Neither party, was a working-class party, although each sought to appeal to the urban working class and poor farmers as well as to the progressive segments of the middle class. The Party of *Minjung* entered the general election in 1988, but the result was dismal; entering in fifteen electoral districts, the party received an average of only 4.3 percent of the vote. In 1990, the *Minjungŭi dang* merged with the *Hankyŏre minjudang* to form the *Minjungdang (Minjung* Party). In the fourteenth general election in 1992, the *Minjung* Party performed a little better, but the result was equally humiliating; the party ran fifty-one candidates and received an average of 6.5 percent of the vote (Roh Hoe-chan 1999). Having failed to obtain the minimum requirement for official recognition—at least one elected congressional seat—the *Minjung* Party disbanded. A preparatory committee was formed in 1992 to form a bona fide labor party, but failed to move ahead with the plan.

Thus, the first attempts to politically represent the working class proved to be a total failure. Many factors are responsible for this, including the continuing influence of security ideology, conservative political culture, unfair electoral procedures for minority parties, laws prohibiting union involvement in politics, as well as an internal division in the labor leadership concerning labor's involvement in electoral politics. In the 1990s, a dominant view in progressive labor movement circles was that organized labor should refrain from electoral politics until it achieved a solid organizational base in the working class and a high level of working-class solidarity and consciousness through militant economic struggles. It took several more years of political experience and internal controversies before labor groups finally established the first labor party, the Democratic Labor Party, in January 2000.

The General Strike

As if to prove that the Korean labor movement was not destined to go down the drain, Korean workers rose up again ten years after the Great Worker Struggle of 1987. The nationwide general strike that occurred in winter 1996–1997 took everybody by surprise and demonstrated the militancy of South Korean labor to the world.

In the early morning on December 26, 1996, a special headline news bulletin hit the streets in Seoul. At dawn, ruling party legislators had met secretly at the National Assembly, with no opposition members present, and passed new labor laws along with the National Security Planning Agency laws in seven minutes. The new labor laws were designed to give more power and flexibility to employers in laying off workers and hiring temporary workers or strike replacements, while disallowing the formation of multiple unions for another few years.

No sooner was the news released, than a furious labor response followed. The leaders of the Korean Confederation of Trade Unions (KCTU) met immediately on hearing the news and decided to call a general strike. By afternoon of the same day, some 145,000 workers had walked out, led by workers at the two large auto plants of Hyundai and Kia. The next day, the FKTU also voiced its outrage and called a limited strike among its 1.2 million members. On the third day of the strike, some 372,000 workers were on strike, shutting down most of South Korea's auto industry, shipbuilding industry, and other large industries. Thus, began the first nationwide general strike in South Korea since the end of the Korean War.[5]

The strike was suspended for a few days because of the New Year holidays. Government leaders hoped that the strike would fizzle out after the holidays and, in fact, this seasonal factor had played an important part in their political calculations when they had decided to railroad the bill through at the end of the year. Labor leaders also feared that it would be difficult to resume the general strike once the momentum had been lost over the long holidays. Surprisingly, however, worker participation in the strike did not dampen at all after the holidays, and the general strike became more extensive and broader as white-collar workers in the insurance industry, banks, hospitals, and broadcasting services joined the strike. The general strike continued for three more weeks in a stop-and-go fashion under the joint leadership of the KCTU and FKTU, mobilizing some three million workers and demonstrating an impressive level of class solidarity. On January 21, Kim Young Sam met with the heads of opposition parties and indicated that the government was willing to withdraw the controversial labor laws and rework them.

A main reason for the successful mobilization of workers against the labor legislation was that it concerned the vital issues of the day for many

5. The first and only previous general strike had occurred in 1946 during the turbulent post-liberation period. It was organized by the militant leftist union, the National Council of Korean Trade Unions (Chŏnpyŏng).

Korean people. As the South Korean economy continued to falter in the global economy and as Korean employers sought various ways to reduce their labor costs, the long tradition of lifetime employment for white-collar workers became frayed and the threat of layoffs became a reality for many workers. Not only were manufacturing workers threatened by unemployment, but many white-collar workers and middle-level managers faced the same problem. Job security had a special social meaning in a society where workers had been expected to devote themselves wholly to the company in return for long-term job security. Laying off workers because of temporary company financial difficulties was widely believed to be unfair and morally unjust because such behavior violated the important social value of reciprocity that had been at the base of institutional practices of Korean companies. Furthermore, in a society where only an extremely meager security net existed outside the family, losing a job is likely to mean losing the only source of one's livelihood as well as a main basis of one's social identification. Thus, by fighting to defend those values that concerned people in general, the labor movement regained the moral ground that it had lost in the previous years.

The general strike also received strong support from external sources. The ILO, OECD, and the International Confederation of Free Trade Unions (ICFTU) protested against the new labor legislation by sending their delegations to the South Korean government. Labor and human rights organizations held rallies in twenty-two nations and 223 letters of support came from various foreign labor organizations and workers. The ICFTU even organized a global campaign to boycott Korean products to increase pressure on the South Korean government (Sonn 1997).

Given such favorable conditions and the successful national mobilization of workers, it is somewhat surprising that the January 1997 strike achieved very little in the end. After the strike ended, the controversial labor laws were returned to the legislative process, while unions staged half-day strikes to continue their pressure on politicians. New labor laws were drafted in a relatively short time and were approved by majority vote in the National Assembly on March 10. But the newly revised labor laws differed only slightly from the ones that labor groups had opposed so vehemently. They retained the employers' right to lay off workers, to be exercised after a two-year deferment (as in the earlier controversial laws). The "no work, no pay" rule and no payment for full-time union leaders were also written into the new laws, as was the flexible workday policy aimed at reducing real wages. In return, organized labor obtained the immediate authorization of the KCTU and the right to form multiple unions at the industry level (but not at the workshop level until the year 2002). The new laws, however, continue to disallow union formation among schoolteachers and public servants (KOLIAF 1999, 178).

In order to adequately understand the irony of the successful strike ending with such a dismal result, it is necessary to place the strike in the context of globalization. It was the impact of global capitalism and South Korea's deteriorating position within it that had initially created the structural impetus for the labor-market reform, and it was the imperative of the global economy and its hegemonic ideology of neoliberalism that predetermined the result of the 1997 general strike in South Korea. The state-led and *chaebol*-dominated South Korean economic structure revealed many problems when it was exposed to fierce global competition, including a low level of technological development, outdated financial institutions, overexpansion of the *chaebol* groups, huge debts carried by most large firms, endless bureaucratic red tape, high costs of production, and declining rates of productivity.

Korean capitalists were particularly concerned about losing competitiveness in the labor market because their hitherto unhampered power on the shop floor had been severely damaged by growing union power and because Korean wages were no longer competitive in the world market. Their demand for labor-market reform became more vociferous as the liberalization and globalization of the Korean economy made them more insecure in competition with global capital. In the age of the post-Fordist regime of production, when flexibility had become a synonym for competitiveness and economic success, a call for an institutional framework that allowed a more flexible economy naturally carried great intellectual authority. Against this seemingly self-evident logic of market freedom, the demands of the workforce for fairness and economic justice sounded increasingly quaint and irrational. As South Korea's declining economy produced an increasing number of business failures in 1996 and 1997, policy makers were more convinced by the capitalist argument that it was more important to save the companies than to protect a few jobs for workers. Thus, the changing economic reality and the power of neoliberal ideology set the limits of what the Korean labor force could achieve against its own capitalists and the state.

The Impact of the Economic Crisis

The South Korean economy's inability to adapt successfully to globalization became more apparent in 1997. On November 24, 1997, the Kim Young Sam government requested a bailout from the International Monetary Fund (IMF) and received $57 billion in December. Apart from the deep humiliation it brought to Koreans, the IMF bailout had devastating consequences for their livelihoods, causing a staggering number of business failures, massive unemployment, sharply reduced incomes, and spreading problems from family breakdowns. The number of jobless workers tripled from 658,000 in December 1997 to 1.7 million in December 1998. The yearly unemployment rate increased from 2.6 percent in 1997 to 6.8 percent in 1998. This was clearly the worst economic crisis Koreans had experienced since the Korean War.

Following the IMF bailout, Korean labor became the focus of attention from all sides—from the Korean government, business owners, international lending institutions, and prospective investors. All parties seemed to agree that labor held the key to overcoming the current economic crisis because the IMF-mandated economic restructuring inevitably necessitated massive layoffs and an institutional change toward a flexible labor market. Flexible layoffs were deemed essential to carry out the extensive corporate restructuring through bankruptcies, mergers, and acquisitions, as well as to induce foreign equity investments. Thus, the success of the structural adjustment under the IMF regime depended, to a great extent, on forcing Korean labor to accept the sacrifices without causing industrial or social instability. Maintaining industrial peace in the process of economic restructuring was thus defined as a major task for the newly elected president, Kim Dae Jung.

One of the first things that Kim Dae Jung proposed was to form a labor-management-government tripartite body following the social corporatist model. The Labor-Management-Government Council was formed on January 14, 1998. On January 20, this Tripartite Council issued the first labor-management-government joint communique, in which the three parties agreed on the basic principle of fairly sharing the burdens and pains of economic restructuring. Subsequently, after much arduous negotiation, the labor-management-government council produced a historic Tripartite Accord on February 6. The accord included an agreement on allowing the earlier implementation of redundancy layoffs in an emergent situation of the company (the revised labor laws in March 1998 had disallowed layoffs until the year 2000). In compensation, the accord endorsed collective bargaining rights among schoolteachers and civil servants as well as rights for unions to participate in political activities.

The Tripartite Accord was welcomed and praised as a historic compromise both inside and outside the country, but workers were not at all happy. Although rank-and-file criticisms were relatively mild inside the FKTU, the KCTU leaders were severely criticized by its rank-and-file members for accepting the layoff clause. On February 9, the KCTU convened an extraordinary meeting of delegates and adopted a resolution denouncing the accord. They also voted to oust their incumbent leaders and elected a hard-line president of the Hyundai Heavy Industries union, Lee Kap-yong, as their new president. The Tripartite Council thus set off on a rocky road, littered with several protest walkouts and reluctant returns to the committee by KCTU representatives (see Kim Yong Cheol 1998).

Thus, we can see that the economic crisis had conflicting consequences for Korean labor. The financial crisis devastated the lives and livelihoods of the Korean workers, but at the same time it helped elevate the political and social status of organized labor. The establishment of the Tripartite Council under the direct authority of the president meant that for the first moment in Korean history labor was invited into the national decision-making body as a bona fide member, a major achievement for Korea's organized labor. But the irony of the empowerment of Korean labor at this juncture was that with the enhanced status and power, union leadership was given the task of accepting an institutional change that would seriously impair and destabilize workers' labor-market position. With the political inclusion that labor had fought for so long, labor leaders were now required to pacify their workers and to cooperate to maintain the industrial peace during economic restructuring. Thus, the current trend of the South Korean labor movement converged with the situation common in other advanced industrial economies. As Hyman describes, "In most countries the economic climate restricted the scope for substantive achievements. Unions had to settle increasingly for procedural and symbolic outcomes, while often being expected to perform a restraining and disciplining role" (1992, 157). South Korea was not an exception to this general pattern.

Nevertheless, the political inclusion of labor in the new corporatist framework succeeded in maintaining a relatively high level of industrial stability in 1998 in the midst of the mounting problems of unemployment and unfair labor practices in the industrial arena. Overt labor conflicts were restricted, more or less, to large-scale firms where there were strong unions, and the focal point of conflicts was the issue of layoffs. Workers in smaller firms, especially in the labor-intensive sector, were unable to resist corporate restructuring or plant relocation. The strong unions were concentrated in large conglomerate firms, but the rest of the unions were mostly very small and fragile and could easily disappear with the collapses of their companies. As the effects of the economic crisis on jobs were felt more deeply, most unions became preoccupied with the immediate problems of protecting jobs and preventing wage cuts for their own members and could ill afford to concern themselves with broader issues pertaining to other workers.

Concerning the general trend of South Korean unionism, there is one interesting comparative point to consider. Unlike the experiences in other newly industrialized countries, the South Korean labor movement did not develop as what Seidman (1994) calls "social-movement unionism." On the basis of her excellent comparative study of the "new unionism" in Brazil and South Africa, Seidman argues, "Both movements developed in the 1980s into 'social-movement unionism': shop-floor organizations, originally formed by semi-skilled industrial workers to press employers on wages and working conditions, began to articulate broader working-class demands in conjunction with community groups in poor neighborhoods" (28). She further argues that "these cases suggest that state-led, authoritarian industrialization strategies in late industrializers may tend to produce militant working-class movements whose demands go well beyond the factory gates" (12). Consequently, she speculates, the South Korean labor movement may reveal the same pattern.

However, that was not the case in South Korea. Although there were several similarities to the ways labor militancy occurred in Brazil and South Korea, South Korea's "new unionism" after 1987 clearly did not develop into social-movement unionism. More specifically, the democratic union movement in South Korea both before and after the 1987 labor insurgence did not seek to articulate and represent the broad interests of the working people in general or to assist protest movements in poor neighborhoods. The links between the shop floor and community organizations were tenuous, although not completely absent. This is an interesting divergence, not only because South Korea experienced the same pattern of state-led, authoritarian industrialization, but also because church organizations and students, who played an instrumental role in linking factory and community in Brazil and South Africa, also played a crucial role in fostering the Korean labor movement.

What accounts for this divergence? To answer this question satisfactorily, we need more thorough empirical research, but I can suggest some possible reasons for the failure of the South Korean labor movement to develop into social unionism. The first concerns the legal and political constraints on enterprise unionism in South Korea. The South Korean labor regime since the Park *yushin* period consistently tried to confine the labor movement within the boundaries of enterprises. The state used both legal means, such as the law prohibiting the involvement of third parties, and security agencies to prevent the union movement from moving beyond the factory gates.

A second possible reason for the divergence is that the level of unemployment was much lower and the size of the informal sector was much smaller in South Korea than in Brazil or South Africa, where high unemployment and high inflation served as important connecting mechanisms between workplace and community. In Brazil, as Keck argues, "the spread of unemployment has also blurred the lines between worker and non-worker, forcing the definition of class identity to move outside State-structured relations and into the sphere of common experience" (1989, 286). The more successful performance of the South Korean economy reduced this structural source of factory-neighborhood linkages and of active community movements in poor neighborhoods.

A third reason concerns the nature and objectives of the grassroots union movement in South Korea. Korean workers fought for independent unions not primarily to increase their wages or standards of living but to demand humane treatment and human dignity. Although demands for honor and dignity seem to be a common theme in all national labor movements, Korean workers put an extra emphasis on these values, largely because of the excessively despotic industrial relations in Korean factories. It is possible to argue that the situation was not so very different in other countries, but the point I would like to stress is that South Korean workers were preoccupied with their factory-specific problems and were less interested in, or could not afford to divert their attention to, consumption-related problems in the community. In short, it was probably not so obvious to Korean workers that neighborhood and factory were "two sides of the same coin," as it seemed to be, according to Seidman (1994, 39), for their counterparts in Brazil and South Africa.

In short, a variety of economic, political, and social factors contributed to shaping the South Korean labor movement as economic unionism rather than as social unionism, despite the important role played by outside groups and women workers in fermenting labor struggles. The failure of the labor movement to address community issues opened the door for a blossoming of citizens' movements after the democratic transition. The active civic movements were led by progressive intellectuals, many of whom had been active in the labor movement during the pre-1987 period (Cho Hee-Yeon 1998; Kim Sunhyuk 2000). This led to the separation of the working-class movement and the middle-class-led social movements in the 1990s, further restricting the scope of the labor movement.

Internal Differentiation of the Working Class

A distinct characteristic of the South Korean working class until the mid-1980s had been its homogeneity, both in terms of sociodemographic characterisitics and market position. The great majority of workers were semi-skilled and engaged in mass production under what might be called the "peripheral Fordism" (Kim Hyung-ki 1988; You 1995). Not only was there little differentiation in terms of skills (as well as age and family background), there were also few differences in terms of wages, job security, and welfare benefits. Wage differences between large and smaller firms were very modest, and so were the wage differences between unionized and non-unionized workers (Song 1991, 107–36; Kim Hyung-ki 1988, 378–417). Working conditions were uniformly poor and hazardous across industries and across firms of various sizes. In these aspects, South Korean factory workers constituted a very homogeneous working class, close to the ideal type of the industrial proletariat.

But after the 1980s, the South Korean economy began to move beyond peripheral Fordism. Led by the *chaebol* firms, large manufacturing firms strove hard to move up the technological ladder in world production and out of the sandwich position between the advanced industrial economies and the new tiers of export economies. Escalating wages and the growing power of the trade unions in South Korea were major contributing factors to the capitalists' endeavor to move beyond the low-wage-based mass production system, or what Krugman (1994) calls a growth strategy based on "perspiration" rather than "inspiration". The general strike in winter 1996–1997 occurred in this context, as Korean capitalists tried to restructure the legal framework to be more compatible with the post-Fordist regime of capital accumulation.

Even before this legal battle, Korean capitalists had actively sought to increase the flexibility of their use of the labor force. Since the mid-1980s, subcontract production increased rapidly in Korean manufacturing, as large-scale firms farmed out an increasing proportion of their production processes to external and internal subcontractors in order to save on labor costs and discourage union formation. In the 1990s, large firms in both the manufacturing and service industries employed the strategy of reducing the number of regular employees and hiring instead a large number of temporary, part-time, and home-based workers. The financial crisis in 1997 accelerated this trend. Thus, the internal structure of the Korean working class began to converge with the common pattern found in the other industrial societies, with the overall improvement of working-class material conditions, as indicated by their increased wages and change in lifestyle, and the increasing disaggregation of the working class by a polarizing labor-market structure.

The internal differentiation of the Korean working class in the 1990s occurred along several dimensions. First, significant differences in job conditions and wages appeared between employees at large firms and those at small- and medium-size firms. Since the late 1980s, workers at large firms, especially at the *chaebol* firms, have obtained substantially greater wage increases than those working in small factories, resulting in a widening economic gap between the two categories of workers. In 1980, the average wage for workers employed in small firms with 10–29 workers was 92.9 percent of the average wage at large firms (500 or more workers), but the ratio decreased to 87.5 percent in 1987 and to 72.3 percent in 1997 (KOILAF 1999, 133). The average wage at firms with 30–99 workers was 99.1 percent of that at large firms in 1980, but declined to 90.7 percent in 1987 and to 73.6 percent in 1997. Greater economic disparities between small and large firms developed in their provision of company welfare measures. Although this difference had existed to a certain extent before 1987, the disparity greatly increased after that as large firms tried to buy workers' cooperation and company loyalty by offering them generous welfare services, including housing subsidies, commuter buses, medical insurance, children's tuition support, funeral expenses, and other family-related supports.

Another critical axis of cleavage in the working class that has become more important in the 1990s was between those who were regularly employed and protected by legal contract and by unions and those whose employment status was irregular, unstable, and easily disposable. This is the well-known problem of the core-periphery, formal-informal, or insider-outsider division of the labor force in advanced industrial societies (see Hyman 1992). In South Korea, this division in the labor market was not serious until 1987, partly because there was a generation of continuous employment thanks to rapid economic growth, and partly because there was no pressing need for capital to hire many temporary workers because regular employees did not enjoy much bargaining power either.

One of the most significant changes that occurred in the Korean labor market in the 1990s was the rapid growth in the number of these irregular workers. The labor statistics indicate that between 1988 and 1997 the number of full-time employees increased from 5,348,000 to 7,133,000 (a 3.3 percent annual increase), while the number of irregular workers increased from 2,766,000 to 4,204,000 (a 4.8 percent annual increase) (KOILAF 1999, 41). The growth in the number of irregular workers increased more sharply in the second half of the 1990s, especially after the financial crisis in 1997. It is estimated that in 1999 more than half of all employed workers (approximately 52 percent) were either temporary or daily workers (Pulanjŏng nodong yŏngu moim 2000, 43). Most probably, the actual size of the irregular workforce was larger than this because government labor statistics excluded those employed in tiny enterprises with fewer than five employees. Also, many workers who were classified as full time might have been in short-term contract positions.

Not surprisingly, women were the main victims of this flexibility strategy. In 1999, regular employees constituted only 31 percent of the female labor force, compared to 69 percent of the male labor force (Pulanjŏng nodong yŏngu moim 2000, 47). With a severe labor shortage in the labor-intensive sector since the late 1980s, a large number of married women were encouraged to enter the labor force, but a majority of them found themselves working in temporary, part-time, or dispatched positions. The impact of the financial crisis in 1997 was much harsher on the female labor force. In most firms, women were the first to be laid off, and this was particularly the case for white-collar workers. Blue-collar women also suffered severely because many of their employers (most of whom were in the competitive sector) did not survive the financial crisis or had to scale down their business operations.

   The development of this structural cleavage within the working class inevitably exerted a deleterious effect on the working-class solidarity. As
noted previously, an important structural source of the rapid growth of the
Korean labor movement had been the homogeneity of the working class—
predominantly semi-skilled, low paid, unprotected, and suffering the same
social degradation. Worker solidarity was much easier to achieve with this
high degree of homogeneity, especially because of the accompanying high
degree of geographic concentration. But in the 1990s such structural conditions no longer prevailed. As Song Ho Keun argues, "Workers, who were
comrades in the past struggle, became more self-interested competitors in
the intensified market competition. Divided workers with pragmatic
concerns took the place of working-class solidarity in the early phase of
democratic consolidation in Korea" (1994a, 16). Increasingly, the different
market positions began to be reflected in union orientations. Unions representing the privileged core workers became increasingly pragmatic and
trade-unionist, whereas the NCTU, representing peripheral workers,
adhered to political unionism. Thus, the general trend of the South Korean
union movement in the 1990s was to become more pragmatic and in-
wardly oriented within the confines of enterprise unionism. This tendency
was generally stronger in unions at *chaebol* firms.
   There occurred, however, a countermovement to this dominant tendency. The devastating impact of the economic crisis in 1997–1998
triggered novel efforts to organize vulnerable workers and defend their
interests. There were efforts to organize temporary and part-time workers
in the construction industry, and in the sales and service sectors. The
KCTU also adopted an official policy of increasing unionization among
temporary workers and the unemployed.
   Another important development in the late 1990s was the attempt of female workers to organize their own unions separate from the male-dominated unions. In the 1990s, feminist consciousness grew noticeably among
women activists. Within the KCTU and the FKTU, women unionists demanded a greater voice for women and and secured greater women's representation in the leadership positions in the organizations. Yet many
women found these changes too slow and felt the need to organize
women's own unions. In early 1999, they organized women's trade unions
in nine geographical regions, incorporating both regular and temporary or
part-time workers across industrial and occupational categories. In the
same year, these nine regional unions formed a national umbrella organization, the National Federation of Women's Trade Unions. The dominant
orientation of the women's unions was well expressed in the inaugural
statement of the Seoul Women's Trade Union: "We organized women's
trade unions in order to achieve women's rights with the women workers'
power. Despite the fact that a large number of women workers have been

laid off and pushed into temporary jobs with no rights, the existing unions are losing their ability to fight back. Also, the patriarchal hierarchy within the present unions became an obstacle to organizing women workers" (Pulanjŏng nodong yŏngu moim 2000, 270).

Given that a majority of women workers are temporary, part-time, or subcontracted workers, women's unions were formed on a regional basis, including diverse categories of workers, and addressing not only employment issues but also other feminist issues such as gender discrimination at work, sexual harassment, and the lack of child-care services. Thus, from its beginning, the women's trade union movement exhibited the characteristics of social unionism more than the male-dominated conventional unions. The future of the women's trade union movement in 2000 was very uncertain, but it showed some promise of stimulating the South Korean labor movement to broaden its constituencies and community concerns. So, women workers' unique inclinations to and capabilities of linking workplace and community, which Seidman (1994, 38) suggests in the context of Brazil, began to express themselves in South Korea in the post-democratic-transition period, although not in the earlier authoritarian phase of industrialization.

No More Goliat Workers

During the early decades of export-oriented industrialization, the collective identity of Korean factory workers was more or less defined by outsiders. Workers were either called the industrial warriors, or *kongsuni* or *kongdoli*. If industrial warriors was the image created by the state in order to exhort workers to hard work, discipline, and sacrifice for the nation, *kongsuni* or *kondoli* was the product of society's stigmatization of factory workers based on the traditional Confucian status system. In both cases, the dominant ideology and traditional culture were employed to simultaneously mobilize and demobilize, extol and deride, factory workers.

The Great Worker Struggle of 1987 represented an outburst of the deep-seated resentment and anger of the Korean workers against the way they were treated and looked on by those in positions of power in society. It was a struggle not simply for economic gain but for human dignity and respect from society. The 1987 labor offensive was powerful and momentous enough to bury the facile identities of industrial warriors and *kongsuni* or *kongdoli*. And it brought a new worker identity. The labor struggle during the period of political transition, as we have seen, was militant, aggressive, and emotionally charged. The new worker identity of labor militancy that emerged during this period was most clearly demonstrated in the image of the *Goliat warriors*. The strikers at the Hyundai Heavy Industries in 1990 who climbed up the Goliat crane, eighty-two meters above the ground, symbolized the militant, combative, and class-conscious workers in the post-1987 period. As the strikers claimed, it was a struggle for workers' pride and respect, "a big fight with a dictatorial regime with the trust and pride of 25 million workers at stake."

The image of the "Goliat warriors" was clearly a product of the past years of harsh oppression and exploitation. It was a counteridentity to those hollow and stigmatizing identities of industrial warriors and *kong-suni* or *kongdoli*. The image of the Goliat warriors expressed workers' militant determination to end the "long years of servile submission" to managerial despotism. And it expressed workers' deep anger against "those long years of slave-like life."

The dominant slogan in the South Korean working-class struggle during this period of militancy was the "liberation of labor." Never clearly defined even among activists, this new discourse implied at least two things: liberation from oppression and inhumane treatment, and a more positive desire to create "a society in which workers are the masters." Most labor activists admitted that this was a rather abstract phrase and was not widely used among the masses of workers, but it nevertheless had a certain appeal to workers in the post-1987 period because it expressed their strong desire for justice and respect in the workplace and in society (based on interviews with several labor activists, including Roh Hoe-chan, Kim Ho-kyu, Lee Sang-do, and Kim Hae-yoon). The other, more positive meaning of the "liberation of labor" as a socialist transformation of society seemed to have appealed primarily to *sŏnjin nodongja* (workers with advanced class consciousness). In any event, the Goliat struggle more or less symbolized the struggle for the "liberation of labor" and thus received wide support from workers nationwide.

In 1999, a dozen years after the Great Worker Struggle of 1987, the Goliat workers had by and large disappeared from the South Korean industrial scene. Those radical, resistant, and class-conscious workers now represented a shrinking minority in most large heavy industries. The workers at Hyundai Heavy Industries and other similar large industrial firms had become increasingly pragmatic, individualistic, selfish, and apolitical. This is what both union leaders and managers at Hyundai Heavy Industries told me of the rank-and-file union members in their company.[6] "Workers support the militant leadership," one manager told me, "because they like to see them fight for their pride and ego, but they can quickly dump radical leaders if they fail to produce good results. They are very pragmatic and selfish." Union leaders also complained that rank-and-file union members

6. I made two visits to Hyundai Heavy Industries, in 1995 and 2000. Both union leaders and company managers were more emphatic in June 2000 in describing their workers as having become more pragmatic and individualistic.

liked them to take a tough stance, but were not very willing to participate in actions themselves when their support was needed. They also said that their workers were primarily interested in issues internal to their company and were rather unwilling to participate in strikes over broader issues removed from their immediate interests. They are no longer the Goliat warriors who were willing to lose jobs and go to prison for the sake of "pride and loyalty" to the working class.

A 1997 study by the Hyundai Heavy Industries union of their activist members is instructive in revealing the changing attitudes and consciousness among their members.[7] "It is said," the report acknowledges, "that Hyundai Heavy union members are no longer the Goliat warriors of the past. On the surface, they own apartments, drive their own cars, and rather than attending union meetings after work they would prefer to work overtime in order to earn more to meet the expenses of their children's tutorial lessons, or to return home early to pursue familistic and individualistic happiness" (Hyundai Heavy Industries Union 1997, 77). It also notes that union leaders at the Hyundai Heavy Industries had generally become passive, cautious, and somewhat pessimistic about assertive unions. This is partly due, this report suggests, to a noticeable improvement that occurred in the economic status of their members and the generous company welfare system, which made them more conservative and individualistic. Hyundai managers seemed to believe that their employees had no reason to be dissatisfied with their conditions because the company took care of them very well. Indeed, Hyundai Heavy Industries provided apartments for most of its employees; full college tuition for the first child and half for the second child; health insurance; and first-class gymnasium, theater, and other recreational facilities for their families (Lee Kyun-Jae 1997). Increased wage levels and access to these facilities allowed workers' families to partake in a middle-class lifestyle.[8]

From the workers' point of view, however, a more important factor dampening worker interest in union activities was the sophisticated technique of managerial control. The "new management strategy" intensified control on the shop floor using a variety of methods, including the increased power of foremen, team-based organization of work, performance-based pay system, and personalized approach by managers to individual workers to discourage activism. Workers complained that they were con-

7. I would like to thank Kim Ho-kyu, a union leader at Hyundai Heavy Industries, for giving me his personal copy of this report as well as other important materials. He and his wife, Lee Soo-kyung, herself a previous labor activist, helped my research in many ways. (Lee Soo-kyung now acts as a leader of a feminist social movement, Ulsan Women for Egalitarian World.)

8. Several surveys of industrial workers in large-scale heavy industries, conducted in the late 1980s and early 1990s, indicate that more than one-third identified themselves as belonging to the larger middle class (see Lim Young-il and Lim Ho 1993).

stantly watched and were under pressure to compete with their fellow workers. Unionists at Hyundai Heavy Industries told me that it was this new technique of control and financial inducement that has made their fellow workers selfish and individualistic and increasingly apathetic to collective actions.

Whereas the managerial strategy became ever more sophisticated, union strategy hardly changed at all. This was another very important reason, as the Hyundai union report admits, for the decline in their union movement. "The union members are fed up [with the union strategy] because it does not keep up with the changing masses and repeats the same things of the past." The study also notes, "The present method of union activities that repeats the simplistic slogan of former days, 'Down with Capital' cannot but have distance from the union members' attitudes which are being reshaped by the diversified capitalist strategy" (Hyundai Heavy Industries Union 1997, 48). Union leaders at Hyundai and elsewhere seemed to agree that one of the most serious problems facing the Korean labor movement in the late 1990s was the huge imbalance between capital and labor in their abilities to devise strategies. "Over the last ten years, capital has prepared themselves thoroughly and has dealt with us with a long-term strategic plan, but what we activists have done was to approach union members with the same simplistic logic of taking capital and the state as objects to destroy" (48). In part, this imbalance was due to an organizational problem. While managers remained in their positions for a long time, union leaders served only two years or often even less. With this constant change in union staff, there was no group in the enterprise union structure that could study and develop a long-term strategy.

So, the core of the Korean working class in the late 1990s were no longer Goliat warriors. The worker identity born out of intense resentment against managerial despotism and from the oppressed feeling of *han* against injustice in the workplace and in society seemed to have faded away with democratization in both the political and industrial arenas. This change must not be interpreted, however, as a simple retrogression in the working-class identity of Korean industrial workers. As students of working-class formation understand well, working-class identity and consciousness are complex and variable phenomena. Class consciousness does not grow in a linear fashion and, at any moment, working-class consciousness tends to include inconsistent and contradictory elements within itself (Mann 1973, 46–47; Marshall 1983; Fantasia 1988, 5–6). We would expect that this is particularly so in South Korea because of the adverse political and ideological environment that suppresses working-class consciousness.

It is useful to review analyses of several attitude surveys conducted in large-scale heavy industry from the late 1980s to the early 1990s. Kim Hyung-ki, for example, argues that "After the 1987 great worker struggle, the consciousness of the workers employed in the large-scale monopoly sector advanced significantly in terms of their militancy, democratic orientation, solidarity, political consciousness, and all other aspects" (1997, 230). Similarly, Lim Ho argues that "during this period, the masses of workers came to realize the importance of class solidarity and have acquired a firm working-class identity" (1992, 145). Also, Lim Young-Il and his colleagues write about "the amazing changes and development in the workers' consciousness within one and two years" since 1987. They further argue, "We can confirm that in comparison with other classes or groups, core workers in large-scale firms in the heavy and chemical industry have reached a very high level of healthy and critical social consciousness in almost every aspect" (Lim et al. 1989, 252).

These survey data, however, reveal another aspect of the workers' consciousness. A large majority of the respondents in these surveys demonstrated a conservative and traditional attitude toward industrial authority and industrial relations, as well as concerning the role of collective actions. For example, although three-quarters of the respondents agreed with the statement, "Workers must engage in aggressive struggles against employers in order to improve their situations," an equal proportion agreed with the statement that "Labor-management cooperation is beneficial to the workers" (Kim Hyung-ki 1997, 218). Also, workers had less trust in their own actions than in the government's role in bringing about desired changes in their economic status. Responding to a survey question concerning the most important thing that would improve their living standards, a large proportion (37 percent) of the respondents stressed the "government's role," and many others (32 percent) said that a "structural change in society" was necessary. A relatively small proportion of the respondents (14 percent) emphasized "workers' collective actions," and still smaller proportions mentioned "individual efforts" (12 percent) or "better economic performance by the company" (5 percent) (Kim Hyung-ki 1997, 315).

More important in Korean working-class consciousness was the continuous influence of family ideology and paternalism. A surprisingly large proportion of the respondents (67 percent) agreed with the statement that "Employers and workers belong to one family," even in the late 1980s. Furthermore, one-quarter of the respondents expressed a stronger deferential attitude toward managers by endorsing the statement that "Workers must treat the employer and managers like elders in our family" (Lim et al. 1989, 210). This traditional attitude was more common among older and less educated workers. But it also seems clear that the ideological campaign by the state and capital equating company with family and industrial harmony with prosperity, had made an enduring impact on the consciousness of the Korean workers.[9]

Thus, as far as the consciousness of the masses of factory workers is concerned, there was probably no significant change in the 1990s. As before, their consciousness was still complex, inconsistent, and contingent. Although it is true that they became more pragmatic and individualistic, they did not seem to lose their strong anti-capitalist feeling and deep sense of affinity with other industrial workers. Nor had the memory of the Great Worker Struggle of 1987 and of the general strike in 1996–1997 disappeared from their minds. Although the workers lost their bitter resentment against inhumane treatment, they obtained a stronger sense of rights consciousness. They demanded not only justice but the right to participate in the decision-making process in many spheres of factory life. And their rights consciousness was directly linked to union consciousness. Furthermore, a growing number of workers came to believe they needed a working-class party. In general, the political consciousness of Korean industrial workers increased steadily during the process of democratization.

No less important, and probably more important, than the consciousness of the rank-and-file union members, however, was the consciousness and political disposition of the activists. After all, the Goliat warriors represented not the mass of workers, but a minority of highly politicized and class-conscious workers. The political consciousness demonstrated during the 1987 Great Struggle and during the 1996–1997 general strike was in fact the consciousness of these *sŏnjin nodongja*. The significance of these two large-scale struggles is that the consciousness of these *sŏnjin nodongja* spread to the mass of workers and awoke in them a heightened sense of class solidarity and political consciousness. This advanced consciousness, of course, did not remain with the masses for long, but it did not disappear completely. Nor did the *sŏnjin nodongja* disappear. In almost every large factory, there were a significant minority of *sŏnjin nodongja*. In many of these factories, they were organized into several informal shop-floor organizations (*hyŏnjang chojik*) and exerted a powerful influence on the official leadership of the unions. These activist shop-floor organizations were linked through national networks and prevented the South Korean labor movement from becoming a narrow economic enterprise unionism. The search for ways to revitalize the Korean working-class struggle and to push

9. Thus, it seems prudent to conclude, as Lim Young-Il and Lim Ho argue, that in the years following the 1987 great struggle "workers' consciousness represents in many aspects healthy 'incipient class consciousness' but at the same time reveals the infiltration of dominant ideologies" (1993, 48). Choe Jae-Hyun's earlier study (1991) suggested the same conclusion.

it in the direction of political and social unionism was still alive and will continue in the new millennium.

Conclusion

The working class struggle in South Korea in the 1990s was shaped by two larger forces, democratic transition and globalization. Like all larger social processes, both processes had complex and contradictory consequences on the labor process, producing many paradoxes and puzzles in the formation of the Korean working class.

The political transition to democracy after 1987 brought important changes in the behavior of the state and capital and, consequently, in industrial relations and factory working conditions. First, democratization and the rising power of workers in this process caused the state to gradually refrain from direct physical intervention in the labor arena and to take instead a more indirect, legalistic approach. The state modified its old anti-unionist approach and assumed a more neutral stance toward enterprise unionism, while suppressing militant union actions. Collective bargaining and union activities were accepted not only in formal legal terms but also in actual practice. Thus, the presence of the repressive state, which had been a major source of worker resentment and politicization, gradually faded into the background. Instead, capital came to the forefront of the industrial relations system. Second, democratic changes in state policies and aggressive labor challenges forced employers to modify their behavior toward their workers. In many factories, the patriarchal and despotic management style slowly gave way to a more subtle form of control. Employers learned that they must live with unions and accepted collective bargaining as part of the normal industrial order.

These changes in state policies and capitalist attitudes led to a gradual transformation of South Korea's industrial system from "despotic factory regime" to "hegemonic regime," to borrow Burawoy's (1985) terms. While the former was based on coercion, the latter was primarily based on consent and the institutional separation of state and factory apparatuses. Although it would obviously take a much longer time to see the end of managerial despotism in Korean industry, especially in small enterprises, substantial improvement was noticed in this regard across industrial sectors since 1987. This change in the factory regime necessarily entailed important changes in Korean workers' daily experiences in the factory. The deep-seated resentment against inhumane treatment, which had provided the springboard for the labor protests of the previous decades, became attenuated; and so did workers' frustration over the status discrimination against manual production workers. In the 1990s, therefore, labor struggles were determined primarily by the workers' desire to enhance their economic status and organizational power rather than by a desperate cry for humane treatment.

Another important consequence of democratization was a gradual separation of the working-class struggle from the broad social and political movements. With the end of military rule, the two movements lost the common enemy that had united the two. In the changed political environment, the democracy movement began to turn its focus away from labor issues to the broader social issues of distribution, environment, gender inequality, consumption, and civic morality. The "new social movements," led by middle-class intellectuals, consciously kept their distance from the organized labor movement and the radical *minjung* movement. Many intellectual labor activists left the labor movement and joined these new social movements or were recruited by conventional party politics. At the same time, the mainstream of the labor movement became more pragmatic and economically oriented, distancing itself from the political and social movements.

As the authoritarian system of labor control gradually ceased to operate as a crucial determining factor of the South Korean labor movement, globalization emerged as a dominant force shaping the new terrain of labor struggles in South Korea in the 1990s. Faced with increasing competition in export markets and faced with empowered unions domestically, Korean capitalists adopted various strategies to enhance labor-market flexibility and to curb labor power on the shop floor. These new corporate strategies had the serious effect of disaggregating the Korean working class. The previously homogeneous working class increasingly became divided into regular and irregular, core and periphery, protected and unprotected workers. The overall economic improvements brought about by the great labor offensive in the late 1980s benefited these two sectors unequally and widened the gap between the two. The resulting fragmentation of the working class had a dampening effect on working-class solidarity and encouraged a tendency toward narrow enterprise unionism.

Yet this economic trend has simultaneously generated new sources of industrial conflicts and new objects of labor mobilization. The central concern of labor disputes in the 1990s was job security, which was increasingly threatened by the impact of globalization. And the dynamism of labor struggles seems to have been shifting from blue-collar workers in the heavy and chemical industries to white-collar workers in the service sectors, which were under heavy pressure due to corporate restructuring, and to the fast-growing groups of irregular and unstable workers. Women workers, who bore the brunt of the flexibilization strategy of capital, also became a major proponent of a new unionism that sought to reach workers who were unprotected by the existing unions. Unlike previous female activists who were practically all young single women, many new activists were middle-age married women working in the service sector. While the frontiers of labor conflicts expanded and new actors were brought into the labor movement, the terrain of labor struggles became restricted to economic problems concerning job stability and wages.

Thus, at the dawn of a new century the South Korean working class finds itself at the crossroads. A newly born class, it may continue to grow into a mature working class possessing a strong and effective class organization and offering a new constructive vision of future to society. Alternatively, current economic problems may force the Korean working class to engage in a narrow trade unionism and to become internally fragmented and externally isolated. Despite its world-renowned militancy and combativeness, the Korean working class is still a weak and vulnerable class—organizationally, politically, and ideologically. It is a class with relatively shallow and ambivalent class consciousness, with no strong political organization or party support, with no clear vision of an alternative social structure, and with only incipient forms of class-based community life and cultural patterns. It is nonetheless a class possessing a strong spirit of resistance, a keen sense of class inequality and social injustice, strong sentiments of solidarity, and a growing sense of political efficacy. It is a fresh-made class whose indentity and political character are to be molded and remolded in the continuous evolution of the capitalist system. The current trend in the global economy and associated political and ideological changes will have a serious impact on the Korean working class; they may lead to the unmaking of this infant-stage working class or may rekindle spirited labor resistance and class solidarity to produce a more cohesive and class-conscious working class. Whatever the course of its future evolution, the South Korean working class will be remembered for its heroic struggle against tremendous oppression during the period of export-oriented industrialization and for its contribution to making the Korean society more just and democratic.

Bibliography

Abegglen, James. 1958. *The Japanese Factory: Aspects of Its Social Organization.* Glencoe: Free Press.

Abelmann, Nancy. 1996. *Epics of Dissent: A South Korean Social Movement.* Berkeley: University of California Press.

Aminzade, Ronald. 1981. *Class, Politics, and Early Industrial Capitalism: A Study of Mid-Nineteenth Century Toulouse, France.* Albany: State University of New York Press.

———. 1993. *Ballots and Barricades: Class Formation and Republican Politics in France, 1830–1871.* Princeton: Princeton University Press.

Amsden, Alice. 1989. *Asia's Next Giant: South Korea and Late Industrialization.* New York: Oxford University Press.

Bae Kyuhan. 1987. *Automobile Workers in Korea.* Seoul: Seoul National University Press.

Bai, Moo Ki. 1982. "The Turning Point in the Korean Economy." In *The Developing Economics,* 20. Japan: Institute of Developing Economics.

Bairoch, P., T. Delycke, H. Gelders, and J. Limbor. 1968. *The Working Population and Its Structure.* New York: Gordon & Breach.

Bang Yong-Suk. 1994. "Mŏritmal" [Introduction]. In *Han'guk nodong undongsa* [History of the Korean labor movement], edited by Han'guk minju nodongja yŏnhap. Seoul: Tongnyŏk.

Bello, Walden, and Stephanie Rosenfeld. 1990. *Dragons in Distress: Asia's Miracle Economies in Crisis.* Harmondsworth: Penguin.

Bendix, Reinhard. 1956. *Work and Authority in Industry.* New York: John Wiley & Sons.

Bergquist, Charles. 1986. *Labor in Latin America: Comparative Essays on Chile, Argentina, Venezuela, and Columbia.* Stanford: Stanford University Press.

Biernacki, Richard. 1995. *The Fabrication of Labor: Germany and Britain, 1640–1914.* Berkeley: University of California Press.

Bourdieu, Pierre. 1977. *Outline of a Theory of Practice.* Translated by Richard Nice. Cambridge: Cambridge University Press.

Brandt, Vincent. 1971. *A Korean Village: Between Farm and Sea*. Cambridge, Mass.: Harvard University Press.

Burawoy, Michael. 1985. *The Politics of Production*. London: Verso.

Castells, Manuel. 1997. *Power of Identity*. Cambridge, Mass.: Blackwell.

Calhoun, Craig J. 1981. *The Question of Class Struggle: The Social Foundations of Popular Radicalism during the Industrial Revolution*. Chicago: University of Chicago Press.

Chakrabarty, Dispesh. 1989. *Rethinking Working-Class History: Bengal 1890–1940*. Princeton: Princeton University Press.

Chang Myung-kook. 1985. "Haebanghu Han'guk nodong undongŭi palchachui" [Trajectory of the South Korean labor movement since liberation]. In *Han'guk nodong undongron I* [On the Korean labor movement I], edited by Kim Keum-su and Park Hyun-chae, 113–45. Seoul: Mirae.

Chang Nam-soo. 1984. *BBaeatkkin Ilto* [The workplace dispossessed]. Seoul: Ch'angchakkwa Pipyong.

Chang Sang-hwan. 1988. "Hyŏnhaeng tojimunje ŭi sŏngkyŏk kwa haekyŏl panghyang" [The nature of the current land issues and the direction for their solutions]. In *Han'guk nongŭp-nongmin munje yŏnku I* [A study of the problems in Korean agriculture and Korean farmers I], edited by Han'guk nongŏchon sahoe yŏnkuso. Seoul: Yŏnkusa.

Chhachhi, Amrita, and Renee Pittin. 1996. "Introduction." In *Confronting State, Capital and Patriarchy: Women Organizing in the Process of Industrialization*, edited by A. Chhachhi and R. Pittin. London: Macmillan.

Cho Hee-Yeon. 1998. *Han'guk ŭi minjujuŭiwa sahoe undong* [Democracy and social movements in South Korea]. Seoul: Tangdae.

Cho Seung-hyok. 1988. *Han'guk ŭi kongŏphwa wa nosa kwankye* [Industrialization and labor relations in Korea]. Seoul: Chŏngamsa.

Cho, Soon. 1994. *The Dynamics of Korean Development*. Washington, D.C.: Institute of International Economics.

Cho, Soon-Kyoung. 1987. "How Cheap Is 'Cheap Labor'? The Dilemmas of Export-Led Industrialization." Ph.D. diss., University of California, Berkeley.

Cho U-hyun, and Yun Jin-ho. 1994. *Han'guk ŭi hwaitŭkala nodong chohap yŏnku* [A study of Korean white-collar union movement]. Seoul: Korean Institute of Labor Studies.

Cho Wha Soon. 1988. *Let the Weak Be Strong*. Bloomington, Ind.: Meyer, Stone, and Co.

Cho, Young-rae. 1991. *Chun Tae Il pyŏngjŏn* [Chun Tae Il's life story]. Seoul: Dolbege.

Choe, Jae-Hyun. 1991. "80 nyŏndae kongŏp nodongjadŭlŭi chŏngchi sahoe ŭishik" [The political and social consciousness of the industrial workers during the 1980s]. In *Han'guk ŭi nodong munje* [Labor issues in South Korea], edited by Nodongmuje yŏnguso. Seoul: Pibong.

Choi Chang-Woo. 1987. "Kuro tongmaeng paŏp ŭi palsaeng wŏnin'e kwanhan chŏngchihakchŏk yŏnku" [A political analysis of the causes of the solidarity strikes in Kuro Industrial Park]. Master's thesis, Korea University.

Choi, Chungmoo. 1995. "The Minjung Culture Movement and the Construction of Popular Culture in Korea." In *South Korea's Minjung Movement: The Culture and Politics of Dissidence*, edited by Kenneth Wells, 105–18. Honolulu: University of Hawaii Press.

Choi Jang Jip. 1989. *Labor and the Authoritarian State: Labor Unions in South Korean Manufacturing Industries, 1961–1980*. Seoul: Korea University Press.

———. 1992. "Han'guk ŭi nodong undongŭn woe chŏngchi chojikhwa'e silpaehako itna?" [Why is the Korean labor movement failing in political organization?]. In *Han'guk ŭi kukawa siminsahoe* [The state and civil society in Korea], edited by the Korean Sociological Association and the Korean Political Science Association, 230–54. Seoul: Hanul.

——. 1993a. *Han'guk minjuchuŭi ŭi iron* [Theory of Korean democracy]. Seoul: Hankilsa.

——. 1993b. "The Working Class Movement and the State in Transition to Democracy: The Case of South Korea." Paper presented at the Conference on East Asian Labor in Comparative Perspective, University of California, Berkeley.

Choi Sang-Chin, and Uichol Kim. 1992. "Conceptual and Empirical Analyses of Han: An Indigenous Form of Lamentation." Paper presented at Center for Korean Studies, University of Hawaii.

Chŏn Y. H. nodong chohap and Han'guk nodongja pokji hyŏpuihoe [Former Y. H. union and Korean Association for Labor Welfare]. 1984. *Y. H. nodong chohapsa* [History of the Y. H. union]. Seoul: Hyŏngsŏngsa.

Christian Institute for the Study of Justice and Development. 1988. *Lost Victory: An Overview of the Korean People's Struggle for Democracy in 1987*. Seoul: Minjungsa.

Chu, Yin-Wah. 1998. "Labor and Democratization in South Korea and Taiwan." *Journal of Contemporary Asia* 28: 185–202.

Chun, Chum-suk, ed. 1985. *Inkan tapke salja: Pusan chiyŏk yahak nodongja kŭl moŭm* [Let's live like human beings: A collection of Pusan-area night school workers' essays]. Chinju: Noktu.

Chun I-du. 1993. *Han ŭi kujo yŏngu* [A study of the structure of han]. Seoul: Munkak kwa Chisŏngsa.

Chun Tae-Il. 1988. *Naŭi chukŭmŭl hŏttoei malla* [Don't waste my life: A collection of Chun's writings]. Seoul: Dolbege.

Chung Hyun-baek. 1985. "Yŏsŏng nodongjaŭi ŭisikkwa nodong sekye: Nodongja suki punsŏkŭl chungsimŭro" [Consciousness and the world of work of female factory workers: analysis of workers' essays]. *Yŏsŏng* [Women] 1:116–62.

Chung I-dam, and Park Young-jung, eds. 1991. *Munye undongŭi hyŏndankyewa chŏnmang* [Present state and prospect of the cultural movement]. Seoul: Hanmadang.

Chung Jin-Sung. 1984. "Ilcheha Chosŏn'e itsŏsŏ nodongja chonchae hyŏntae wa chŏimkŭm" [The living conditions and low wages among Korean workers in Chosun under Japanese rule]. In *Han'guk chabonjuŭi wa imkŭm nodong* [Korean capitalism and wage labor], edited by Hwada. Seoul: Hwada.

Chung, Young-Il. 1984. "Han'guk nongŏp ŭi hyŏnhwang kwa tangmyŏn kwaje" [The state of Korean agriculture and its tasks]. In *Han'guk nongŏp munje ŭi saeroun insik* [New understanding of Korean agricultural problems], edited by Park Hyun-Chae et al., 33–66. Seoul: Dolbege.

Clark, Donald, ed. 1988. *The Kwangju Uprising: Shadows over the Regime in South Korea*. Boulder: Westview Press.

Cole, David, and Princeton Lyman. 1971. *Korean Development: The Interplay of Politics and Economics*. Cambridge, Mass.: Harvard University Press.

Cole, Robert. 1979. *Work, Mobility and Participation*. Berkeley: University of California Press.

Collier, Ruth Berlins, and David Collier. 1991. *Shaping the Political Arena*. Princeton: Princeton University Press.

Cumings, Bruce. 1981. *The Origins of the Korean War: Liberation and the Emergence of Separate Regimes*. Princeton: Princeton University Press.

Das, Dilip K. 1992. *Korean Economic Dynamism*. London: Macmillan.
Daewoo Auto Union. 1985. *Daewoo chadongcha imkŭminsang tujaeng kirok* [Report on wage-hike struggle at Daewoo Auto]. Seoul: Paeksan.
Deyo, Frederic. 1989. *Beneath the Miracle: Labor Subordination in the New Asian Industrialism*. Berkeley: University of California Press.
Diamond, Larry, and Byung-Kook Kim, eds. 2000. *Consolidating Democracy in South Korea*. Boulder: Lynne Rienner.
Dongil pangjik pokjik tujaeng wiwonhoe, ed. 1985. *Dongil pangjik nodong chohap undongsa* [History of Dongil textiles union movement]. Seoul: Dolbege.
Eckert, Carter. 1993. "The South Korean Bourgeoisie: A Class in Search of Hegemony." In *State and Society in Contemporary Korea*, edited by Hagen Koo, 95–130. Ithaca: Cornell University Press.
Economic Planning Board. 1974. *Korean Economic Indicators 1974: Special Labor Force Survey Report*. Seoul: Economic Planning Board.
——. 1983. *Korean Economic Indicators 1983*. Seoul: Economic Planning Board.
——. 1984. *Korean Economic Indicators 1984: Report on the First Employment Structure Survey*. Seoul: Economic Planning Board.
——. 1990. *Korean Economic Indicators 1990: Major Statistics of Korean Economy*. Seoul: Economic Planning Board.
Elson, Diane, and Ruth Pearson. 1981. "Nimble Fingers Make Cheap Workers: An Analysis of Women's Employment in Third World Export Manufacturing." *Feminist Review* (Spring):87–107.
Fantasia, Rick. 1988. *Cultures of Solidarity: Consciousness, Action, and Contemporary American Workers*. Berkeley: University of California Press.
Federation of Korean Trade Unions (FKTU). 1978. *Chochik yŏsŏng nodongja ŭi kŭnrosiltae e kwanhan chosayŏnku pokoso I* [Research report on the working conditions of the organized women factory workers I]. Seoul: Federation of Korean Trade Unions.
——. 1990. *Han'guk nodongja ŭishik yŏngu*. Seoul: Federation of Korean Trade Unions.
Fernandes, Leela. 1997. *Producing Workers: The Politics of Gender, Class, and Culture in the Calcutta Jute Mills*. Philadelphia: University of Pennsylvania Press.
Fernandez-Kelly, Maria Patricia. 1983. *For We Are Sold, I and My People: Women and Industry in Mexico's Frontier*. Albany: State University of New York Press.
Fields, Gary, and Henry Wan, Jr. 1986. "Wage-Setting Institutions and Economic Growth." Paper presented at the Conference on the Role of institutions in Economic Development, Ithaca, N.Y.
Foster, John. 1974. *Class Struggle and the Industrial Revolution: Early Industrial Capitalism in Three English Towns*. New York: St. Martin's Press.
Foucault, Michel. 1979. *Discipline and Punish: The Birth of the Prison*. Translated by Alan Sheridan. New York: Vintage Books.
Freda, James. 1998. "Absent Suffering and Industrialist Dreams: Discourse on *Han* in Postcolonial Korea." Mimeo, University of California, Los Angeles.
Gates, Hill. 1979. "Dependency and the Part-Time Proletariat in Taiwan." *Modern China* 5:381–408.
Goldthorpe, John, D. Lockwood, F. Bechhoffer, and J. Platt. 1969. *The Affluent Workers in the Class Structure*. London: Cambridge University Press.
Gordon, Andrew. 1985. *The Evolution of Labor Relations in Japan: Heavy Industry, 1853–1955*. Cambridge, Mass.: Council on East Asian Studies, Harvard University.
Gramsci, Antonio. 1971. *Selections from the Prison Notebooks*. New York: International Publishers.

Gutman, Herbert. 1977. *Work, Culture and Society in Industrializing America*. New York: Vintage.

Haggard, Stephen. 1990. *Pathways from the Periphery: The Politics of Growth in the Newly Industrializing Countries*. Ithaca: Cornell University Press.

Han Do-Hyun. 1993. "Capitalist Land Ownership and State Policy in 1989–1990 in Korea." *Korea Journal of Population and Development* 22:155–66.

Han Wan-sang. 1984. *Minjung sahoehak* [Minjung sociology]. Seoul: Chongro Sŏjŏk.

Han Wan-sang and Kim Sung-ki. 1988. "Han'e taehan minjung sahoehakchŏk siron" [A preliminary analysis of han from a minjung sociology perspective]. In *Hyŏndae chabonchuŭi wa kongdongche iron* [Modern capitalism and a theory of the community], edited by the Sociology Study Group, Seoul National University, 253–90. Seoul: Hankilsa.

Han Yun-soo, ed. 1980. *Pibaramsok'e piŏnan kkot* [Flowers bloomed in the midst of stormy rain]. Seoul: Chungnyonsa.

Hanagan, Michael. 1989. *Nascent Proletarians: Class Formation in Post-Revolutionary France*. Cambridge, Mass.: Basil Blackwell.

Han'guk kidokkyo kyohoe hyŏpŭihoe [National Council of Churches in Korea (KNCC)]. 1984. *Nodong hyŏnjang kwa chŭngŏn* [The real world of factory life and testimony]. Seoul: P'ulbbit.

Han'guk kidokkyo sahoe munje yŏnguwon [Korean Christian Institute for Research on Social Problems]. 1987a. *Han'guk sahoe ŭi nodong tongje* [Labor control in Korean society]. Seoul: Minjungsa.

——. 1987b. *7–8wol nodongja taejung tujaeng* [The July–August mass struggle of the workers]. Seoul: Minjungsa.

Han'guk nong-ŏch'on sahoe yŏnkuhoe [Research Group on Korean Farming and Fishing Villages]. 1988. *Han'guk nongŏp nongmin munje yŏnku* [Research on problems of Korean agricultural and farmers]. Vol. 1. Seoul: Yŏnkusa.

Han'guk yŏsŏng yukwonja yŏnmaeng [The League of Women Voters in Korea]. 1980. *Yŏsŏng kŭnroja siltae chosa pokosŏ: Kuro-Kumi kongdanŭl chungsimŭro* [Survey report on the conditions of women workers: Centered on Kuro and Kumi industrial parks]. Seoul: Han'guk Yŏsŏng Yukwonja Yŏnmaeng.

Hart-Landsberg, Martin. 1993. *The Rush to Development: Economic Change and Political Struggle in South Korea*. New York: Monthly Review Press.

Heyzer, N., ed. 1988. *Daughters in Industry: Work, Skills and Consciousness of Women Workers in Asia*. Kuala Lumpur: Asian and Pacific Development Centre.

Hirschman, Albert O. 1971. *Exit, Voice, and Loyalty*. Cambridge, Mass.: Harvard University Press.

Hobsbawm, Eric J. 1984. *Workers: Worlds of Labour*. New York: Pantheon.

Hong, Seung-tae. 1994. "Kwangju minjung hangjaengŭi chwajŏlkwa chinpochŏk nodong undongŭi mosaek" [Defeat of the Kwangju minjung uprising and a search for the progressive labor movement]. In *1970-nyŏndae ihu Han'guk nodong undongsa* [Post-1970s history of the South Korean labor movement], edited by Han'guk minju nodongja yŏnhap [Association of Korean democratic workers], 106–53. Seoul: Tongnyŏk.

Huh Sang-Soo. 1989. "Choekŭn sahoe pyŏnhyŏk undong kwa nodong undong" [The recent social movements and the labor movement]. In *Han'guk sahoe pyŏnhyŏk undong kwa nodong undong* [Social movements and the labor movement in Korea], edited by Han'guk kidokkyo sahoe kaebalwon. Seoul: Chungam munhwasa.

Hwang Ŭi-bong. 1985. "Nodong hyŏnjang ŭi chisikindŭl" [Intellectuals in the labor arena]. In *Rŭpposidae 2*. Seoul: Silchŏn munkhansa.

———. 1986. *80-nyŏndaeŭi haksaeng undong* [Student movements in the 1980s]. Seoul: Yejokak.

Hyman, Richard. 1992. "Trade Unions and the Disaggregation of the Working Class." In *The Future of Labour Movements*, edited by Marino Regini, 150–68. Newbury Park: Sage.

Hyundai Heavy Industries Union. 1997. *Hyundai chungkongŏp hwaldongka sangtaewa ŭishik chosa* [Research on the living standards and social attitudes of labor activists at Hyundai Heavy Industries]. Ulsan: Hyundai Heavy Industries Union and Han'guk nodong iron chŏngchaek yŏnguso.

Ilsongjung. 1988. *Haksaeng undong nochaengsa* [History of debates on the student movement]. Seoul: Ilsongchŏng.

Iltŏ ŭi sori: Nodong kwa yesul 2 [Voices from the workplaces: Labor and arts 2]. 1985. Seoul: Chiyangsa.

International Labour Organization (ILO). Various years. *Yearbook of Labour Statistics.*

Janelli, Roger L. 1993. *Making Capitalism: The Social and Cultural Construction of a South Korean Conglomerate.* Stanford: Stanford University Press.

Jones, Gareth Stedman. 1983. Languages of Class: Studies in English Working Class History, 1832–1982. Cambridge: Cambridge University Press.

Jones, Leroy, and Il Sakong. 1980. *Government, Business, and Entrepreneurship in Economic Development: The Korean Case.* Cambridge, Mass.: Harvard University Press.

Jung, Hee-Nam. 1993. "Land, State and Capital: The Political Economy of Land Policies in South Korea: 1960–1990," Unpublished Ph.D. diss., University of Hawaii.

Katznelson, Ira. 1986. "Working-Class Formation: Constructing Cases and Comparisons." In *Working-Class Formation: Nineteenth-Century Patterns in Western Europe and the United States*, edited by Ira Katznelson and Aristide Zolberg, 3–41. Princeton: Princeton University Press.

Kearney, Robert P. 1991. *The Warrior Worker: The Challenge of the Korean Way of Working.* New York: Henry Holt.

Keck, Margaret. 1989. "The New Unionism in the Brazilian Transition." In *Democratizing Brazil: Problems of Transition and Consolidation*, edited by Alfred Stepan, 255–96. New York: Oxford University Press.

Kim, Chi Ha. 1980. *The Middle Hour: Selected Poems of Kim Chi Ha.* Translated by David McCann. Stanfordville: Human Rights Publishing Group.

Kim, Choong Soon. 1992. *The Culture of Korean Industry: An Ethnography of Poongsan Corporation.* Tucson: University of Arizona Press.

Kim, Dae-ho. 1986. "Han'guk nodongja munwha undong ŭi chŏnkaewa sŏngkyŏk" [Development of the Korean working-class cultural movement and its character]. In *Kongdongche munhwa* [Culture of Communal Solidarity], Vol. 3, 126–67. Seoul: Kongdongche.

Kim Dong-Choon. 1995. *Han'guk sahoe nodongja yŏnku* [A study of the Korean working class]. Seoul: Yŏksawa pipyŏng.

Kim, Eun Mee. 1997. *Big Business, Strong State: Collusion and Conflict in South Korean Development, 1960–1990.* Albany: State University of New York Press.

Kim Hyung-ki. 1988. *Han'guk ŭi tokchŏm chabon kwa imkŭm nodong* [Monopoly capital and wage labor in South Korea]. Seoul: Kkachi.

———. 1997. *Han'guk nosakwankye ŭi chŏngchi kyŏngjehak* [The political economy of Korean industrial relations]. Seoul: Hanul.

Kim, Hyun Mee. 1997. "Gender/Sexuality System as a Labor Control Mechanism: Gender Identity of Korean Female Workers in a U.S. Multinational Corporation." *Korea Journal* 37:56–70.

Bibliography

225

——. 1999. "Han'guk nodong undongŭi tamron punsŏkŭl tonghaebon sŏngchŏk chaehyŏnŭi chŏngchihak" [The politics of gender representation seen through the discourse analysis of the Korean labor movement]. Yŏlin chisŏng 6 (Fall/Winter):128–48.

Kim In-dong. 1985. "70-nyŏndae minju nojo undongŭi chŏnkaewa pyŏnga" [Evolution and evaluation of the democratic union movement in the 1970s]. In Han'guk nodong undongron I [On the Korean labor movement I], edited by Kim Keum-su and Park Hyun-chae, 147–75. Seoul: Mirae.

Kim Jang-han, et al. 1989. 80-nyŏndae han'guk nodong undongsa [The 1980s labor movement in Korea]. Seoul: Choguk.

Kim Jin-ok. 1984. "80 nyŏndae nodong undong ŭi chŏnkye" [The evolution of the labor movement in the 1980s]. In Hyŏnjang. Vol. 2, Nodong hyŏnsil kwa nodong undong, 257–340. Seoul: Dolbege.

Kim Jin-young. 1994. Chŏngbo kisul kwa hwait'ŭ kalla nodong [Information technology and white-collar labor]. Seoul: Hanul.

Kim, Keum-su. 1995. Han'guk nodong undong ŭi hyŏnhwangkwa kwaje [The present state and issues of the Korean labor movement]. Seoul: Kwahakkwa sasang.

Kim Kyong-Dong. 1993. Han'guk sahoe pyŏndongron [Korean social change: Theoretical perspectives]. Seoul: Nanam.

Kim Kyŏng-sook, et al. 1986. Kŭrŏna urinŭn ŏje ŭi uriga anida [But we are not yesterday's we]. Seoul: Dolbege.

Kim Moon-soo. 1986. "Ŏnŭ silchŏnchŏk chisikinŭi chaki pansŏng" [A self-reflection of one activist intellectual]. In Hyŏnjang [Real arena], Vol. 6, 125–64. Seoul: Dolbege.

Kim Sa-in, and Kang Hyŏng-chŏl, eds. 1989. Minjok minjung munkakron ŭi chaengchŏm kwa chŏnmang [Issues and prospect of the Nationalist and Minjung literature]. Seoul: Purŭnsup.

Kim, Seok Ki. 1987. "Business Concentration and Government Policy: A Study of the Phenomenon of Business Groups in Korea, 1945–1985." D.B.A. diss., Harvard University.

Kim, Seung-kyung. 1997. Class Struggle or Family Struggle?: The Lives of Women Factory Workers in South Korea. Cambridge: Cambridge University Press.

Kim Sunhyuk. 2000. The Politics of Democratization in Korea: The Role of Civil Society. Philadelphia: Temple University Press.

Kim Uchang. 1993. "The Agony of Cultural Construction: Politics and Culture in Modern Korea." In State and Society in Contemporary Korea, edited by Hagen Koo. Ithaca: Cornell University Press.

Kim Yŏl-kyu. 1980. Wonhan, kŭ chittŭn angae [Rancor, that thick layer of the mist]. Seoul: Pŏmunsa.

Kim, Yong Cheol. 1994. "The State and Labor in South Korea: A Coalition Analysis." Ph.D. diss., Ohio State University.

——. 1998. "Industrial Reform and Labor Backlash in South Korea: Genesis, Escalation, and Termination of the 1997 General Strike." Asian Survey 38:1142–60.

Kim Yong-ki, and Park Sŭng-ok, eds. 1989. Han'guk nodong undong nonchaengsa [The History of the debates on the Korean labor movement]. Seoul: Hyŏnjang munhaksa.

Kim Young-soo. 1999. Han'guk nodongja kyekŭp chŏngchi undong [The class politics movement of the Korean workers]. Seoul: Hyŏnjang'esŏ miraerŭl.

Kim Yun-hwan. 1978. "Kŭndaechŏk imkŭm nodong ŭi hyŏngsŏng kwachŏng" [The formation process of the modern wage labor]. In Han'guk nodong munje ŭi kujo [Structure of Korean labor problems], edited by Kim Yun-hwan et al. Seoul: Kwangminsa.

Kim Yun-hwan, and Kim Nak-jung. 1970. *Han'guk nodong undongsa* [History of the Korean labor movement]. Seoul: Ilchogak.

Kim Yun-hwan et al., eds. 1978. *Han'guk nodong munje ŭi kujo* [The structure of Korean labor problems]. Seoul: Kwangminsa.

Kocka, Jürgen. 1986. "Problems of Working-Class Formation in Germany: The Early Years, 1800–1875." In *Working-Class Formation: Nineteenth-Century Patterns in Western Europe and the United States*, edited by Ira Katznelson and Aristide Zolberg, 279–351. Princeton: Princeton University Press.

KOILAF. 1999. *Labor Relations in Korea*. Seoul: Korea International Labour Foundation.

Kongdongche, ed. 1986. *Kongdongche munhwa* [Culture of Solidary Community]. Seoul: Kongdongche.

Koo, Hagen. 1989. "The State, Industrial Structure, and Labor Politics: Comparison of South Korea and Taiwan." In *Industrial East Asia*, edited by Kyong-Dong Kim, 21–37. Seoul: Seoul National University Press.

———. 1990. "From Farm to Factory: Proletarianization in Korea." *American Sociological Review* 55 (October): 669–81.

———. 1991. "Middle Classes, Democratization, and Class Formation: The Case of South Korea." *Theory and Society* 20 (August):485–509.

———. 1993. "The State, Minjung, and the Working Class in South Korea." In *State and Society in Contemporary Korea*, edited by Hagen Koo, 131–62. Ithaca: Cornell University Press.

Korean Statistical Association. 1991. *Social Indicators in Korea, 1991*. Seoul: Korean Statistical Association.

Krugman, Paul. 1994. "The Myth of Asia's Miracle." *Foreign Affairs* 73:62–78.

Kung, Lydia. 1976. "Factory Work and Women in Taiwan: Changes in Self-Image and Status." *Signs* 2(1):35–58.

———. 1983. *Factory Women in Taiwan*. Ann Arbor: University of Michigan Research Press.

Kuznets, Paul. 1977. *Economic Growth and Structure in the Republic of Korea*. New Haven: Yale University Press.

Kwon Yong-Mok. 1988. "Hyundai gurup nodong undongsa" [The history of the labor movement at Hyundai group]. *Saepyŏk* 1–3.

Lee Chang-Hee. 1998. "New Unionism and the Transformation of the Korean Industrial Relations System." *Economic and Industrial Democracy* 19:347–73.

Lee, Ching Kwan. 1998. *Gender and the South China Miracle: Two Worlds of Factory Women*. Berkeley: University of California Press.

Lee Dal-hyuk, ed. 1985. *Nodongjaka toiŏ* [Becoming a laborer]. Seoul: Hyŏngsŏngsa.

Lee, Eun-Jin. 1989. "Changing Strategies of Labor Control in the Semiconductor Industry in a Peripheral Country, S. Korea: A World-System Perspective." Ph.D. diss., University of California, Los Angeles.

Lee, Jae Hoon. 1994. *The Exploration of the Inner Wounds—Han*. Atlanta: Scholars Press.

Lee, Jeong Taik. 1987. "Economic Development and Industrial Order in South Korea: Interactions between the State and Labor in the Process of Export-Oriented Industrialization." Ph.D. diss., University of Hawaii.

Lee Kyŏng-hee. 1994. "Urinara imkŭm kujo ŭi pyŏnhwa panghyang kwa munjuechŏm: Taeman, ilbon kwaŭi pikyorŭl chungsimuro" [The Direction of change in our country's wage structure and its problems: In comparison with Taiwan and Japan]. *Quarterly Labor Review* 7(3):151–59.

Lee Kyun-Jae. 1997. "Saengsanchŏk nosakwankye silchŏnŭl uihan nosakaldŭng haeso sarye yŏngu" [A case study of reducing industrial conflicts for the achievement of productive industrial relations]. Master's thesis, Ulsan University.

Lee Kyu-uck, and Lee Sung-soon. 1985. Kiŏp kyŏlhap kwa kyŏngjaeryŏk chipchung [Business conglomeration and economic concentration]. Korea Development Institute Research Report 85–02. Seoul: Korea Development Institute.

Lee Myung-sook. 1993. "Nodong hyŏnjang'e pakodŭn tamul minjokjuŭi" [Tamul nationalism that has penetrated into the labor arena]. Kil (February): 160–65.

Lee Sŏn-young, and Kim Eun-sook. 1985. Sone sonŭl chapko—Nodongja somoim hwaldong sarye [Hands in hands—Case reports from workers' small-group activities]. Seoul: Pulbbit.

Lee Soo-won. 1994. Hyundai gŭrup nodong undong: Kŭ kyŏkdong ŭi yŏksa [The Labor movement at Hyundai group: The history of that great upheaval]. Seoul: Daeryuk.

Lee, Tae-ho. 1986a. Choegŭn nodong undong kirok (Records of the recent labor movement). Seoul: Ch'ŏngsa.

———. ed. 1986b. Nodong hyŏnjang ŭi chinsil [Truth in the world of factory work]. Seoul: Kŭmundang.

Lee Won-Duck, and Choi Kang-Shik. 1998. Labor Market and Industrial Relations in Korea: Retrospect on the Past Decade and Policy Directions for the 21st Century. Seoul: Korea Labor Institute.

Lee Young-ki. 1988. "Nongminchŭng punhae ŭi tonghyang kwa kyechŭng kusŏng" [A trend in the polarization and class composition of the agricultural population]. In Han'guk nongŏp-nongmin munje yŏnku I [A study of the problems in Korean agriculture and Korean farmers I], edited by Han'guk nongŏchon sahoe yŏnkuso, 193–217. Seoul: Yŏnkusa.

Lie, John. 1998. Han Unbound: The Political Economy of South Korea. Stanford: Stanford University Press.

Lim Ho. 1992. "Han'guk nodongja kyekŭp ŭisik hyŏngsŏng yŏnku: 1980 nyŏndae nodong undongŭl chungsimŭro" [A study on the formation of the Korean working-class consciousness: With special reference to the Labor Movement in the 1980s]. Ph.D. diss., Pusan National University.

Lim Hyun-Chin, and Kim Byung-Kook. 1991. "Nodong ŭi chachŏl, paebandoin minjuhwa: Kuka, chabon, nodong kwankye ŭi han'gukjŏk hyŏnsil" [Labor's frustration, betrayed democratization: The Korean reality of the state, capital, and industrial relations]. Sasang 3 (Winter).

Lim, Linda. 1978. Women Workers in Multinational Corporations: The Case of the Electronics Industry in Malaysia and Singapore. Michigan Occasional Papers in Women's Studies. Ann Arbor: University of Michigan.

Lim Young-Il. 1998. Han'guk nodong undongkwa kyekŭp chŏngchi (1987–1995): Pyŏnhwarŭl yuihan tujaeng, hyŏpsangŭl yuihan tujaeng [The Korean labor movement and labor politics (1987–1995): Struggle for change, struggle for negotiation]. Masan: Kyungnam University Press.

Lim Young-Il, and Lim Ho. 1993. "87nyŏn ihu nodongjachŭng ŭi ŭishikpyŏnhwa wa nosakwankye" [Changes in workers' consciousness and labor relations since 1987]. Kyŏngje wa sahoe [Economy and society] 17 (spring):29–72.

Lim Young-il, Cha Sung-soo, Park Joon-shik, and Lee Sang-young. 1989. "Tochŏm taekiŏp nodongjaŭi ŭishik yŏngu" [Study of consciousness among workers in large-scale monopoly firms]. In Han'guk sahoe nodongja yŏngu I, 143–257. Seoul: Paesan Sŏdong.

Lincoln, James, and Arne Kalleberg. 1990. *Culture, Control and Commitment*. Cambridge: Cambridge University Press.
Mann, Michael. 1973. *Consciousness and Action among the Western Working Class*. London: Macmillan.
Marshall, Gordon. 1983. "Some Remarks on the Study of Working-Class Consciousness." *Politics and Society* 12:263–301.
Milkman, Ruth. 1993. "New Research in Women's Labor History." *Signs* 18:376–88.
Ministry of Labor. 1988. *1987 nyŏn yŏrŭm ŭi nosapunkyu pyŏngka pokoso* [Research report on the labor unrest during the summer of 1987]. Seoul: Ministry of Labor.
Minjuhwa undong chikjang chŏngnyŏnhoe. 1989. *Samuchik chŏnmun kisulchik nodong undong* [The Labor movement among white-collar, professional, and technical workers]. Seoul: Paiksan sŏdang.
Minjung yesul wiwonhoe [Committee on minjung arts]. 1985. *Sarm kwa mŏt* [Life and flair]. Seoul: Kongdongche.
Moore, Barrington, Jr. 1978. *Injustice: The Social Bases of Obedience and Revolt*. White Plains: M. E. Sharpe.
Nam, Jeong-Lim. 1996. "Labor Control of the State and Women's Resistance in the Export Sector of South Korea." *Social Problems* 43 (August):327–38.
Nam, Jeong-Lim. 2000. "Gender Politics in the Korean Transition to Democracy." *Korean Studies* 24:94–112.
National Statistical Office. *Social Indicators in Korea, 1991 and 1998*. Seoul: National Statistical Office.
Nimura Kazuo. 1997. *The Ashio Riot of 1907: A Social History of Mining in Japan*. Edited by Andrew Gordon. Translated by Terry Boardman and Andrew Gordon. Durham: Duke University Press.
Ogle, George. 1990. *South Korea: Dissent within the Economic Miracle*. London: Zed Books.
Oh, John Kie-Chiang. 1999. *Korean Politics: The Quest for Democratization and Economic Development*. Ithaca: Cornell University Press.
Oh Yoon. 1996. *Tongne saram, sesang saram* [Neighborhood folks and other people]: *Oh Yoon's 10th Year Memorial Woodcut Paintings*. Seoul: Hakoje.
Ong, Aihwa. 1987. *Spirits of Resistance and Capitalist Discipline: Factory Women in Malaysia*. Albany: State University of New York Press.
———. 1991. "The Gender and Labor Politics of Post-Modernity." *Annual Review of Anthropology* 20:279–309.
Park Duk-je. 1986. "Yŏnkong imkŭm kwa han'guk ŭi nosakwankye" [The seniority-based wage system and Korean industrial relations]. *Sanŏp sahoe yŏnku* 1:225–51.
Park Hyun-chae, and Cho Hee-Yeon, eds. 1989. *Han'guk sahoe kusŏngche nonchaeng* [Debates on the social formation of Korea]. Seoul: Chuksan.
Park In-bae. 1985. "Munhwapae munhwa undongŭi sŏngripkwa kŭ panghyang" [Establishment and direction of cultural movement by culture cliques]. In *Han'guk minjok chuŭiron III* [Korean nationalism III], edited by Changjak kwa pipyŏng. Seoul: Changjak kwa pipyŏng.
———. 1991. "Nodongja munhwa undongŭi naeyongkwa palchŏn panghyang" [Content and direction of the workers' cultural movement]. In *Han'guk nodong undong 20-nyŏnŭi kyŏlsankwa chŏnmang* [Results and prospect of the 20-year Korean labor movement], edited by Chun Tae-Il Memorial Committee, 317–32.
Park Jin-do. 1988. "8–15 ihu han'guk nongŏp chŏngchaek ŭi chŏnkae kwachŏng" [Evolution of South Korea's agricultural policies since August 15]. In *Han'guk nongŭp-nongmin munje yŏnku I* [A study of the problems in Korean agriculture and Korean farmers I], edited by Han'guk nongŏchon sahoe yŏnkuso, 221–47. Seoul: Yŏnkusa.

Park, Joon-Shik. 1996. *Saengsan ŭi chŏngchiwa chaköpjang minjujuŭi* (Labor politics and shop-floor democracy). Seoul: Hanul.

Park Ki-nam. 1988. "Yŏsŏng nodongjadŭl ŭi ŭisik pyŏnhwa kwajŏng'e kwanhan han yŏnku: 1970 nyŏndae putŏ 1980 nyŏndae chungbankkaji" [A study of the process of change in the consciousness among women workers: From the 1970s to the mid-1980s]. M.A. thesis, Yonsei University.

Park Ki-Sung. 1991. *Han'guk ŭi nodong chohap. Vol. 2, Nodong chohap ŭi ŭisa kyŏlchŏng* [Korean trade unions. Vol. 2, Decision making in trade unions]. Seoul: Korea Labor Institute.

Park No-hae. 1984. *Nodong ŭi saepyŏk* [Dawn of labor]. Seoul: Pulbit.

Park Young-Jung. 1991. "80 nyŏndae minjung munye yaksa." [A short history of minjung culture in the 1980s]. In *Munye undongŭi hyŏndankyewa chŏnmang* [Current state and prospect of the cultural movement], edited by Chung I-Dam and Park Young-Jung, 241–60. Seoul: Hanmadang.

Park, Young-Ki. 1979. *Labor and Industrial Relations in Korea: System and Practice.* Institute for Labor and Management Studies, no. 6. Seoul: Sogang University Press.

Perry, Elizabeth. 1993. *Shanghai on Strike: The Politics of Chinese Labor.* Stanford: Stanford University Press.

Polanyi, Karl. 1957. *The Great Transformation: The Political and Economic Origins of Our Time.* Boston: Beacon Press.

Pulanjŏng nodong yŏngu moim. 2000. *Sinjayu chuŭiwa nodong wiki: Pulanjŏng nodong yŏngu* [Neoliberalism and the crisis of labor: A study of the unstable labor force]. Seoul: Muhwa Kwahaksa.

Roh, Hoe-Chan. 1999. "10 nyŏnkanŭi chinbo chŏngdang undongkwa saeroun to-chŏn" [The Movement for progressive parties in the past 10 years and a new challenge]. In *Han'guk sahoewa nodong undong* [Korean society and labor movement], edited by the Social Science Institute, Hanshin University. Seoul: Hyŏnjangesŏ miraerŭl.

Roh Joong-ki. 1995. "Kuka ŭi nodong tongje chŏnryak'e kwanhan yŏnku: 1987–1992" [A study on the state's strategy of labor control: 1987–1992]. Ph.D. diss., Seoul National University.

Safa, Helen I. 1981. "Runaway Shops and Female Employment: The Search for Cheap Labor." *Signs* 7(2):418–33.

Sahoe sajin yŏnguso [Social photography institute]. 1989. *Nodongja: Kangchŏlkwa nonmulŭi pit* [Workers: Light of steel and tears]. Seoul: Tongkwang.

Sakong, Il. 1993. *Korea in the World Economy.* Washington, D.C.: Institute for International Economics.

Salaff, Janet. 1981. *Working Daughters of Hong Kong.* Cambridge: Cambridge University Press.

Scott, Joan. 1988. *Gender and the Politics of History.* New York: Columbia University Press.

Seidman, Gay. 1994. *Manufacturing Militance: Worker's Movements in Brazil and South Africa, 1970–1985.* Berkeley: University of California Press.

Sen, Yow-Suen, and Hagen Koo. 1992. "Industrial Transformation and Proletarianization in Taiwan." *Critical Sociology* 19:45–67.

Seoul nodong undong yŏnhap (Sŏnoryŏn). 1986. *Sŏnbong'e sŏsŏ: 6-wol nodongja yŏndae t'uchaeng kirok* [At the vanguard: The records of the June solidarity struggle]. Seoul: Dolbege.

Sewell, William, Jr. 1980. *Work and Revolution in France: The Language of Labor from the Old Regime to 1848.* Cambridge: Cambridge University Press.

———. 1986. "Artisans, Factory Workers, and the Formation of the French Working Class, 1979–1984." In *Working-Class Formation: Nineteenth-Century Patterns in*

Western Europe and the United States, edited by Ira Katznelson and Aristide Zolberg, 45–70. Princeton: Princeton University Press.

Shieh, Gwo-Shyong. 1992. *"Boss" Island: The Subcontracting Network and Micro-Entrepreneurship in Taiwan's Development*. New York: Peter Lang.

Shin, Doh Chull, Myeong-Han Zho, and Myung Chey, eds. 1994. *Korea in the Global Wave of Democratization*. Seoul: Seoul National University Press.

Shin In-ryung. 1988. *Yŏsŏng, nodong, pŏp* [Women, labor, laws]. Rev. ed. Seoul: Pulbit.

Shin, Kwang-Yeong. 1994. *Kyekŭpkwa nodong undongŭi sahoehak* [Sociology of Class and the Labor Movement]. Seoul: Nanam.

———. 1999. *Tong Asiaŭi sanŏphwa wa minjuhwa* [Industrialization and Democratization in East Asia]. Seoul: Munhakwa Chisŏng.

Shindonga. 1990. *Sŏnŏnŭrobon 80-nyŏndae minjok minju undong* [People's and democracy movements in the 1980s seen through declarations]. Seoul: Donga Ilbosa.

"Shinmyong: The Performer and the Spirit of Life." 1988. *Koreana* 2:42–43.

Smith, Thomas C. 1988. *Native Sources of Japanese Industrialization, 1750–1920*. Berkeley: University of California Press.

Song, Byung-Nak. 1990. *The Rise of Korean Economy*. Hong Kong: Oxford University Press.

Song Chan-shik. 1973. *Yicho huki ŭi sukongŏp yŏnku* [A study of handicraft industry in late Yi Chosun]. Seoul: Seoul National University Press.

Song Ho Keun. 1991. *Han'guk ŭi nodong chŏngchi wa sijang* [Labor politics and market in Korea]. Seoul: Nanam.

———. 1994a. *Yŏlin sijang, tatchin chŏngchi* [Open market, closed politics]. Seoul: Namam.

———. 1994b. "Working-Class Politics in Reform Democracy in South Korea." Paper presented at the Association of Asian Studies, Boston, March.

Song, Hyo-soon. 1982. *Sŏulro kanŭnkil* [The road to Seoul]. Seoul: Hyŏngsŏngsa.

Song, Jung-nam. 1985. "Han'guk nodong undongkwa chisikinŭi yŏkhal" [Korean labor movement and the role of intellectuals]. In *Han'guk nodong undongron I* [On the Korean labor movement I], edited by Kim Keum-su and Park Hyun-chae, 177–96. Seoul: Mirae.

Sonn, Hochul. 1997. "The 'Late Blooming' of the South Korean Labor Movement." *Monthly Review* 49 (July–August).

Soon, Jum-soon. 1984. *8 sikan nodongŭl wihayŏ* [For 8-hour work]. Seoul: P'ulbit.

Standing, Guy. 1997. "Globalization, Labour Flexibility and Insecurity." *European Journal of Industrial Relations* 3.

Steinberg, David I. 1989. *South Korea: Economic Transformation and Social Change*. Boulder: Westview Press.

Suh, Doowon. 1998. "From Individual Welfare to Social Change: The Expanding Goals of Korean White-Collar Labor Unions, 1987–1995." Ph.D. diss., University of Chicago.

Suh Kwan-mo. 1987. "Han'guk sahoe kyekŭp kusŏng ŭi yŏnku" [A study of the class composition in Korean society]. Ph.D. diss., Seoul National University.

Suh Kwan-mo, and Shim Sŏng-bo, eds. 1989. *Hyŏndankye Han'guk samuchik nodong undong* [The Korean white-collar union movement at the present stage]. Seoul: Taeam.

Suh, Nam-dong. 1983a. "Historical Sketch of an Asian Theological Consultation." In *Minjung Theology*, edited by the Commission on Theological Concerns, Christian Conference of Asia. London: Zed Press.

———. 1983b. "Towards a Theology of Han." In *Minjung Theology*, edited by the Commission on Theological Concerns, Christian Conference of Asia. London: Zed Press.

Suk Jung-nam. 1984. *Kongjang ŭi pulbbit* [The light in the factory]. Seoul: Ilwŏl Sŏkak.

Thompson, E. P. 1963. *The Making of the English Working Class*. New York: Vintage Books.

———. 1966. "The Peculiarities of the English." In *Social Register 1965*, edited by Ralph Miliband and John Saville. London: Merlin Press.

———. 1967. "Time, Work-Discipline, and Industrial Capitalism." *Past and Present* 38:56–97.

Tongil pangjik pokjik t'ujaeng wiwonhoe [Tongil Textile workers' strike committee for reinstatement]. 1985. *Tongil pangjik nodongjohap undongsa* [The History of the Tongil Textile labor union]. Seoul: Dolbege.

Tsurumi, E. Patricia. 1990. *Factory Girls: Women in the Thread Mills of Meiji Japan*. Princeton: Princeton University Press.

Uh Soo-Bong. 1999. "Employment: Structure, Trends and New Issues." In *Labor Relations in Korea*, edited by KOILAF, 25–51. Seoul: Korea International Labour Foundation.

Ulsan nodong chŏngchaek kyoyuk hyŏphoe. 1995. *Ulsan chiyŏk nodong undong ŭi yŏksa, 1987–1995* [The History of the labor movement in the Ulsan area, 1987–1995]. Seoul: Ulsan nodong chŏngchaek kyoyuk hyŏphoe.

Ulsan sahoe sŏnkyo silchŏn hyŏpŭihoe. 1987. *Ulsan chiyŏk 7-wol nodongja taejung tujaeng charyochip* [Documentary materials on July mass labor struggles in Ulsan area]. Ulsan: Ulsan sahoe sŏnkyo silchŏn hyŏpŭihoe and Nodong munje sangdamso.

Um Hyun-young. 1986. "Ijen ulji malaya handa" [Now we must stop crying]. In *Sŏnbong'e sŏsŏ*, edited by Seoul nodongundong yŏnhap (sŏnoryŏn). Seoul: Dolbege.

Wallerstein, Immanuel. 1983. *Historical Capitalism*. London: Verso.

Wells, Kenneth, ed. 1995. *South Korea's Minjung Movement: The Culture and Politics of Dissidence*. Honolulu: University of Hawaii Press.

Williams, Raymond. 1977. *Marxism and Literature*. London: Oxford University Press.

Willis, Paul. 1977. *Learning to Labor: How Working-Class Kids Get Working-Class Jobs*. Westmead: Saxonhouse.

Wolf, Diane. 1992. *Factory Daughters: Gender, Household Dynamics, and Rural Industrialization in Java*. Berkeley: University of California Press.

Wonpoong mobang haeko nodongja pokjik tujaeng wiwonhoe. 1988. *Minju nojo 10 nyŏn: Wonpung mobang nodong chohap hwaldong kwa tujaeng* [Ten years of the democratic union movement: The activities and the struggles of Wonpoong Textile Labor Union]. Seoul: P'ulbit.

Woo, Jung-en. 1991. *Race to the Swift: State and Finance in Korean Industrialization*. New York: Columbia University Press.

World Bank. 1985. *World Development Report 1985*. New York: Oxford University Press.

———. 1993. *The East Asian Miracle: Economic Growth and Public Policy*. New York: Oxford University Press.

Yang Seung-jo. 1990. "70 nyŏndae minjunojo undongŭi pyŏngkawa kyŏhoon" [Evaluation and lessons of the 1970s democratic union movement]. In *Han'guk nodong undong 20 nyŏnŭi kyŏlsankwa chŏnmang*, edited by Chun Tae-Il Memorial Committee. Seoul: Sekye.

Yŏn, Sŏng-soo. 1989. "89-nyŏn imtunŭn tankyŏl t'ujaeng changjohanŭn nodongja munhwa wa hamkke" [1989 wage struggle in line with the working-class culture, which creates solidarity and struggle]. In Nodongja munhwa [Working-class culture]. Seoul: Hyŏnjang Munhaksa.

You, Jong-Il. 1995. "Changing Capital-Labour Relations in South Korea." In Capital, the State and Labour: A Global Perspective, edited by Juliet Schor and Jong-Il You, 110–51. Aldershot: Elgar.

Yu, Dong-wu. 1984. Ŏnŭ dolmaengi ŭi oichim [The cry of one stone]. Seoul: Chŏngnyŏnsa.

Yu Jae-chun, ed. 1984. Minjung [People]. Seoul: Munhakwa jisung.

Zolberg, Aristide. 1986. "How Many Exceptionalisms?" In Working-Class Formation: Nineteenth-Century Patterns in Western Europe and the United States, edited by Ira Katznelson and Aristide Zolberg, 397–455. Princeton: Princeton University Press.

Index